WETBACK NATION

WETBACK NATION

*The Case for Opening the
Mexican-American Border*

PETER LAUFER

IVAN R. DEE
Chicago

WETBACK NATION. Copyright © 2004 by Peter Laufer. All rights reserved, including the right to reproduce this book or portions thereof in any form. For information, address: Ivan R. Dee, Publisher, 1332 North Halsted Street, Chicago 60622. Manufactured in the United States of America and printed on acid-free paper.

www.ivanrdee.com

The paperback edition of this book carries the ISBN 1-56663-670-1.

Library of Congress Cataloging-in-Publication Data:
Laufer, Peter.
  Wetback nation : the case for opening the Mexican-American border / Peter Laufer.
    p. cm.
  Includes bibliographical references and index.
  ISBN 1-56663-592-6 (alk. paper)
  1. Mexican-American Border Region. 2. United States—Emigration and immigration—Government policy. I. Title.
F786.L325 2004
972'.1—dc22

2004051915

Para ti, Sheilita, como siempre.

Gracias por tu ayuda.

CONTENTS

ACKNOWLEDGMENTS

I LOOK BACK to well over thirty years of fascination with the Mexican-American border when I reflect on those who have helped me better understand the borderlands. Thanks first to Mark Allen and Chris Slattery for joining me on our coming-of-age trip to Rosarita back in our high school days. When the Mexican authorities would not let us journey south of Ensenada because we were underage and traveling without parental permission, I first started thinking seriously about political borders.

My initial professional forays into Mexico took place during my years working as an NBC News correspondent, often covering border and immigration stories. I thank my boss at NBC, Jim Farley, for the assignments and my producers, Lynne Peterson and Pete Michaels, for their support. I am indebted to *Penthouse* magazine editor Peter Bloch and to the National Geographic Society for further news reporting assignments about Mexican-U.S. relations.

I continued to study Mexico, Mexican immigration, and Mexican-American relations while working as a consulting researcher for Internews, and I thank the David and Lucile Packard Foundation for the grant that funded my Internews Mexico project, with a special tip of the *sombrero* to Packard's Mark Valentine, who encouraged me to write this book. My project manager at Internews, Deborah Mendelsohn, was another early advocate of the book, and I thank her for her companionship and assistance during our time in Mexico together. My Mexican colleague Pedro Enrique Armendares has been perpetually gracious sharing his sources with me. Veronica Melgoza provided me easy entrée to Chiapas, introducing me to her intimate contacts with critical newsmakers there. I very much appreciate the efforts of Dean Graber, project manager at the Knight Center for Journalism in the Americas at the University of Texas in Austin, who assisted me reconstructing some notes I lost in Veracruz.

Thanks to my longtime friends and colleagues Robert Simmons, Terry Phillips, and George Papagiannis for help with interviews in Texas, California, and Washington, D.C., respectively; and to my wife, Sheila Swan Laufer, for help with interviews in Kentucky. Phillips provided additional value reading the manuscript in progress, as did Mark Valentine. Journalist Alisa Roth forwarded important border and immigration stories to me while I was writing. My late friend Milan Melvin, who became a Mexican in his latter years, saved valuable Mexican newspaper clippings for me. I'm most grateful to Carmen Landa, who toils in the media relations section of the U.S. embassy in Mexico City, for introducing me to a long list of important sources. *Köszönön* to Michael Laufer for securing the Laufer Ellis Island records, and thanks to Tal Morris for his creative studio work on the Internews Mexico project audio report and on my radio documentary, "Border Wars," a project funded by the RIAS Berlin Commission. Another radio comrade-in-arms, Peter Morris, infused his enthusiasm into my work as I wrote.

Ivan Dee saved me from myself repeatedly with his skillful editing, and kept careful watch to make sure my words were not laden with *manteca*.

A special thank you is in order for my friends Eleni and Markos Kounalakis, who offered me use of their Barcelona pied-à-terre as an oasis in the ur-Mexico, a place where I was able to complete the manuscript free from routine distractions. Markos took time from his work as publisher of the *Washington Monthly* to conjure up the title *Wetback Nation*. *Gracias, amigo*.

Of course I thank the scores of Mexicans and Americans who agreed to talk with me and share their life histories on both sides of the border. I appreciate their confidence that I would treat their stories with fairness, even when I disagree with their points of view. And speaking of Americans, we're all Americans here in Mexico and the U.S.A. But on both sides of the border we've become accustomed to using the identifier "American" to mean Gringos. I so use it in this book while remaining aware that Mexicans are Americans too.

Finally, I wish to thank my mother for always reminding me what Mr. Pavlak said: "There's no law against enjoying yourself."

P. L.

Sonoma County, California
June 2004

PREFACE:
BIENVENIDOS,
AMIGOS

I AM PREJUDICED to favor immigrants. How can I not be? My father came through Ellis Island. I have the page from the logbook where his arrival was recorded by the immigration officer on duty. He answered all the questions to the satisfaction of the inspector.

"Whether a polygamist?"

"No."

"Whether an anarchist?"

"No."

And Question 24: "Whether a person believes in or advocates the overthrow by force or violence of the Government of the United States or of all forms of law, or who disbelieves in or is opposed to organized government, or who advocates the assassination of public officials, or who advocates or teaches the unlawful destruction of property, or is a member of or affiliated with any organization entertaining and teaching disbelief in or opposition to organized government or which teaches the unlawful destruction of property, or who advocates or teaches the duty, necessity, or propriety of the unlawful assaulting or killing of any officer or officers, either of specific individuals or of officers in general, of the Government of the United States or of any other organized government because of his or their official character?"

"No," my father answered. It was 1923, and America was still more worried about immigrating anarchists from Europe than Mexicans coming north.

"You're an American by birth," my father repeatedly reminded me. "I'm an American by choice."

A few years ago my wife and I spent days searching the bowels of the La Porte County courthouse in Indiana, finally finding her grandfather's naturalization papers.

"It is my bona fide intention," he swore to the clerk of the La Porte County Court in 1913, "to renounce forever all allegiance and fidelity to any foreign prince, potentate, state, or sovereignty, and particularly to Francis Joseph, Emperor of Austria and Apostolic King of Hungary."

We secured the address of the house in what used to be called the Poletown section of La Porte, where her mother lived before moving to California. Poletown is still on the wrong side of the tracks in La Porte. The railroad bisects the town. South of the ornate courthouse, gracious Victorian mansions line Michigan Avenue under a canopy of well-established trees. But east of downtown and north across the tracks the boxy houses are humble, packed into the rusting factory and warehouse district. For immigrants, the wrong side of the tracks is the usual entry point in an American city. And in La Porte, Poletown is filling up with Mexicans, Mexican restaurants, and Mexican grocery stores.

In the summer of 2001, just weeks before the September 11th attacks, I wrote the following essay for the *San Francisco Chronicle*, a strident call to open the southern border of the United States to Mexicans who wish to come north:

> We Americans work hard to keep Mexicans out of the United States, Mexicans who want to wash our dishes and pick our crops. Those crops need picking and those dishes need washing, so workers come north despite our best efforts. America ought to open and demilitarize our southern border immediately, welcome our Mexican neighbors to come and go

with the ease of Canadian travelers to this country, and finally put an end to a sordid and shameful chapter in our national history. Not only is such a change in policy the proper moral and logical course of action for us to take, there will be no negative effects to the lives of most Americans.

The current border, from its Berlin Wall–like ghastliness against cities such as Tijuana, to the equally harsh deserts to the east, doesn't keep Mexicans from coming north and working here illegally. The heavily armed Border Patrol, equipped with the latest hi-tech magic, can't stop this surge of money-motivated migration. We all know that. Just look in the kitchen of your favorite restaurant, or along the roadside at one of the ad hoc hiring stations where desperate manual laborers congregate all over the United States. Mexican workers are everywhere north of the border, especially in California. The only Mexicans who choose to come north illegally and don't are the unlucky who get caught. And many of them just try again moments after they are deported.

Since the passage of the 1996 Illegal Immigration Reform and Immigrant Responsibility Act, the U.S. Border Patrol has grown into the nation's largest uniformed law enforcement agency, with nearly ten thousand officers. Nonetheless our southern border remains porous.

A friend of mine who works in gardens and construction in Marin County commutes—illegally—from his home in Sinaloa. He's practiced at the journey, telling me that jumping the border at Nogales, hitchhiking up to Tucson, and grabbing a Southwest flight to Oakland is just a necessary part of his work routine. Another friend simply walked into the United States past overworked border guards at a bridge between Ciudad Juárez and El Paso. Once on the U.S. side, she piled her hair up high on her head, made up her face, and with her short shorts and entitled attitude, she sashayed to the airport for a flight further north, sure no one would mistake her for a desperate Mexican peasant. She was right, and she's lived in rural California ever since, raising a family of American-born children.

I have traveled the artificial line between our two countries with Border Patrol officers, and many have acknowledged that they cannot keep determined Mexicans from crossing north.

It's time to try a new approach.

Let's begin by opening the border to all Mexicans who wish to travel north. Supporters of guns, guards, and fences argue that if the border were open, the United States would be smothered by Mexicans escaping their poverty-stricken homeland. Yet there is no restriction on immigrants coming to California from Mississippi or West Virginia, and California is not inundated with a parade of workers from those poorer states. They cannot afford to live here without working, and they apparently don't want the jobs that are available. As long as those agriculture, construction, restaurant, and other positions are vacant, workers will come north. But that's good. We need the help. Our economy depends on its Mexican workforce. Economically driven immigration ultimately is self-regulating. When and if enough migrants fill the jobs that U.S. citizens refuse to take, there will be little motivation for Mexicans to leave home. There is no restriction on the movement of labor within the European Community. When the German economy was humming, the Portuguese, for example, moved north to better paying jobs from Stuttgart to Berlin. When stagnating growth then created high unemployment in Germany, the Portuguese went home or sought jobs elsewhere.

Critics argue that unrestricted traffic north from Mexico will result in increased demands on schools, health care, and welfare. But that's also a fatuous worry. Few workers from Mexico who do not qualify legally for such benefits attempt to secure the services. They are afraid of being caught. And if workers earn a living up here and do qualify for benefits, it does our social service systems no harm for them to collect.

Historically there is no basis for keeping Mexicans south of the frontier. Aside from the fact that much of the West was once half their country, there were no restrictions on the movement of Mexicans back and forth across the current border until relatively recently. Controls were first placed at the border in the late nineteenth century to keep out Europeans and Asians who were denied legal access to the United States. Well into the twentieth century, Mexicans continued to enjoy free passage back and forth from their country to ours. U.S. authorities found that most of these border crossers traveled for work, and they were therefore treated as commuters.

Restrictions began to be enforced during the Mexican Revolution of 1910, when Mexicans were forced to pass a literacy test and pay a one-time eight-dollar fee to cross legally into the United States.

Today Mexicans are treated as a threat, and futile attempts continue to keep them on their side of the line. Some proponents of a closed border fear problems associated with overpopulation. Others worry that an open border will encourage employers to pay even less for entry-level jobs because of a growing and anxious labor pool.

Perhaps these concerns could be rationalized if our border controls worked. But in addition to the fact that most any determined Mexican eventually can get north and find a job, the borderlands have become a tragic gauntlet for them to run. Violent robbers, cheating *coyotes* [the smugglers of illegal immigrants], murderous desert heat, and cruel vigilantes all compete to victimize those crossing the border illegally. For many, the Border Patrol is the least of their problems. Its officers may end up providing lifesaving rescue from the other threats.

Yet despite these miserable conditions, a Mexican who really wants to come north, comes north. Most just want to come work, make some money, and go home. After the Berlin Wall fell back in 1989, there was an initial rush of East Germans west. Then they went home. They did not enjoy the West German culture, they missed their families and friends. They went home.

So let's stop this deadly nonsense—at least as a test—and replace the failed barrier we've erected with a banner reading *Bienvenidos*. Let's make it as easy for a Mexican to come north as it is for a Canadian to come south.

Timing is everything, they say. Shortly after my call to open the border was published in the *Chronicle*, the World Trade Center and the Pentagon were attacked. Immediately following those tragedies there were few takers for the idea of opening the southern frontier to Mexicans. But as the years pass since the September 11th events, the validity of eliminating the futile attempts to keep Mexicans out of the United States only seems greater. Not only would such free passage for Mexicans end a deadly charade along the borderline, it would make it much easier for the United States to secure its southern border against aliens who are genuine threats to its security.

Consider these points. Most everyone agrees that the current border policy is a fraud. Mexicans come north despite U.S. law restricting their migration. The U.S. government spends enormous amounts of money and human resources chasing millions of Mexicans. If these migrants crossed into the United States in an orderly fashion, unafraid of deportation, the numbers of people trying to cross illegally would be dramatically reduced. The Border Patrol would be in a much better position to apprehend those undocumented OTMs (Other Than Mexicans, to use the Border Patrol's parlance) who pose a much greater potential threat to national security than the Mexicans who eventually get across to the other side despite U.S. efforts. Fringe benefits to such a policy would include a radical decline in the abuse of Mexican labor by U.S. employers. They would no longer be able to take advantage of workers afraid to stand up for a fair wage and decent working conditions. Predatory *coyotes* would be all but put out of business.

The best arguments for eliminating attempts to control Mexican migration are that such a policy is counterproductive to attempt and impossible to achieve. Instead, open the border to Mexicans. These people are coming north despite U.S. laws. Open the border to Mexican workers so that the bad guys cannot hide in their shadows as they sneak across the border. Open the border to Mexicans the United States wants and needs, and then the Border Patrol will know that the people trying to break into the country—the ones in the tunnels, those running across the desert and jumping the fences—are the real villains. Open the border to Mexicans, a significant fuel for the U.S. economy, and make it easier for the Border Patrol to keep out the drug traffickers and the terrorists.

To find fact, opinion, and experience to bolster my argument, I've traveled the U.S.-Mexican border, meeting with the victims and the perpetrators of current U.S. government immigration policy, contemplating alternatives. I'm a journalist, so I've looked at the border wars through the prism of news and news reporting, broadcasting, and publishing. Stories related here of my Mexican colleagues fighting bribery—long institutionalized as a tool to manipulate Mexican journalism—offer glimpses into the rot in the Mexican economy, rot that emboldens frustrated workers to look to Gringolandia for a better life. I've wandered deep into Mexico to observe, experience, and record the poverty and hopelessness that drive migrants to leave their homes and risk their lives on the long journey north. I've talked with undocumented immigrants living the American Dream, walked the beat with cops frustrated by unenforceable immigration laws. I've interviewed immigration lawyers and those ultimately responsible for enticing Mexicans north: their employers in *El Norte*. On my journey I've avoided the obvious border trip, that crooked line from San Diego and Tijuana east to Matamoros and Brownsville, the line that marks the artificial national frontier between Mexico and the United States. Instead I've traveled the extended border, crisscrossing our melded cultures from Niagara Falls to Chiapas, from Mexico City to Washington, D.C., studying the borders that exist in our heads and hearts, searching for sane and humane solutions to the problems and conflicts plaguing our two countries.

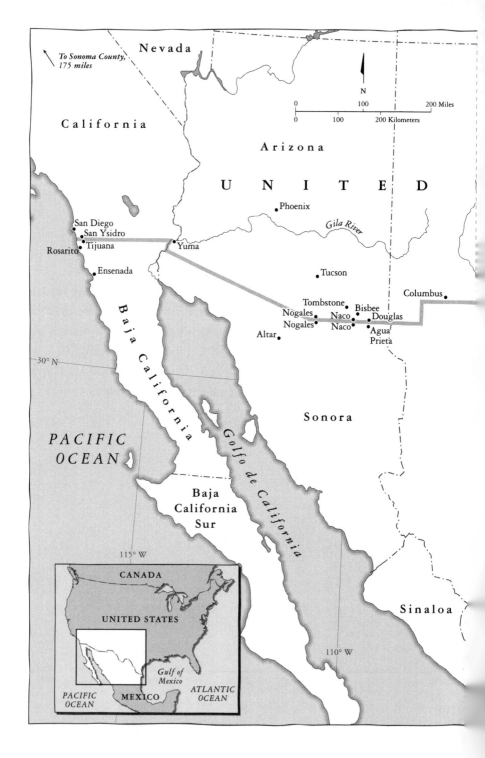

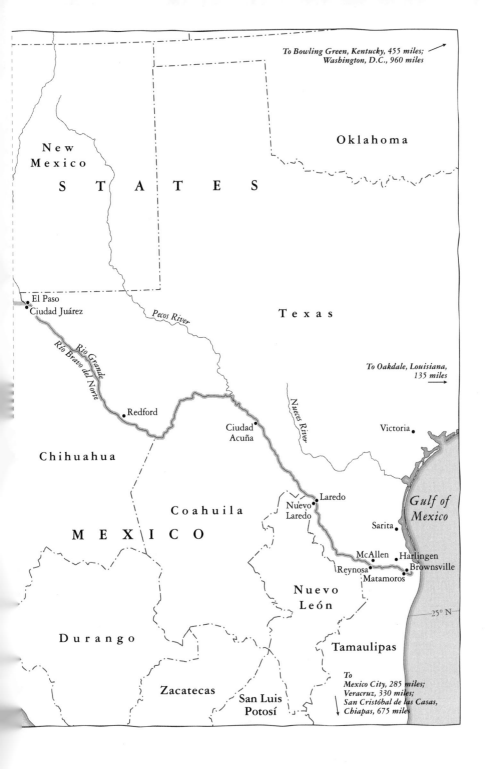

*To Bowling Green, Kentucky, 455 miles;
Washington, D.C., 960 miles*

Oklahoma

**N e w
M e x i c o**

S   A   T   E   S

El Paso
Ciudad Juárez

Pecos River

T e x a s

Rio Grande

Río Bravo del Norte

*To Oakdale, Louisiana,
135 miles*

Redford

Nueces River

Ciudad
Acuña

Victoria

C h i h u a h u a

Laredo

Nuevo
Laredo

*Gulf of
Mexico*

C o a h u i l a

Sarita

M   E   X   I   C   O

McAllen Harlingen

Reynosa   Brownsville

Matamoros

**N u e v o
L e ó n**

25° N

D u r a n g o

Tamaulipas

*To
Mexico City, 285 miles;
Veracruz, 330 miles;
San Cristóbal de las Casas,
Chiapas, 675 miles*

Z a c a t e c a s

**San Luis
Potosí**

WETBACK NATION

1

ILLEGAL ALIEN
OR CLEVER
NEW AMERICAN?

LET ME INTRODUCE YOU to that friend of mine who crossed into the United States from Ciudad Juárez over to El Paso. Juana María is a bright and bubbly woman in her late thirties. Her toddler daughter is in the living room learning English from a television program when we sit down in her kitchen to talk about her trip across the border more than thirteen years ago. Her two boys are in school. She offers me a cup of tea.

"Do you have anything decaffeinated?" I ask.

She does. Her bicultural kitchen cupboards include *mole*, tortillas, and decaffeinated mint tea. I've heard Juana María's* border-crossing story often, but in bits and pieces. Today she's taking time out of her schedule to recount it from start to finish.

It was 1990 when Juana María first came to the United States. She had waited patiently in line at the U.S. consulate in Guadalajara and applied for a tourist visa, which she received. Eight months earlier her husband had crossed into California, looking for work. A hardworking mechanic, he found a job easily—on a ranch where his pay included living quarters in a trailer.

---

*Juana María's name is changed for this book, and I've excised the name of her new hometown from her story.

She remembers all the dates precisely. "I came on May 27th in 1990, that's the first time I came to the United States." Juana María speaks English with a thick Mexican accent and only rarely drops a Spanish word into the conversation. Her English vocabulary is more than adequate for her story. She's spent the last several years studying English, working with a volunteer tutor, and her boys bring English home from school and into the household. "I flew from Guadalajara here to California." In addition to her three-month-old first son, she traveled north with her mother-in-law and her thirteen-year-old brother. She was twenty-three. Stamped into her Mexican passport was her prized tourist visa.

When she reached the immigration officer at the airport, she was asked a few key questions. "He asked, 'How much money do you have to spend in the United States?' I had only five hundred dollars. My mother-in-law didn't have anything. He said, 'That is not enough money for three people to visit the United States for two months.'" The Immigration and Naturalization Service officer asked the next crucial question, and she now knows that her honest answer doomed her trip. "He asked, 'Why are you coming here?' And I told the truth, 'I come to visit my husband. I want to stay with my husband, and I want my child to grow up with his father.'" Despite the valid visa, Juana María and her family were refused entry. It was obvious she was no tourist; she was an immigrant.

"We stayed all night, like we were arrested. We didn't go to jail because we had two little boys. But we stayed all night in one room in the airport."

The officer was Latino, she says, and told her, "Oh, I'm so sorry. I feel so bad about what I'm doing." She says she remembers the moment vividly when he took her cash. "He bought a ticket. The next day we flew back to Mexico on another airplane. One officer went with us into the airplane and made sure we were sitting down in the airplane. And he never gave me my money back. He bought that ticket with my money."

A month later Juana María was shopping for a *coyote*. "I didn't want to stay in Mexico. My husband was here." Her older brother convinced her to avoid the Tijuana crossing into San Diego, scaring her with stories of rape, robbery, abandonment, and murder in the hills along *la frontera*, the border. She decided on a crossing from Ciudad Juárez into El Paso. She bundled up her baby, and, once again accompanied by her mother-in-law, she flew from Guadalajara to Juárez. This time she didn't tell her husband of her travel plans. "I didn't tell him because if something happened he would have worried about me and my boy. I wanted to give him a surprise."

Her brother confirmed arrangements with the *coyote* and secured the address of a house for the rendezvous with the guide. Juana María took a cab at the Juárez airport, but when the three travelers arrived at the Juárez house, they were unable to find their contact. And they quickly realized that they had left a suitcase in the cab. "We were missing in the big city," she says. "In the suitcase we had diapers and the formula." They told their story to whomever they could find around the address that would listen. Luck was with the migrating trio. A mechanic knew their *coyote* by a different name but didn't know how to find him. The taxi company insisted on buying formula for the baby; when the company found the missing baggage, it delivered it to their hotel.

Juana María called her brother. He contacted the *coyote* and sent him to the hotel, and there they made their plans. "I was nervous, but he told me to relax." In those pre-September 11th days, Mexicans routinely crossed the bridge into El Paso to shop. The crowds were so great and the traffic so important to the local economy that immigration officers only spot-checked border crossers walking north. Juana María was told to dress like a typical Mexican housewife, carry a shopping bag, and act confident. "We looked like people from Mexico who were shopping and going back home." They agreed to make the crossing during the noon rush hour. The *coyote* figured inspectors would be eating lunch and that the throngs crossing the bridge would camouflage his clients.

The next morning a car came to the hotel for Juana María. She was dropped near the border and walked north. "We crossed, walking"—Juana María, the baby, her mother-in-law, and the *coyote*. "I was wearing a dress to look like a Mexican woman. We crossed at the border and walked for maybe ten or fifteen minutes into El Paso." As the migrants walked north, homeless persons living on the street kept the *coyote* informed that the street was free of *Migra* (Spanish slang for the INS, the Immigration and

Naturalization Service); they were tipped a dollar for the intelligence. "Finally we stopped at a McDonald's, because it was 104 degrees."

She ate her first American meal in the cool of the McDonald's—a hamburger, of course—and the *coyote* called a taxi. They drove to a house where a friend of her brother lived, and there they spent the night. The easy part of the journey was over. Now the job was to get Juana María out of the borderlands and up into the interior and on to her husband in California. A further masquerade was needed. She no longer had to look like a Mexican housewife; she had to look like a Mexican American. "That's when they made me look like a teenager. They put me in shorts with a lot of flowers. They put me in a blouse—phosphorescent orange. And they put my hair up, like a *chola*!* They colored my eyes black, and red lipstick! Oh, my goodness." Juana María is a pretty woman, but she dresses conservatively and wears only minimal makeup. She was happy to play dress-up "because I needed to look like the girls from El Paso, Texas. The teenagers in El Paso look different from the teenagers in Mexico. That's why they changed my looks."

They flew to Dallas with no trouble, the baby disguised as an El Paso infant sporting a Hawaiian shirt. Her mother-in-law was still with them, not worried in "a dress like a North American girl" because her hair is blonde. "I felt nervous," Juana María admits, but more than just nervous. "I felt embarrassed to look like that. When I looked at myself in the mirror I said, 'Oh, my God. No!' But I needed to relax and look normal, like all the other people in the airport."

When they arrived at the Dallas–Fort Worth airport they waited for another brother to pick them up. "He passed me three times and didn't recognize me." Finally she said to him, "Hi, honey! I'm Juana María." He was shocked at her appearance. "Well, I looked like a *chola*! He told me, 'If your husband sees you looking like that, immediately he will divorce you.' We left the airport and went right to Sears to buy makeup and a dress, to wash my face and change clothes. We went to my brother's house,

---

Cholo(a) is a Mexican term originally used to describe a person of mixed Spanish and Indian heritage. On the north side of the border it's been used as a derogatory identifier for Latino street gang members and often implies the specific attire favored by the subculture.

and then we called up my husband and I said, 'Honey, I'm here!' He said, 'No, you are joking.' I told him I was serious and that I had another surprise—I had his mother with me."

The mother-in-law had told her husband she would go only as far as Ciudad Juárez, but she went across into the United States, says Juana María, on a lark. "The *coyote* said, 'It's fun. You can cross. It's not dangerous.' So she crossed to have one more adventure in her life. My brother paid only $500 for all three people. Very cheap."

The date of her arrival in *El Norte** is fixed in her mind. "I crossed the border June 24, 1990." After a week visiting her brother, she flew to California for a reunion with her husband. It was July 1, just in time for the Fourth of July festivities at the ranch where he worked. "My husband told me I needed to buy clothes for the celebration. I got blue jeans and a red and white blouse, because those are the three colors of the American flag."

Juana María's parrot is chirping. Her daughter takes a break from the television to listen, eat some corn chips, and make a mess on the counter trying to pour some 7-Up into a glass. Outside cattle are feeding at the trough. Her dogs occasionally bark. Through her kitchen windows I see the bucolic California hills that surround her home. "I haven't been back to Mexico for thirteen years." She looks pensive when I ask her why. "Because I don't have a Green Card, and now I am worried about crossing the border. I hear a lot of bad stories. It costs $2,500 for each person."

Living without proper documentation for thirteen years has been nothing much more than an annoyance for Juana María. "I don't do anything illegal. I live a good life and take care of my kids. The only effect of not having a Green Card is that we cannot have a driver's license." Juana María does carry an official California identification card. Until 1996 these were available from the Department of Motor Vehicles with no questions asked, based only on a birth certificate. The law changed that year, and aliens without Green Cards were no longer eligible for driver's licenses or

---

*Mexicans use many different terms for the United States, including *El Norte*, the North. *Gringolandia* is another. *Gringolandia* tends to be used disparagingly, whereas *El Norte* is simply an identifier. And the United States is often just referred to as *el otro lado*, the other side.

official identification cards. But immigration officers rarely show up in her rural neighborhood, and when they do patrol places that she frequents in the nearby urban district, she says she's warned and just avoids them. "When the INS* is around here they say so on the radio station: don't go out to Wal-Mart or Sears or whatever shopping center because the INS is around. So I don't go there. After one or two days, they're gone."

I ask Juana María what she would do if an immigration agent approached her. "If he asks me for a Green Card, I can't do anything," she says about this perpetual threat to her domestic tranquility. "If you don't have the Green Card, they only arrest. They say, 'You have a right to call a relative, but you're going to jail.' If I don't have a Green Card, they'll deport me to my country, to Mexico. That's what they do. They don't ask for identification, they ask for a Green Card, or your permission to stay in the United States, like a passport. If I don't have anything with me, they'll arrest me, and they'll take me out to the border."

But life was more uncertain for her when Pete Wilson was governor of California and he rallied voters to pass Proposition 187, the referendum that limited the rights of undocumented migrants and was ultimately struck down by the courts. During the anti-immigrant climate of those years in the mid-1990s, just picking the kids up at school was cause for concern. "The INS came to the schools and arrested illegal parents. For more than a week we didn't send our boy to the school when I heard that the INS was here in my county."

Juana María figures that about 70 percent of her Latino friends in California are in the state illegally. She hopes to legalize her status in the United States. Perhaps there will be another amnesty for immigrants who entered without documentation. Perhaps when her second son, who was born in the United States and consequently is an American citizen, becomes an adult he will be able to establish legal residency for his parents and his older Mexican-citizen brother. Meanwhile she and her family

*Juana María still says INS, using the acronym for the Immigration and Naturalization Service. The new nomenclature of the Department of Homeland Security and its Bureau of Immigration and Customs Enforcement had not replaced her jargon. She also doesn't use the slang word *Migra.*

thrive. She works hard at the local PTA, organizing fund-raising dinners of rich Mexican food to pay for the rehabilitation of the playground. Her daughter is christened at the local Catholic church in a Spanish-language ceremony, followed by a block party crowded with friends and relatives, food and music. Her husband goes off to work each day; she works part time. They pay their taxes. She is an American by every definition except for her paperwork.

A few days after we talked at her home, it was Mexican Lunch Day at the local elementary school. Juana María brought together a group of the Latino mothers to prepare burritos. The women were lined up in the kitchen, the first ladling out the rice, the next passing out a tortilla, the third the beans. The burritos were topped off with lettuce and sour cream and salsa. Juana María was proud of the healthy ingredients, far from her Mexican roots. "I didn't use lard in the beans," she told the other mothers. The money raised by the lunch was used to provide child care for Latino mothers at the school who were taking classes to earn a high school equivalency certificate.

In one important way Juana María suffers because of her illegal status in the United States. "I feel sad because I cannot go to Mexico and come back again. I cannot visit my relatives. My friends who have Green Cards, they do that every year or every other year. I want to go to Mexico. But how can I cross? Maybe I'd be lucky and not have any problems, like the first time. Or maybe I'd have a lot of problems." She has reason to worry; she's heard the horror stories. "I have friends who came here two months after I came to the United States. Two years later they went to Mexico." The return trip to the states was a disaster. "One of the ladies," she says with a combination of sadness and a matter-of-fact reporting of the news, "the *coyote* killed her. With a screwdriver. In Tijuana. I say no. I'm not going. I love my relatives. But I don't want to put my life in between. My life is first, and my kids too.

But when Juana María's father-in-law was dying, her husband decided to chance a trip back to Mexico. In just over ten years the price of a *coyote* had increased fivefold. He paid $2,500 for help crossing from Tijuana to San Diego. He crossed with a false Green Card—not counterfeit but stolen. *Coyotes* prowl border nightclubs, Juana María explains, looking for drunk Latinos with legitimate identification papers. They steal their Green Cards. Her husband sat down at a table with a *coyote* who displayed a stack of stolen Green Cards. Together they searched through the cards for a picture of a Mexican who looked enough like her husband to satisfy a border guard. He crossed the border with someone else's Green Card. The system isn't perfect: he crossed successfully three times, "but the last time," she tells me, "the officer said, 'You don't look like him!' They arrested him and sent him back to Mexico. He called me from Rosarita and said, 'I am here because they caught me and sent me back to Mexico.' I called the *coyote* and said, 'You promised me my husband would come back to California safely. If my husband is not here in my house, I will not pay you anything.' The *coyote* went to get my husband at Rosarita, and he crossed again at Tijuana with the same stolen Green Card! That day was lucky."

"Sometimes the *coyotes* have business with the immigration officer," she said, "and they give him money under the table. My husband flew home from San Diego. When he was on the airplane, I sent the money by Western Union to the *coyote*."

That's Juana María's theory, that the *coyote* bribed the guard. It's hard to imagine a U.S. immigration officer jeopardizing his career and pension— not to mention risking prison time—for a cut of a $2,500 *coyote* fee. Hard to imagine but certainly possible. U.S. officials along the border have been arrested for conspiring with smugglers. Corruption is not limited to the Mexican side of the border.

The Border Action Network is an Arizona-based group founded in 1999 that documents charges of abuse against the Border Patrol and other government agencies involved with securing the Mexican border. The list they post on their website of charges against Border Patrol agents gives credence to Juana María's theory. Here are a few excerpts from that list:

> Off-duty Border Patrol agent William Varas faces charges that he lied to authorities in July 2002 when he claimed that he fired his gun at immigrants only after they had first shot at him. Agent Matthew Hemmer was arrested in August 2000 on state charges of kidnapping, sexual assault,

and sexual abuse. A criminal complaint said Hemmer took an undocumented woman, then 21, to a remote location and sexually assaulted her before allowing her to return to Mexico. Agent Dennis Johnson, a former supervisor, was sentenced to seven years in prison for sexual assault and five years (concurrent) for kidnapping in connection with a September 28, 2000, incident. Johnson sexually assaulted a 23-year-old El Salvadoran woman who was in custody, naked and handcuffed. Agent Charles Brown, a 23-year veteran, was arrested in November 2003 for allegedly selling classified information to a drug cartel. Brown worked in the agency's intelligence unit.*

The Bush administration's 2004 election-year proposal offering temporary worker status to Mexicans in the United States illegally is no solution to the border wars for Juana María. Offering Green Cards is all well and good, she says, "but I feel bad that he wants to give permission for three years to work here, and then after three years you go back to your country." She looks puzzled and disgusted by the suggestion. "You're living your life here, you work so hard," she points out with hurt pride, "now, go back? No. This is not an option."

What is the solution for Juana María and the millions of others living without documentation in the United States? "Amnesty for good persons," she says. "So many persons come here for work, to have the best life . . ."

But why should someone who broke the law be given amnesty and the opportunity legally to pursue the American dream? "Because we work hard and we are important to the country, to help the country grow. And we grow too, because we have the best life."

What about the long-term solution, I ask. Any determined Mexican who wants to come to the United States can figure out a path.

"No problem," she agrees, "they can come."

*A summary of the work conducted by The Border Action Network can be seen at www.borderaction.org.

But if it is an illegal crossing north, they must perpetually fear deportation. Does she favor an open border?

"Yes. Open the border."

Her reasons are clear and come from personal experience.

"No business for the *coyote*. No people dead along the border. Then people in Mexico can come here and work, and the United States has cheap workers. That's simple. Open the border and you have no problems. Then Mexican people can feel free to come here, like Americans go to Mexico."

If the border were open, where would Juana María prefer to live, in Mexico or California?

"I love the life in California, but I miss my family," she says, sounding a little dreamy. "Especially at Christmastime, or New Year, when we make family parties. The traditions are so different here and there. In Mexico we eat beans and cheese and tortillas, but every family is together. Here we have turkey with everything, but I don't feel happy. . . . I mean, I feel happy because my kids have the best school, and we stay together with my husband. But I have a heart, and my heart is in Mexico."

2

STILL LIFE

ON THE BORDER

ON THE POOR and dirty streets of Nuevo Laredo, just across the border from Laredo, Texas, huddled masses listen to *mariachis* and wait for nighttime without much concern for the Border Patrol on the other side. "I'm not worried about the *Migra*," says one worker poised to cross the Rio Grande. "*Cuando el estómago tiene hambre, no piensa en dificultades.*" When the stomach is hungry, you don't think of difficulties. The men eat sardines from tins, sip orange soda, trade stories.

"I usually go to Florida with the tobacco, or North Carolina for the tomato."

How many times have you crossed?

"Well, I've crossed a lot of times. Maybe fifty or sixty." A laugh.

On the Day of the Migrant each year since 1999, local Catholics lead a procession in Nuevo Laredo from the central park, where many migrants gather before making the crossing, across town to the International Bridge. They walk in silence and carry white crosses to commemorate the Mexicans who have died trying to get into the United States. Nuevo Laredo priest Leonardo López calls the deaths "executions by unemployment, the economy, and the persecutions of migrants."[1] Advocates for migrants' rights blame U.S. border policies and the unsuccessful Mexican economy for the desperation that drives them to cross the border illicitly. "These immigrants that have died are not only victims of a dream but also of their desire to get ahead, of the frustration of not having money or stability," says López.

On the Mexican side of the border, pueblos along the migrant trail are making *migradollars* as staging points for the trek north. Places such as Altar, 160 miles southwest of Tucson, have filled with travelers as the U.S. Border Patrol has tightened security at urban crossing points. From Altar north into the United States there is nothing much more than desert. In addition to small merchants selling food and water, organized smuggling gangs are at work, providing temporary housing in marginal *casas de huéspedes*—guest houses—and offering guided trips into the United States at prices that increase as U.S. efforts make the border more difficult to cross.

It is not against Mexican law to cross from Mexico into the United States, but it is illegal to smuggle undocumented foreigners. Consequently Mexican law-enforcement officials can chase the smugglers because plenty of their clients come from countries south of Mexico's border. The interior secretary of Mexico, Santiago Creel, watched the smuggling business grow rapidly after the United States instituted its Southwest Border Strategy in 1994, forcing migrants into the desert. "We are talking about international mafias of extremely dangerous groups that have caused great pain to many families," Creel said of the smuggling operations. "The great problem we face is a humanitarian one," agreed the head of the Organized Crime Unit of the Mexican attorney general's office, José Luis Vasconcelos.[2]

Travelers too poor to afford the guest houses and the smugglers' fees camp outdoors. The local Catholic church at Altar tries to help the indigent migrants. There Father René Castañeda Castro presides over a dormitory for scores of the overexposed, and a kitchen to feed them. He and his crew try to convince the desperate migrants to turn back, telling them stories and showing them videos of the dangers ahead. "It's not a desert anymore," he tells them, "it's a cemetery."[3]

The free market adapts quickly on the Tijuana–San Diego border. Immediately after the September 11th attacks, legal border crossers were faced with extraordinary delays as U.S. agents carefully checked documents and searched cars. Those walking across the border also were subject to increased scrutiny, their papers checked thoroughly and their possessions sent through airport-style X-ray machines. Lines were hours long. But in addition to motor vehicles and pedestrians, there was a third line: for bicyclists. And very few border crossers were heading north by bicycle. There was virtually no waiting.

Thus a group of Mexican entrepreneurs set up shop just south of the border with a haphazard collection of bicycles, offering them for rent to anyone standing in the hot sun waiting to pass the U.S. control point. I was in that line and jumped at the opportunity to speed up my passage, happy to rent a bicycle ludicrously too small for me. Riding was not an option; I couldn't fit on it. I gave the new businessman five bucks and took temporary custody of my bike. He instructed me to push the bike up to the crossing point, passing the hundreds of pedestrians sweltering in the sun.

"What do I do with it once I'm on the other side?" I asked him.

He smiled. "There's another *bandito* at the other end who will take the bike."

And indeed there was. As soon as I cleared U.S. immigration minutes later, his partner grabbed my bicycle and sent it south to earn another five dollars.

My wife and I were en route to Dallas when we made a typical tourist stop along the border. We parked the car in the shade in El Paso and left a window cracked open and plenty of water for the dog. Then we walked over to Juárez just to see it, before the long drive across Texas. (As a popular postcard says, "The sun is riz, the sun is set, and we ain't out of Texas yet.")

We were strolling down the streets of Juárez, just walking around looking at the sleazy honky-tonk joints that hug the border, when my wife said, "Why don't we go into this one?" She'd never been in a strip club before. Inside were Formica tables lined up theaterlike in front of a stage. The place was all but empty; it was still early in the afternoon. We sat down and ordered a couple of beers, asking for Carta Blanca. "Okay," nodded the waiter. He disappeared into a back room and returned with a couple of bottles of beer with labels identical in design to the Carta Blanca trademark. Except they said Carta Cruz. It tasted terrible, watery. He charged us top dollar, which we paid because the floor show was included.

We nursed the beers, waiting. Finally the waiter climbed up on the stage and announced, "And now," dramatic pause, "the world famous Miss Lola Brigetta!" From out of the wing, stage left, Miss Lola slouched out onto the boards. She was wearing a green-sequined dress that looked a little worn, as did she.

On the stage, perched on a stool, was an old portable record player. Wires trailed across the floor to speakers set up on the edge of the stage, facing the audience. Miss Lola turned on the record player, plopped the needle onto the spinning vinyl, and began walking around the stage, more or less in time to the burlesque music. She made it abundantly clear that she was not just disinterested but utterly bored. Quickly she claimed center stage and began unzipping her dress, not as a stripper but as if she were getting ready for bed and no one was watching. Underneath were her bra and panties. The music bumped and ground. She pranced around in her underwear. Then she took off her bra and dropped it on the stage next to her dress. She meandered around some more in her pasties and panties, stopped, and looked at her watch. She called off into the wings what we guessed must have been a message to the manager, something like, "I've been out here long enough, okay?" He must have said okay, because she quickly pulled off the panties, giving us a look at her thong while she tapped her foot waiting for the record to end. Then she picked up her clothes and walked off the stage. The whole affair lasted the amount of time it takes to smoke a cigarette.

More than fifty thousand cars, trucks, and buses roll through the main crossing point between Tijuana and San Diego every day. The Homeland Security Department admits it stops and searches only about a thousand of them. Because of these odds, plenty of migrants take the gamble and come north through the official crossing point, hidden casually under sleeping bags and baggage or carefully stashed in secret compartments.

This type of human smuggling is catching the fancy of freelance Anglo *coyotes*, students, and other cash-strapped San Diegans who are discovering that a quick trip over the border and back can earn them at least several hundred tax-free dollars or more. And the risks are minimal. Prosecutors admit that they rarely pursue these ad hoc smugglers if their human cargo is not mistreated and if they are not dealing with more than a few migrants.

"The number of cases exceeds the available resources in the criminal justice system," is how the San Diego director of the Bureau of Customs and Border Protection, Adele Fasano, puts it. "We prioritize and prosecute the most egregious ones."[4]

These Gringo *coyotes*, often high school students, don't necessarily need to arrange for their cargo in advance. Savvy Mexicans solicit the Gringos where they're frolicking, at Tijuana bars and dance clubs.

3

ON GUARD

IN 1993 the U.S. government imposed what it called Operation Gatekeeper along the border at San Diego. A high gash of concrete replaced ad hoc and sometimes minimal fencing while the Border Patrol expanded with new hires. But Operation Gatekeeper did not keep Mexicans out of the United States, it simply pushed them from the urban crossing point at Tijuana east to the rural deserts of California and Arizona. The Immigration and Naturalization Service claimed it was not surprised that the migrants moved to the more dangerous deserts and continued to cross. "Our national strategy calls for shutting down the San Diego sector first, maintaining control there, then controlling the Tucson and South Texas corridors," explained INS spokeswoman Virginia Kice. "We recognize that traffic will increase in other sectors, but we need to control the major corridors first."[1] It was a failed policy. Traffic across the border only grew, with deadly results.

In the first few years of Operation Gatekeeper, and the similar Operation Hold the Line at El Paso, the number of Mexicans who died en route north increased markedly. The University of Houston Center for Immigration Research, citing what it called conservative estimates, reported that well over a thousand undocumented immigrants died trying to cross the border from 1993 to 1996. "For every body found there is certainly one that isn't," said the center's co-director, Nestor Rodriguez.[2]

"It's a shocking number of deaths," was the response from Roberto Martinez, director of the U.S.-Mexico Border Project for the American

Friends Service Committee. "It sets us back on the human rights issue. It can't be ignored by the governments on both sides of the border."[3] Yet in the years since, the border has remained heavily fortified at San Diego and other urban centers, and the death toll in the deserts keeps climbing. By 2003 the official body count was well over two thousand, with the wilds of the desert undoubtedly providing the resting place for unclaimed and uncounted more.

In 2001 a report by the U.S. General Accounting Office had already condemned the so-called Southwest Border Strategy, the name used by the Border Patrol for its scheme to dissuade illegal crossings by hardening urban ports of entry. By that time the Border Patrol had doubled its agent roster over a period of some seven years and had seen its annual budget quadruple to well over $6 billion. The result? "The primary discernible effect," stated the GAO, a "shifting of the illegal alien traffic."[4] And the deaths of more than two thousand migrants.

The Southwest Border Strategy was the brainchild of El Paso Representative Silvestre Reyes. Reyes holds unique credentials for his job. He is the only member of Congress with working experience as a Border Patrolman. He retired after twenty-six years with the Immigration and Naturalization Service, thirteen of them as Border Patrol chief in Texas. "The chaos of illegal immigration, uncontrolled and unaddressed, as it existed before I implemented Hold the Line in El Paso, was unacceptable," Reyes testified. "It was unacceptable to the officers and it was unacceptable to the community." Even as the deaths mounted in the deserts far from El Paso, Reyes expressed pride and confidence in the strategy. "I have firsthand knowledge of not only the difficulties and struggles we face on the border, but also of the success we have had with initiatives such as Operation Hold the Line, Operation Gatekeeper, and Operation Safeguard. While our Border Patrol has made progress, we all agree that we have a long way to go before we establish control of our 2,000-mile border with Mexico."[5]

The Border Patrol requires that its agents speak fluent Spanish. That prerequisite is at least partially responsible for the fact that more than a third of the agents are Latino. Some were born in Mexico and became U.S.

citizens; some were born in the United States and have lived in Mexico. Others have parents or grandparents who came north illegally. The veteran agent Marco Ramirez was raised in Mexico but says he does not let his heritage interfere with his work. "The way I see it," he explains, "you carry the badge in one hand, and in the other hand you carry your heart."[6]

Immigration invaded presidential politics during the 1996 campaign, with both political parties inciting fear. First Bob Dole blanketed television with ads accusing Bill Clinton of being soft on illegal immigrants. The pictures accompanying the aggressive narration were of migrants clandestinely crossing into California. Clinton was on the air in retaliation with pictures of a brown-skinned man handcuffed by the Border Patrol, inflammatory images that were punctuated by text claiming a 40 percent increase in Border Patrol ranks during Clinton's first term, along with record numbers of deportees.[7]

More Border Patrolmen on the frontier, of course, resulted in more encounters with Mexicans trying to cross into the United States. Over a weekend in late September 1998, Border Patrol agents twice reacted with guns to what they said were threats from Mexicans armed with rocks who refused orders to stop. Agents shot both migrants dead. The official Border Patrol explanation was terse, impersonal, and clinical: "Fearing for his life, [the agent] brings out the weapon and shoots this person, striking the person in the torso area," said Border Patrol spokeswoman Gloria Chavez about one of the shootings. Her colleague, Border Patrol spokesman Mario Villarreal, said about the other, "The agent ordered him to drop the rock and stop. [The man] went on in an aggressive manner. The agent discharged his service firearm in self-defense, striking the individual in the torso."[8]

"Something is going wrong," was the response of the Mexican consul general in San Diego, Luis Herrera-Lasso, who explained that rock throwing was commonplace along the border and that the Border Patrol need not use deadly force to combat it.[9]

In 1989 the U.S. government sent regular army troops to the Mexican border to fight drug traffickers. On July 30, 1997, it suspended these border operations, two months after a Marine corporal shot and killed eighteen-year-old Esequiel Hernandez, Jr., as the high school student was herding goats near his hometown of Redford, Texas.

Redford, understandably, was shocked.

"The only thing we know is that a good kid is dead who shouldn't be," said Hernandez's English teacher Kevin Stahnke immediately after the killing.[10]

The teacher and the rest of Redford—the population in 1997 was 107—soon learned that Esequiel was herding his family's goats down near the Rio Grande, as usual, on the afternoon he was killed. He was carrying his grandfather's 1910 rifle, as usual, to protect the goats from wild dogs.[11] He apparently shot a few rounds in the direction of brown shapes moving near his goats.

Those shapes were four Marines, covered in brush for camouflage, their faces blackened. They were deployed on the border for surveillance duty, assigned to track suspected drug smugglers and report on the traffickers' whereabouts to the Border Patrol. These Marines were a unit of something called Joint Task Force Six, a federal agency set up to coordinate operations between the military and the Border Patrol. The U.S. military is proscribed by law from performing domestic police work, a prohibition established in 1878 with the passage of the Posse Comitatus Act. But in 1981 federal law was changed to allow for *cooperation* between the military and civilian police, specifically for the purpose of stopping drugs at the border.

Joint Task Force Six, known as JTF-6, was the work of then Secretary of Defense Dick Cheney, who—along with then Joint Chiefs of Staff chairman Colin Powell—wanted to militarize the border as part of the so-called War on Drugs. Part of their strategy was to deploy the Marines without informing local townspeople. Since Esequiel and the rest of Redford were not informed of the patrol, they also could not know the orders for the Marines' tour in their neighborhood. Unlike domestic police, the Marines were not to identify themselves. They were not to fire warning shots. And if they felt threatened, they were expected to shoot to kill.[12] These were their "rules of engagement." As the months passed following young Esequiel's death, that term, "rules of engagement," infuriated the citizens of Redford.

"What are these 'rules of engagement?'" questioned a neighbor of the Hernandez family, Diana Valenzuela. "We had no idea we were being engaged in the first place. I was amazed when I heard that the military was walking around the hills in our backyard."

Another Redford schoolteacher, Leonel Ceniceros, agreed. "It seems crazy to me now that they were even here. When you think about it, these are young Marines brought in here from out of state. They've probably been told there are drug dealers all over the place, you're in enemy territory, protect yourself. But the result is, this good young man is dead."[13]

"They say they are trained to kill," Esequiel Hernandez's older brother said about the Marines. "They should kill in war, not in towns."

The Marines essentially said the same thing in their initial official response to the killing. Marine Col. Thomas Kelley told a news conference, "If you reach the point where you fire for fear of your lives, then you usually fire to kill."

After Hernandez fired his grandfather's old rifle, the Marines radioed to their Border Patrol associates that they were the targets of his shots. They tracked Hernandez and say he again raised his rifle and aimed at them. That's when twenty-two-year-old Corp. Clemente Bañuelos fired a single round from his M-16 and saw Hernandez fall. The Border Patrol recovered his body over twenty minutes later. The Marines did not try to save his life after he was shot; their orders did not require such follow-up. According to the autopsy, Hernandez bled to death.

"These people had no right to be here," said retired Episcopal priest Melvin La Follete about the Marines. A friend of the Hernandez family, La Follete organized Redford citizens to protest the militarization of their border town. "The Marines left their observation post, they stalked him, they came onto private property. And then they killed him. We were going blithely about our business, not knowing that Congress had handed away the civil rights of people on the border."

Eventually the Hernandez family received $1.9 million dollars from the federal government in compensation for the loss of Esequiel. In return, the government admitted no fault.

"This was a tragedy, not a criminal act," said Jack Zimmermann, a lawyer for the shooter, Corporal Bañuelos. But the Texas Rangers were not convinced. After a review of the record, Ranger Sgt. David Duncan said, "The federal government came in and stifled the investigation. It's really depressing."

Esequiel Hernandez, Jr., dreamed of a career in law enforcement. On his bedroom wall hung a U.S. Marine Corps recruiting poster.

Months before Hernandez was killed, the JTF-6 troops had reported their first Mexican casualty. A Green Beret veteran on duty east of Brownsville, Texas, took aim at a figure climbing out of the Rio Grande. Eleven shots later Cesario Vásquez, en route to Houston to look for a job, was dying.

As Mexicans continued to die along the border from attacks by the U.S. military and the Border Patrol, at the hands of bandits and cheating *coyotes*, and from the extreme heat and cold of the desert, the United States continued its efforts to slow the flow of migrants. In 1998 the Arizona border became the path into the United States with the greatest number of illegal crossings, according to the Border Patrol, outstripping Tijuana where extensive patrols and the wall convinced migrants that the Arizona desert was a better risk. The next year the Border Patrol caught nearly half a million intruders in Arizona, a doubling of their caseload in just five years.[14] By the year 2000 the radical wall along the Tijuana–San Diego line was replicated in the Arizona desert at Douglas, across from Agua Prieta. But five miles of floodlights and cameras, sheet metal and iron were able only to complicate the crossing and make it more expensive and dangerous for illicit travelers, pushing them away from the urbanized Douglas–Agua Prieta twin cities and into the unforgiving wilds of the desert.

Agua Prieta *presidente municipal* Daniel Fierros could see from the changes in his city how futile the Southwest Border Strategy and its new strip of wall in the desert north of his town were to U.S. goals of securing the border. "People who didn't have income rent their houses," he said about the economic boom that new migrants brought to his part of the border. "People sell fast food and things to cook with. Taxis get more business. And the *coyotes* do very well. We don't condone it, but it's a business as lucrative as drug trafficking, without the risks."[15] By 2000 hundreds of guest houses—just homes with rooms to rent—were operating in Agua Prieta, catering to border crossers waiting for the right moment to head north.[16]

In 1994 there were fifty-eight Border Patrol agents working out of the Douglas station. By 2000 their ranks had soared toward six hundred. And still the migrant trail was filled with Mexicans on the move.

The people-smuggling business thrived as the border became harder to cross. *Coyotes* raised their prices for a guided crossing; they fought with one another for the lucrative human cargo. Warfare between smuggling syndicates spread from Mexico and the border farther north into U.S. cities. More expensive and sophisticated smugglers promised to get migrants far from the border into safe houses where they could rest and make plans before disappearing into American crowds. Again the U.S. government responded with force, doubling the number of immigration agents in Phoenix, for example, to one hundred. "We're dealing with ruthless individuals who view human life as nothing more than cargo for profit," said Michael Garcia, acting assistant secretary for the Bureau of Immigration and Customs Enforcement.[17] "Smuggling-related violence in the Phoenix area has reached epidemic proportions."

Phoenix police reported instances of traffickers kidnapping migrants from rivals and holding them for ransom. Day laborer Anna Roblero said she was one of those kidnap victims when she arrived in Phoenix after paying a *coyote* $400 for passage across the border. "We walked for three days and three nights through the desert," she told National Public Radio during an interview on a Phoenix street. "When we got across the desert, the smugglers told us to wait for some men to pick us up, but they never came. We didn't know where we were." Different smugglers then took custody of the group and demanded more money. Anna said she called a cousin, who was able to raise the money, but it took over a week, a week she spent confined in a house. "I just cried and cried. I thought I was never going to see my kids again. They had guns, and I thought they were going to kill us. Thank God my cousin came and gave them the money."[18]

Since a conviction for people-smuggling usually results in a much less severe jail sentence than a conviction for drug smuggling, law-enforcement authorities are convinced that experienced criminals from the drug trade saw a business opportunity with human cargo and moved into trafficking in human beings.

4

DEATH ALONG
FOR THE RIDE

TEXAS SUMMERS BAKE. I know; when we lived in a stuffy Dallas bungalow, my wife and I periodically treated ourselves to relief from the heat and humidity by spending time in the company car. We'd just sit in the driveway, air conditioner cranked up high, listen to the radio, and cool off.

On a hot May 13, 2003, well before summer, down by the Mexico border near Harlingen, smugglers guided as many as a hundred immigrants into a freight trailer. They had just crossed the border illegally, wading across the Rio Grande as so many millions of Mexicans and others had done before that hot night. The doors to the long van were shut, and the truck headed north through the night toward its destination, Houston.

Not three hours later, just outside Victoria at a Harris County gas station, the driver stopped his rig, opened the back doors of the trailer, and abandoned it and its devastated cargo.[1] Nineteen of his hundred or so passengers were dead or dying, killed by heat stroke and dehydration, greed and incompetence, desperation for a better life, and unenforceable U.S. immigration laws. One of the dead was a five-year-old Mexican boy.

"No sheriff likes to be called at two o'clock in the morning to be told he has multiple deceased people in his community," Sheriff Mike Ratcliff says when he recalls that miserable night.

"Upon arrival at the location we discovered there were multiple victims on the ground. Then, of course, we had to deal with the victims who had dissipated into the woodlands surrounding the area—snake-infested terrain that we had to worry about." Sheriff Ratcliff tends to speak in official-sounding jargon, with words such as "dissipated" and "co-victims." But after just a few minutes talking with him about this worst case of human smuggling in American history, his compassion is obvious.

"We had some witnesses, co-victims, if you will, who described the number of people in the vehicle. We could estimate that as many as sixty to ninety people were on the ground in our community. We had to deal with that problem as well."

While the Bureau of Customs and Immigration Enforcement and its special ICE* team raced to Victoria to take over the federalized investigation, Ratcliff's detectives hunted down the truck driver, Tyrone Powers, finding him a few hours after he ran from the tragedy.

The sheriff is still shaken six months later when he retells the story of that dreadful night. His deputies called him to come quickly, which was no problem. His home is just a mile and a half from the crime scene. He feels no mercy for the ring of smugglers and their driver.

"It's difficult for me as a twenty-six-year veteran of law enforcement to consider that a person doesn't know the cargo in his van," he says about Powers's initial defense tactic. "Human cargo is unacceptable. The thought of human beings trapped, encapsulated in that trailer and brought to our country, or taken anywhere in hundred-degree weather is totally . . ." His voice trails off for a few seconds. "Well, it's just unacceptable."

What's the correct penalty for such a crime?

"Should a person be put to death for the death of nineteen people?" he considers the question. "I would tell you in my estimation, if they did it one time, they could do it again, because greed seemed to premise everything. If greed allowed them to do it that one time to nineteen people, and that little boy, then the opportunity for them to do it again would not be changed by anything but death."

*ICE is the Immigration and Customs Enforcement division of the Homeland Security Department.

Driver Powers finally did open the trailer door. Was that an act of humanity? No, says the sheriff, it was a result of stupidity. "His stupidity ran out when his human resources came into play and he decided to buy water for some of the victims and he opened the doors to the trailer. That was when stupidity was overcome by human nature. But the one factor to be considered is that if he did this one time, there is the potential that he could do this again. And the world can't stand that loss of life. Our community will not overcome that tragedy. We are now the site of the most tragic immigrant loss of lives in our nation's history."

Oil and cattle made Victoria famous during its booming past. Back in the 1930s ranchers around Victoria began discovering oil and natural gas under their rangeland. By the 1950s Victoria boasted more millionaires per capita than any other American city. Today memories of those times are enhanced by the stately Victorian homes still scattered throughout the city. The sheriff's office is in the heart of the old downtown, a modern concrete and glass building just off the old city square. Sheriff Ratcliff clearly wishes a truckload of dead immigrants had not replaced oil and cattle as his city's reason for notoriety.

"As sheriff of the county, I will do whatever I can to ensure that our community and our state and our nation never have to undergo that type of tragedy again. We are a caring people. We love fellow human beings. If they come to the country illegally, we will deal with them under the appropriate law."

But Ratcliff is convinced the laws should be changed, and changed fast. "We need to come up with laws that would help these people. We need to create the legal method for people to enter our country to work or go to school or do other things that they feel they need to do to help their families and themselves."

The sheriff is in his forties. He's a mix of Irish, English, and Hispanic ancestry, nicely matching the population he serves. He projects the confident manner of a public servant who wants to see justice and a safer, more orderly world.

Inside that trailer coffin, suffocating with his brother, was Guillermo Cabrera from Veracruz, Mexico. He was on his way to the rolling hills of south central Kentucky, promised work on a dairy farm.

"The heat started really by nine," he says about the ride north. "By eleven, twelve you can really feel it. Hot. Some people were already fainted, six or seven. Some friends started to faint. Very strong heat, like in hell, an inferno."

Cabrera and I are sitting at a plastic table in what he calls *la tiendita*, the little store, Paul's Minute Market at the Key Stop gas station in Temple Hill, Kentucky. Cabrera survived the inferno; his brother died.

"We were both there, but I never saw my brother during the whole crisis. I never saw him again. I couldn't find him. Where was he? When they opened the door, there were a lot of people lying on the floor of the trailer because it was really hot inside, very hot. I do not know how I got out of there; many of us have no idea how we got out of there. We realized that we were alive because God is great."

Guillermo Cabrera's eyes tear. He looks away but continues his story.

"Seven days later I learned that my brother had died. I was in the hospital. I was there for four days, almost dying. I was really sick. I didn't know what was going on. Everything was erased."

Cabrera is wearing a baseball cap announcing "Branson, Mo. The Ozarks." His T-shirt is more specific: it's a rendition of the Liberty Bell featuring the words, "America" and "Let Freedom Ring." He drove to the Minute Market in an old faded red Ford Ranger pickup truck. We met at seven in the morning. Three old-timers were nursing their coffee behind a sign in the window announcing, "We sell and recommend Coon Hunter's Pride."

"Is it okay to talk here?" I asked him quietly in Spanish, not knowing his immigration status.

He assured me it would be no problem as he casually greeted the regulars. Cabrera is one of the lucky ones. Not only did he survive the inferno, the U.S. government rewarded his trauma by granting him the legal right to stay north of the border.

Whose fault was the disaster? I ask him.

"Well, you pay for them to bring you here safe and alive," he says about the smugglers. "But they don't know how you are going to arrive. If they are going to put you into a trailer, they should give you fresh air. Since everything is closed, you don't know what is going to happen in there."

He soon knew something was very wrong. "With all the heat, your head is not working well. Many things start going on in your head. I thought of God, my family, everybody. Many of us survived. We tried to take apart a piece of the wooden door. My brother was one of those who were taking apart the door, because he was really desperate. His hands were all destroyed from that."

Once the doors opened, Cabrera climbed over dead bodies to the fresh air. "I walked over many people and got down. And then I just collapsed. The ambulance came and they took me to the hospital. I was there for four days, and then they took me to jail for six days. They worked on the permits to allow us to stay in this country legally. They gave me one of those after the accident."

I suggested a solution so that others need not fear sharing his fate in the future: an open border between the two countries so that workers could travel north freely. His answer surprised me.

"No, that would not be possible. All of Mexico would be here."

Particularly grating for Sheriff Ratcliff is that the trailer tragedy scarcely put a dent in the abuse of migrants on the road. "Nineteen people perished on May 14, and on May 15 eighteen people were stopped approximately ten miles north of that point, and of those eighteen people who had stopped at a roadside park, two had to be carried into a hospital—just two days later! They were compacted into a trailer that could not sustain them. They were taken to a local hospital and kept overnight for dehydration."

Washington Post reporters Kevin Sullivan and Mary Jordan noted that in the same week as the trailer tragedy, at least eleven other people died trying to cross the border—without the headlines accorded to the trailer deaths, because the eleven others were part of the now-routine tally of lost lives on the frontier. Sullivan and Jordan recorded drownings in the Rio Grande and heat exhaustion in the deserts of Texas and Arizona, deaths that occurred one or two at a time, quietly, without notice.[2]

Sheriff Ratcliff expresses no patience with the standard anti-immigrant lines. "The borders are being screened for drugs and weapons. Certainly I want our country rid of drugs and weapons. But look at what's going on, adverse to what our nation is all about. To me, optimum consideration should be given to the presence of human beings in those very cargo vehicles that travel our nation daily. When we lose sight of that, we lose sight of a lot of very important matters. I thought about it several times that day in our command center. I think the intensity of what is perceived as a threat really doesn't exist." He says it is an illusion that Mexicans take jobs and opportunities from U.S. citizens. He is disgusted with the argument that immigrants abuse the social services available in the United States. "And who wouldn't want to? That's my answer. Who wouldn't want to come to the most wonderful country in the world? Can you blame them?"

Change the laws, insists the sheriff, to encourage migrants to pay taxes. Of course, migrants without papers already pay plenty of taxes. They pay sales tax. They pay indirect property tax when they pay rent. Those who use fake Social Security numbers lose salary to money withheld that they never collect, money that helps fund the overall Social Security system from which legal residents profit. It's difficult for the undocumented to use Medicare and other services both because of the registration process and their fear of discovery of their illegal status.

Opportunity is what America is all about, says the sheriff, again invoking the memory of the lost five-year-old boy. "What would he have done in our country? Who could he have become? These people came to our country looking for opportunity. You can talk about the Statue of Liberty and what it represents all day long, and say that it's a hill of beans. But it's true! These people come into our country looking for exactly that. One word. Opportunity."

The law needs to be changed, says the sheriff, to reflect reality. "Use history. Approach the current day with what America lives upon and should: its own history. Examine what we have done in the past. Look at and give weight to the open arms of the east. Carry the Statue of Liberty to the borders of Mexico and Canada and create laws that identify with what the French gave to America. You can't open the doors to a country just by etching in stone the words that welcome you. You have to create law that represents what's etched in stone."

And Mexico, he says, shares the responsibility. "We need to eliminate human cargo. We need to ensure this does not happen again. President Fox needs to educate his folks as to what is legal. These people come to our country not knowing what is appropriate and what is not. And they pay $2,000 for a ride in a conveyance that cattle wouldn't be carried in. Because they don't know any better. If we welcome people to our country, let's do so legally and let's make sure they know how to get to our country legally. Two thousand dollars would have bought somebody a Green Card all the way in. But they don't know that."

5

A LEGAL VIEW

AS THE CASE against the Victoria smugglers developed, Texas-based immigration lawyer Barbara Hines was surprised to find herself representing one of the migrants who was packed into the truck trailer that headed north with a load of human cargo just the day after the Victoria disaster. Hines had gone to law school specifically motivated to work for social justice. After passing the bar in the mid-1970s, she had expected to join the cadre of lawyers inspired by the women's liberation movement and engage in women's rights issues. She remembers drifting into immigration law by chance.

"I showed up at a legal aid office in 1975 and someone said, 'Do you speak Spanish?' and they handed me twenty immigration cases. At the time there were no immigration courses. Very few people were practicing immigration law, and people used to say, 'You're a *what* kind of lawyer? What in the world do immigration lawyers do?'"

It turns out that immigration lawyers fall into two basic categories: those who help people coming to the United States legally, and those who help people already in the United States who are facing problems with the authorities. It's the latter type of law that Barbara Hines practices, a specialty known as family-based immigration and deportation law. Her clients are trying to legalize their status in the United States. They're seeking work permits, temporary visas, or the famous Green Card—the ticket to legal permanent residency, and a first step toward U.S. citizenship. Often she deals with crises. She represents Green Card holders facing deportation for a crime or a bureaucratic misstep. And she works with asylum seekers, those who escape to the United States fearing persecution at home.

Over her thirty years of practice, she has seen greater enforcement of increasingly restrictive immigration laws. "In an ironic way, it's reduced our work because there's so little we can do for people."

In addition to her private immigration law practice, Barbara Hines teaches law at the University of Texas in Austin where she is director of the Immigration Clinic. The clinic represents clients without funds and otherwise without access to legal representation. Work at the clinic concentrates on the needs of immigrants facing deportation and those seeking political asylum. Clients include battered immigrant women.

"I think it's really all about the haves and the have-nots," she says about migration into the United States. "I had an immigration judge come to my class and say, 'You know, if I were in the same situation as most of these people, I'd come too.' If you're starving, or even if you're in search of a better life, why wouldn't you move? It's the historical phenomenon of migration. Why do people migrate? They migrate because they want something better. People don't voluntarily leave their home surroundings unless there is a push factor."

Airplanes and the internet only make the global population more mobile. "Twenty years ago the only people who could get to the United States were the Mexicans and the stowaways and the people who could get tourist visas, because how were you going to get to the United States from China? Now, because of more sophisticated smugglers, people from China can get on a boat, and they can beach the boat in Mexico and come up the exact same way the Mexicans have come for years. People are more aware that you might be able to get here from Eastern Europe and China. You have to pay a lot of money, but now somebody can get you here."

Hines and her students visit Texas lockups near Austin where undocumented migrants are held during deportation proceedings. They look for prisoners who might benefit from legal representation, and they offer their services. It's a scattershot approach to social work, looking for the mostly destitute migrants picked up by the Border Patrol and other law-enforcement agencies. But it's better than nothing in a judicial system packed with potential clients where only a few independent lawyers are willing to represent them pro bono.

"If people happened to be brought in that day and their luck was good, they would get us as their lawyers," Hines says about her periodic visits to jails and prisons. "Just by chance we happened to find someone who was on that truck trailer. What was really shocking to me was that it was discovered just after the one in Victoria. The second one was called Operation Pick Axe by investigators. I said to my client, 'Didn't you hear about the other truck before you left? How could you have gotten on this truck?' My client told me [one of the smugglers] said, 'Don't worry. Here's a pick axe. If there are any problems, just bang on the cab and I'll hear you.' That's why investigators named it Operation Pick Axe." Hines's client, intent on finding work north of the border, climbed aboard. "It's very sobering to me to think about how desperate people are."

Over the last thirty years Hines has watched as people-smuggling along the Mexican border has become big business and a sophisticated operation. Much of it used to be informal. An experienced border crosser would help his friends and family cross to *El Norte* and maybe take some money for his trouble. When others in his village heard of the successful trip, they'd ask for help and offer to pay him a fee. Today the smuggling is professional and expensive. "All of a sudden it got taken over by the cartels, the gangs. In Arizona immigrants are being held hostage between warring smuggling gangs. Fifteen years ago that was unheard of. It's like drug wars, trafficking in persons, and it's very, very lucrative. That's the reason it's moved into boxcars and trucks. There's just so much more human smuggling on a much larger scale going on in the last ten years. There's just been a really notable shift in the way people come. It used to be you just paid some little smuggler right at the border a couple hundred bucks. But it's not like that anymore."

Hines is working to get her trailer victim legal status in the United States based on the suffering he experienced crossing the border and then being herded into another potential death truck. The U.S. government does allow for sanctuary as a humanitarian gesture when a border crosser suffers extreme trauma en route. License to stay in the United States is also offered when prosecutors feel confident that the migrant can provide valuable testimony against traffickers. Beginning in 2002, two new types of visas were established to help such victims, T and U visas. T visas are for victims of inhumane trafficking. They're offered to those migrants forced into prostitution and indentured servitude. U visas are offered to other crime victims. Those who hold T and U visas are allowed to stay in the United States for three years, and work.

Working with undocumented migrants, teaching law, living along the extended border—all add to Barbara Hines's conviction that the current immigration laws are a travesty. "Unless we're going to put up the Berlin Wall, and as long as people are starving and can't feed their kids and want a better life, people are going to keep coming. All these really, really strict immigration laws do is create a population of more and more undocumented people. One of the ironic things about September 11th is that there is a much stronger argument now to say, 'Why would you want this entire population that's underground? Isn't the idea that we're supposed to know who's here so we can be looking for the real terrorists?' The policy is a failure. Increased enforcement on the border hasn't stopped the flow. All it's done is made the price much higher, because what happens now is that immigrants are pushed out into the desert because of increased enforcement in the urban areas. So there's a greater risk to life—but it hasn't stopped people from coming."

Hines believes the United States must at least adopt a temporary worker program to cover the millions of undocumented laborers who come north. "We make you risk your life to get over here. You may die in the desert. But once you get here, we'd love to have you. That's what's so ridiculous about this policy. It's not that once you get across the desert nobody will hire you. People are dying to hire you. I don't think there's any workable solution unless we understand why people immigrate."

Obviously most people come north from Mexico for work. Until the 1986 immigration law was passed by Congress, it was not against the law to hire illegal immigrants. But after 1986 employers were subject to fines for failing to determine the legal status of their workers. That policy is a failure. Authorities cannot begin to check all places of employment, and workers are clever about obtaining false documents once they are safely north of the border. Barbara Hines says pressure from industry put a stop to initial attempts to enforce the new law targeting employers.

"There was a lot of political pressure," Hines says about INS raids in the early 1990s on the meatpacking industry in the Midwest. "The meat-packers and their senators and representatives put pressure on the government to stop doing this. They said, 'We need people. So leave us alone.' So the authorities have really backed off on employer sanctions." She says the raids, and the threat of them that exists as long as the employer sanctions law remains on the books, merely prompted a new industry. "It spawned an interest in fake documents. You just go to a flea market, and for fifteen dollars you buy your fake Green Card. An employer is not an immigration expert. He can't know whether this is a fake card or a real card. The only enforcement now is against employers who are also involved in the trafficking of people, where employers are not only hiring people but are involved in recruiting people illegally in Mexico."

Any improvement in the situation would please Barbara Hines, who doesn't favor one or the other of the many propositions for immigration reform that continue to percolate through Congress. "Obviously I would like the best bill possible. But I don't like to have to tell my clients, 'No, you cannot go to your father's funeral. No, you cannot go home to see your mother before she dies. . . . Well, you can go home—but you can't get back.' I'm sure my clients would be willing to have any temporary worker permit that would allow them to cross the border and not have to come back through the desert or the river.

"Right now you're spending all your resources patrolling the borders for most people who have absolutely nothing to do with terrorism. Sometimes I feel sorry for this agency," she says about the Homeland Security Department and their impossible task of securing the border. "Although I have spent most of my life suing this agency, I kind of feel sorry for them."

6

WHAT IS A

BORDER?

GET UP in the morning and stumble to the bathroom. There is probably a door on that bathroom. Do you close it? That probably depends on
who is in the house with you. If you've been sleeping with a friend or a
lover, or just sharing a bed for convenience, you've faced a border even
before the bathroom. "Get back on your side of the bed," you may have
mumbled if your companion disturbed your sleep. Or, "You've got all
the covers!"

We are surrounded by borders. They provide us with security and
comfort, limits and definitions.

Once in the bathroom, perhaps you decide to close the door. You
might want some privacy while you go about your morning routine. Or
maybe you don't want to disturb your companion with the noise you
make, so closing the door creates a sound barrier. If the door is equipped
with a lock, you face another decision.

There are plenty of other borders in your home. "Stay out of my
room," you may instruct your kids. Perhaps you've got some secrets in
the dresser, or you just don't want them sitting on your clean sheets with
their dirty jeans. The kids may want to keep you out of their rooms too.
House rules create borders without walls and doors. You may not allow
food in the living room, or you may forbid roller skates on the rugs. A
particularly unruly friend of one of your kids might be barred from

spending the night in the family home, or even forbidden from visiting under any circumstances.

Of course if your own child is a tad mischievous, he may let that blacklisted friend in through his bedroom window in the middle of the night and shove him out at dawn. You might never know that the troublemaker was in your house. And while you're at work, someone might be watching TV in the living room, eating a peanut butter and grape jelly sandwich, in violation of your house rules. As long as there are no crumbs on the floor, or purple stains on the carpet, you might never know it was transformed into an after-school snack room.

Is there a fence around your house? If so, why is it there? Perhaps it keeps your dog in your yard. Perhaps it keeps other dogs out of your yard. Maybe you built it just to define the border of your property, to give you a sense of what is yours and how far into the distance that legal ownership extends. Or your fence may block a view you don't want to look at: the neighbors' turquoise house, or their '67 Dodge Charger up on blocks. Your fence may provide a sequestered playground for your children, a safety zone from which they can't escape if they're still toddlers.

Is there a lock on your gate? Is there a lock on your front door? If you live in a metropolis, there are probably several different types of locks on your door—a spring lock, a couple of deadbolts, and a chain to allow for some restricted communication or exchange of goods without actual entry. This crucial border between your sanctuary and the rest of the world may be equipped with a peephole to check on the identity of visitors, along with all the locks installed, in an attempt to ensure that no one violates your person or property. Apartments in rough neighborhoods are now often equipped with a steel bar that fits into a hole in the floor and braces against the front door, creating an obstacle to those who, frustrated by the locks, may attempt to break down the door and cross the border— uninvited—into your house.

Where else are there borders—protected and unprotected—in your daily routine? One fellow I know cites what he calls "the five-second rule" when he drops food on the floor. As long as he picks it up within five seconds, he considers it fit to eat. An old married friend of mine long ago explained away his girl friends with his arbitrary hundred-mile border from home. As long as the locale of his dalliances exceeded that self-imposed limit, he believed he was doing his marriage no damage.

If you drive to work or school in your own car, you create a rolling castle with that car, its borders the obvious and rigid exterior steel panels of the automobile. But unlike your house, you can't hide very well in your car. The borders you count on for protection and privacy do not include visual borders. On the contrary, especially as the driver, you are highly visible to an enormous number of mostly anonymous other people. You may count on the steel and glass to protect you from this horde. In worrisome neighborhoods, you probably hope the engine doesn't fail and that you don't run out of gas, forcing you to abandon your car and cross its border into a world you were expecting just to pass through. Perhaps you carry a cell phone to summon help in the event that someone attempts to breach the borders of your movable container. Carjackings are not common; the physical barrier of the automobile door rarely is molested. We drive through the streets with the windows down, enjoying the breeze, expecting that no one will reach into the car at a stoplight and throttle us. Yet it's common to flick the door locks for an extra sense of security that the border into our car is secure.

At work and at school there are more borders. Metal detectors at the doors. Identity cards to allow passage past guards into buildings. Codes to punch into door-lock keypads. Old-fashioned keys to offices. Areas off limits to the unauthorized. Even executive washrooms. Cops and guards and closed-circuit televsion cameras patrol these borders.

Many of these borders at home and at work need no enforcers. As a society we accept each other's signals and respect and obey them. Few of us want to barge into a bathroom and disturb a friend or relative engaged in behavior he or she would prefer to keep private. We don't want to participate, nor do we want to violate the established border. We appreciate the signpost of the closed door, just as the housekeeper in a hotel walks on past the rooms where a Do Not Disturb sign is hanging.

Public transport is a maze of borders. Most buses, streetcars, and subways require a payment to ride. Without paying the fare, you can't get on the bus. Or at least you're not supposed to get on the bus. The driver is usually the enforcer, demanding cash (exact change only, another barrier to entry) or a transfer, or a prepaid pass. Getting on via the back door may not be allowed. If a passenger attempts to ride without paying, the driver must decide whether to attempt to eject the freeloader. In today's short-fused society, such a challenge may seem to the driver too risky to bother with.

Buses, streetcars, and subways often operate on an honor system. You are expected to buy a valid ticket before you cross the border and get on the train. But it's not really an honor system. Random checks by guards encourage payment, because if you're caught with no ticket the fine is severe, and for some the very public embarrassment of being caught is humiliating.

These unpatrolled borders all around us—the unlocked bathroom door, the sanctity of the camera left on the car seat, the subway ride—usually are respected, their rules enforced by our ethics and honesty, our fear of the consequences if we violate them, and our continuing contract with a supposedly polite and civilized society.

We create borders to define our personal space, and we devise techniques to patrol and enforce them. How close do we stand to others in a line? Where do we keep our hands in a crowded subway car? Do we kiss or shake hands meeting someone? All these decisions mark borders.

San Diego Union reporter Sandra Dibble, who covers the U.S.-Mexico border beat for her paper, tells a personal border story that echoes my own childhood: how she and her brother fought for space in the backseat of the family car. I recall that my sister and I drew an imaginary line across the backseat of our family's 1957 Oldsmobile on long car trips. Sandra says of the Mexicans and Americans who live along the border, "We're stuck in the backseat of this car that someone else is driving, and we're annoying each other."

I arrive at Schipol Airport in Amsterdam and am intrigued to see the billboards not just at the airport but all over Holland, sultry ads for Peter Stuyvesant cigarettes. The graphics are dark and mysterious, featuring a big-busted woman showing off everything but her nipples as she stands half turned from a row of urinals. She's looking with a smirk into the middle distance, cigarette in hand. The headline announces, "There are no borders."

"Excuse me, can I have something to eat?" I watched as the bum asked a couple at a sidewalk café. "Some of the cheese maybe?"

Polite—not stumbling drunk, not drooling—he was an inoffensive bum. He dressed for the warm day in shorts and a shirt that looked clean enough.

The scrubbed couple had finished eating before he made his request. He had already made one pass by their table, slowly inspecting the possibilities, before he edged back toward them, interrupting their lazy Sunday morning. He saw the basket still filled with bread and the barely tasted jam waiting in a silver dish. There was plenty of butter, and on her plate she had ignored several tomato wedges, apple slices, a handful of cherries, and much of the main course: various cheeses and meats.

The couple had been murmuring at each other, shaded under the café's umbrella. The silence between their words was accompanied by languid, satiated looks. And she would run her hands through the perfectly cut bristle of hair on the back of his head. They would kiss and smile and kiss again. She wore a silver hoop earring in one ear and in the other a wire ornament that balanced horizontally and moved as if it were a mobile.

"No," she told the bum and dismissed him with her hand.

He moved off, and they prodded at the food they had forgotten until his intrusion. Another bite of cheese, a few cherries. They kissed some more.

But breakfast was over, and she pushed her plate away, still with cheese on it, just a minute or two after the bum made his request. She reached into her bag, pulled out a Gauloises Blondes, and lit it. He continued to pick at the leavings on his plate and stroked her hair a couple of times. They were distracted now. A cop paced slowly past the café. The traffic was noisy; brakes shrieked.

Why did she say no to the beggar? He was not disgusting, not stinking from drink or filth. But his was a dirty intrusion, with two or three days' beard, leaning over her varnished wooden table, leering over her breakfast, violating her border. Why should she have said yes?

They no longer talked much, and the kissing stopped. About ten minutes after the bum asked for the cheese, the waiter cleared their plates from the table. They paid their bill and headed into the summer Sunday.

Borders in the bed, the bedroom, the bathroom, the home. Borders around the yard or at the lobby door of the apartment building. Borders in the car or around your body in the bus and on the subway. Borders at the office and the school, at the restaurant keeping bums from the leftovers. All these personal borders lead to state-created and state-controlled borders. In some cases—prisons and East Germany come to mind—state borders are created to keep us from escaping. But most state borders are designed to keep others—the bums—away from us.

When the Chernobyl nuclear power plant in Ukraine spewed radiation, the prevailing winds blew the worst of it north into Belarus. There were no nuclear power plants in Belarus. Ivan Kenik, the Belarus government official in charge of dealing with the problems the incident caused, observed, "The Chernobyl disaster taught us there are no borders to the modern world."[1]

"A border," wrote Ambrose Bierce, "is an imaginary line between two nations separating the imaginary rights of one from the imaginary rights of the other."

7

FAILED

BARRIERS

I'M AT THE FOOT of La Rambla in Barcelona, circling the Mirador de Colón, the monument to Christopher Columbus. He stands on a column, high above a traffic circle at the old port, pointing out to sea. The monument was built in 1888 and displays the architectural flourishes of the era. Columbus is guarded at the base of his column by regal-looking lions, and the column is decorated with filigree, angels, and anchors. A band around it near the top announces Gloria Colón. The man himself is gigantic, pointing not west to the hemisphere he claimed for Spain but south, out to the Mediterranean Sea and Africa. Columbus sailed back to Barcelona on his first voyage to and from the New World, a land with no fixed borders until the European settlers who followed Columbus carved it into colonies. He arrived in 1493 and showed Ferdinand and Isabella the loot he had brought back from America: gold, spices, strange animals, and a sampling of the natives he caught and subjugated. "Good work," said the king and queen, who sent him off on two more trips to explore and settle, or plunder and conquer, depending on your point of view.

The pointing Columbus statue made me think of California artist Yolanda Lopez's poster of a Native American in an Aztec headdress pointing an accusing finger. The image is captioned, "Who's the illegal immigrant, pilgrim?"

Spain and Morocco are separated by ten miles of the Strait of Gibraltar and by their status as First and Third World countries. Desperate Moroccans and other Africans brave the waters of the Strait nightly, trying to smuggle themselves into Spain and the rest of the job-rich European Community. People-smugglers offer expensive and dangerous rides across in overcrowded and barely seaworthy boats. Those who don't drown en route may be seized by the Spanish Civil Guard. But enough migrants make it safely to shore to convince others desperate for a better life to take a chance. "You don't want to know what I went through to reach this city," said a young Moroccan who managed to get to Barcelona. "Do you know how many people die every day trying to cross the Strait? Why do we come here? We come because we want to work, to send money back home."[1]

Tunisians sail north and land illegally in Sicily. Albanians cross over to Bara in Italy. African immigrants complain of prejudice in a Europe where they often live as second-class citizens. Many Europeans consider the Africans and the culture they bring with them a threat. The story is replicated wherever a poor country is within reach of a rich one where cheap labor is needed. In today's world of efficient travel, that match can come from across the globe.

Dover, England, is an example. I was there in the summer of 2000, just after a truck filled with tomatoes arrived on a ferry from the Netherlands. Customs inspectors decided to check the cargo. They pulled open the rear doors and found bodies. The truck had been hired by smugglers to bring a load of Chinese into the United Kingdom. Behind the crates of tomatoes they found more dead, a total of fifty-eight asphyxiated in the refrigerator truck. The sole air vent had been closed for unknown reasons. Two of the migrants miraculously survived.

"Those two have been fortunate because as people are dying, there is that person's air to breathe," said Dover coroner Grahame Perrin, explaining their macabre good fortune. "Those two have been very lucky."[2]

I walked up the Folkestone Road from the docks where the death truck was opened, and stopped for a drink at a seedy pub called The Engineer. The jukebox was blasting in competition with the loud television.

The tables were messy with overflowing ashtrays and dirty beer glasses. It was late afternoon. A woman was feeding a slot machine while her boyfriend chatted with the barkeep. I sat outside, nursed a Guinness, and watched the street parade. White Englishmen and women were coming home from work, pouring out of buses. Darker people shared the neighborhood, many of them asylum seekers who had managed to get to the English shores and were waiting in Dover while their cases were adjudicated. Two were in a nearby phone box, studying official-looking papers and talking on the phone. A glazier was busy repairing the broken front plate-glass window of a kebab shop. Dover is another border city dealing with the push of immigration from south to north.

"We're not rednecks," Dover mayor Gordon Cowan found it necessary to announce after the *London Times* followed its reports of the Chinese immigrants' deaths with a story charging that Dover was filled with racists and bootleggers. The local paper *Express* responded with a picture-postcard photo of Dover Castle and the subheadline, "MAGNIFICENT!" In an interview with the mayor, he insisted, "Dover is a very pleasant, safe place in which to live, work and visit. We love our town and we are very proud of its national and international importance."[3]

I left The Engineer as the Beatles' "Michelle" blasted out of the jukebox, mixed with the equally loud strains of Middle Eastern music coming from the open window of an upstairs flat across Folkestone Road.

Come with me to Cairo, Egypt—not Cairo, Illinois, which is filling up with Mexican immigrants—but Cairo, Egypt, teeming with some seventeen million people in the greater Cairo region. No one even tries to keep a credible official count. Jammed streets, deafening traffic noise, perpetual horn honking. Dirty. Filthy. A devastated infrastructure: rusting, cracked, crumbling, broken, shattered. Most buildings and roads in desperate need of repair. I'm here working on a journalists' exchange program funded by the U.S. Agency for International Development. We're bringing Egyptian journalists to the United States for intensive training in American-style journalism.

It's the fall of 2003, two years after the September 11th attacks.

I hail a cab at my oasis at the Marriott Palace in Zamalik along the Nile. I jam myself into the tiny and ancient Fiat taxi that's been repainted so many times it appears the car body is made out of enamel, not metal. We head out to the fashionable suburb of Maazir. The USAID fortress is up a blocked road in Maazir, looming like a cross between a Hyatt Regency and a maximum-security prison. Behind the barriers, the U.S. bureaucracy labors. The Cairo mission dishes out half a billion dollars in aid to Egypt each year, more than to any other country in the world, save Israel.

I give up my passport, step through airportlike security, and make my way to a meeting with the administrators of the journalism training program. We have a problem. Only fifteen of the twenty-five students we selected to bring to the United States were granted visas by the U.S. government, and thirteen of the fifteen were women, creating an odd imbalance in the classroom. A few months earlier, when we submitted the twenty-five names for clearance, young and unmarried Muslim men were being flagged for detailed background checks by the American embassy in Cairo—on instructions from the State Department in Washington—and the lag time for visas was interminable for most of the men in our group while they were being investigated. Washington was trying to make sure that no terrorists were granted visas.

There was no such trouble for the women; all but one received a visa promptly. When the group—the thirteen women and two men—arrived at passport control at O'Hare airport in Chicago, the women all sallied through the gates with a cheery "Welcome to the United States" from immigration officers. The two men were pulled from the line, ushered away for mug shots and fingerprinting, questioning and extra paperwork.

Shortly after our students arrived in the United States, the Middle East was plagued with a series of suicide bombings perpetrated by women. "Don't expect it to be easy for the women either this time," a USAID staffer tells me about our second group. Since the September 11th attacks, she says, the rules are constantly changing as Washington scrambles, trying to figure out how to control U.S. borders. "Sometimes we issue visas in the morning and have to hold the passports because the rules change before the Egyptians come to pick them up in the afternoon."

Remember, according to most reports the September 11th hijackers all came to the United States legally, and only two overstayed their visas.

USAID's advice: invite 35 to 50 percent more journalists than we can accommodate for this next round, because that many probably will fail to secure approval. Imagine all the detailed work going on in Cairo regarding these fifty journalists, multiply that by all the exchange programs processed by this active USAID mission, add the rest of the USAID offices around the world, and factor in all the other foreigners seeking admission to the United States at consulates worldwide.

It is an extraordinary bureaucratic operation. And it is understandable. The U.S. government wants to control the country's borders and decide who enters. Yet because of the dysfunctional attempts at control on the U.S.-Mexico frontier, all of this effort overseas is of questionable value. The people who are screened out can simply go to Mexico and walk into the United States with all the farm workers and cooks, maids and mechanics. Many Middle Easterners could even pass as Mexicans, blending into the swarthy, dark-haired crowd pushing north.

If the United States really wants a secure post-9/11 border, fixing the U.S.-Mexico boundary is a much more constructive goal than denying male journalists with jobs and close family connections at home in Egypt a two-month stay at an American university.

I'm sitting on the steps from the lobby down to the basement restaurant in my hotel in Athens, the Hotel Divani Palace Acropolis. The hotel is just blocks from the Acropolis; when I sit out on my balcony I can glance up from my newspaper to see the Parthenon. In the early morning it slowly appears through the fog. At night it's lit like the jewel it is.

But here on the basement steps where I'm writing now, I'm looking at the remains of the Themistocles Wall. The hotel foundation is built around portions of the wall. These remnants were carefully preserved and are displayed behind a glass wall adjacent to the steps.

The Themistocles Wall is an early example of how hard it is to keep the "other" out. It dates to 479 B.C., built by the Athenian military strategist Themistocles, designed to protect Athens from invasion threatened by Sparta. Despite it, the Spartans jumped the wall and attacked.

The section I'm looking at is made up of rows of blocks—formidable looking, several yards wide. Almost 2,500 years later the remainder lie here, solid and substantial but worthless then and now as a barrier.

While I'm gazing at these ancient ruins, CNN and the *International Herald Tribune* are filled with the latest attempt to wall people off from each other: Israel's stark wall inside the West Bank. Panoramic television pictures cannot help but conjure up memories of the Berlin Wall. The scar of concrete is the same, as is the cleared no-man's land. In the newspaper the human scale of the wall is made clear in a photograph of a Palestinian man, stereotypically showing stubble on his chin, peering—is it furtively or with despair?—through a narrow gap in the wall at an Israeli soldier. The contrast is clear. The clean-shaven soldier sports a sharp military haircut. He's wearing aviator-style sunglasses, the wires of his walkie-talkie are obvious on his crisp uniform. The Palestinian is wearing a rumpled shawl.

The architect of the Israeli wall is Dany Tirza, who says of the barrier, "It gives order to space."[4]

"Good fences make good neighbors" is a cliché overused when attempts are made to rationalize barriers. The prestige of Robert Frost is often invoked along with this mantra. The line comes from his poem "Mending Wall," and the suggestion when using the quote is that Frost endorsed such borders. Ariel Sharon cited Frost's line when he was first attempting to explain away his wall separating the West Bank from Israel.

In fact Frost's poem is a meditation on a day he was working with his neighbor, the two of them repairing a common rock wall that marked the connection of their properties. As they labored, it was the other man who insisted, "Good fences make good neighbors." Frost then reacted, "Before I built a wall I'd ask to know what was I walling in or walling out, and to whom I was like to give offense. Something there is that doesn't like a wall, that wants it down."

At Checkpoint Charlie in 1987 I was locked in a holding cell for several hours one day as I was returning to West Berlin from East Berlin. I was working on a report about the origin of the story that AIDS was the result of a runaway CIA experiment. I had traced the story back to what appeared to be its source, an old East German university professor living out his retirement in a high-rise apartment near the east side of the Wall.

With my satchel of notes from the interview and a tape recorder, I walked back toward the border crossing. The guardhouse sat like some sort of misguided, oversized tollbooth on the line that separated East and West. That's what it was for many years, a tollbooth. The East Germans charged curious tourists five marks for a day visa to enter the country in addition to the twenty-five West German marks spending money they were forced to exchange for twenty-five of the vastly less valuable East German marks. It was like an admission ticket to the Communist Disneyland.

The passport officer sat up above the waiting visitors, looking down through a glass window in his cage. A solid, locked door blocked entrance into East Germany. The area was lit up brightly with irritating fluorescent tubes. A mirror placed at a forty-five-degree angle above the guard made it possible for him to see into the back pockets of waiting travelers.

The drill was always stern—no smiles or casual exchanges. The guard took your passport, looked at the visa and your picture, then studied your face to make sure you were you. Then the procedure was repeated, to make really sure.

The same process, in reverse, applied when you exited East Germany. If all your papers were in order, the solid metal imitation wood door buzzed. The lock was now open and you passed into the customs inspection zone. On this trip the customs officer decided to look inside my bag.

When he found the tape recorder, I was charged with practicing journalism without a proper permit and led into the holding room. My bag and papers were taken, the door was locked, and I was left alone.

The room was empty except for a desk and a couple of chairs. Periodically, one guard or another would come back with a scrap from my papers and we'd converse briefly.

"What's this?"

"A credit card receipt for gasoline."

And he'd be gone again.

Finally my things were returned intact, and I was allowed through to the West after being cautioned to get approval before I attempted another reporting job in the East. The fact that the professor I had interviewed on my forbidden tape recorder was part of their propaganda machine probably speeded my release.

The other crossing point for Westerners into East Berlin was the Friedrichstrasse train station. I was stopped by an East German border guard at Friedrichstrasse on one of my trips to the East because I was carrying that day's edition of the *International Herald Tribune*. He walked me over to a garbage can and told me to dump it, making an overt public display indicating that he was not just confiscating it himself to take home.

Then I was escorted to a windowless cubicle and told to empty my pockets.

"What's this, hashish or heroin?" The guard was fingering pocket lint that clung to my wallet. Again, credit card slips were fascinating to the inspector. This time the delay was only a few irritating minutes.

But even the strict East German border failed to keep Germans from crossing, and eventually it too failed completely.

Not long after the Wall collapsed I visit Checkpoint Charlie, where there remains meager evidence of the vicious concrete barrier that divided East and West. Instead of watchtowers and a no-man's-land, a forest of construction cranes dominates the cityscape. Workers with forklifts and surveyor's tripods cross paths with camera-laden tourists searching for some evidence of what was one of the world's most starkly demarked borders.

A beat-up guard tower remains on the site, as a souvenir. One of the familiar four-language border signs is still posted: "You are entering the American Sector." Both the tower and the sign now are owned by the Checkpoint Charlie Museum.

Looking down at the sidewalk and street, searching for the actual line of the old frontier, I wander between parked cars and contractors' trucks and find a red line on the sidewalk. That must mark the spot. A Ford truck is parked over it, but I follow it out to Friedrichstrasse and look over to where the guard tower sits. Yes, this unceremonious red (who chose the color?) strip is clearly the line. Now I'm on the east side. I take a step.

Now I'm on the west side. The murder and misery the Wall caused is erased from daily routine, except at the T-shirt shop just over the west side of the line that offers Wall posters, Coca-Cola, Häagen-Daz ("America's No. 1 super premium ice cream"), and, of course, alleged pieces of the Wall encased in plastic for 9.90 deutsche marks (small) up to 29.90 deutsche marks.

Despite the failure of border walls over the centuries, in the first years of the twenty-first century the United States certainly wasn't the only country trying to protect its interests with a physical barrier.

India looked at its 1,800-mile border with Pakistan and decided a fence might help keep out militants seeking to solve the Kashmir crisis with violence. The Demilitarized Zone in Korea separated the North and South, lined with 148 miles of barbed wire. When I visited the DMZ in the 1980s the barbed wire was fresh and shiny, the paint on the guard posts fresh and new, all spiffed up for an upcoming visit by President Ronald Reagan, who famously said in Berlin not long after, "Mr. Gorbachav, tear down this wall!" Cyprus was bisected by a 112-mile fence keeping the Turkish and the Greek Cypriots apart.[5]

Eventually these barriers open. In the spring of 2003, for example, Turkish Cypriots allowed day trips across the line between the two Cypriot political entities for the first time since 1974. In the first few days after the checkpoints were opened, thousands of Greeks and Turks took advantage of the breach in the fortifications between them to visit the other side of the island. At one border crossing point a Turkish Cypriot looked at the long lines on both sides waiting to cross and observed, "People are like rivers; you can't stop them."[6]

The severe Communist-era decor of the main meeting room in the Frankfurt-on-der-Oder city hall failed to dampen the enthusiasm of a group of marginalized Germans, Poles, Mexicans, and Arizonans who gathered in the mid-1990s to share information along the Poland-Germany border. Far from the notice of news reporters or their own state and federal governments, these representatives of border towns met to compare common cross-border complaints and challenges, from cultural and trade issues to drug and immigration crises. The meetings I attended with them along the Oder River in Germany and Poland followed a first such grassroots get-together the year before on the Arizona-Sonora border.

The participants were engaged in a direct challenge to their respective central governments in Washington, Warsaw, Mexico City, and Bonn. At meetings in somber Frankfurt-on-der-Oder, Germany, and dirty, dusty Slubice, Poland, frustrated borderland pioneers were discussing the creation of semi-autonomous border regions where borderlands communities would devise their own pragmatic rules and regulations for cross-border interaction, which their national governments would feel compelled to accept.

"We need to move, we can't just sit," says the energetic mayor of Yuma, Marilyn Young. Mayor Young passes out Yuma-boosting lapel pins as she celebrates the official establishment of a sister-city relationship with Frankfurt-on-der-Oder. "We're both becoming sophisticated," she says about the two cities, both suffering from some 25 percent regional unemployment and both convinced that their strategic locations ought to produce success stories.

Her newfound awareness of the global economy translates into ideas that bubble out of her with American enthusiasm. "They grow white asparagus here," she says, "and it's very popular." Late spring is asparagus season in Central Europe. Restaurants promote asparagus soup, asparagus and potato main courses; roadside stands are packed with asparagus. "They can only grow it during about a three-month period. In Yuma we grow three crops of asparagus a year." Mayor Young sees hope for Yuma unemployment as she ponders, "Why can't we grow it there and ship it here?"

Nogales, Mexico, businessman Jorge Sandoval Mazón is studying similarities along the various borders, such as the struggle to create a working cross-border relationship in spite of the meddling interference of central governments. "A lot of times what is considered unrealistic by a government is not unrealistic for a community," he says. "They have to understand that the health of a border region is also the health of a central government."

The Polish vice governor for the Slubice region, Boguslaw Bil, agrees with his Mexican colleague that their two emerging economies can learn lessons from each other about dealing with big, powerful neighbors. Cross-border businesses are forcing some de facto autonomy along his border with Germany, says Governor Bil, despite the centralized nature of Polish government. "They are one step ahead," he says gesturing to the flourishing outdoor market and shopping district in his border town. "We have the signal from people who want to do business that we must change laws."

Even Governor Bil, an official appointed to his job by the prime minister in Warsaw, sees decentralization as the future. "Ruling from Warsaw is quite difficult. One cannot see everything that's happening in the border regions. We have done a lot already to decentralize, and we are still working on it."

Standing on the Whirlpool Rapids Bridge just downstream over the Niagara River from Niagara Falls, looking through the girders of the railroad bridge next to me, I can see the falls in the distance. It is a gorgeous midsummer day, clear blue sky except for a few puffy clouds. Now I'm at the railing, resting my notebook high over the gorge, and there is just enough gusting wind to activate a sense of vertigo. A metal plaque announces "International Boundary Line," and it exhibits an actual line with "United States" written on one side in raised steel lettering and "Canada" on the other. I'm on the Canadian side.

A few cars are backed up waiting to clear border formalities. But no little farouche Canadian kids are trying to sell me Chiclets.

The rushing Niagara River is a much more formidable river than the Rio Grande. But there is no barbed wire separating these countries and no crowds waiting to cross from one to the other. I head over to the immigration officer's hut.

"*Buenas noches.*" I'm sure that's what the guard said to me. I expected a "Howdy" or maybe a "*Bon nuit,*" but not "*Buenas noches*" up here, especially in the middle of the afternoon. He ambles out of his office to the counter. I'm his only foot traffic.

"Excuse me?" I say to his Spanish greeting.

"Where are you from?" he asks.

"California," I tell him, showing my passport. He just glances at it and waves me into fortress America with a congenial "Okay!"

It's not much more difficult for a Canadian to come south into the United States, and travel around the fifty states. Canadians are allowed to enter with no paperwork other than proof of Canadian citizenship. They can travel the country with no geographic limitations and may stay as long as six months with no need for a visa. Mexicans, by stark contrast, are not allowed to travel beyond twenty-five miles of the U.S.-Mexican border (except for those who enter at certain ports on the Arizona-Mexican border) and can stay only seventy-two hours unless they carry visas allowing for a longer stay with further travel. Mexicans who wish to take advantage of even the restricted border visits must produce a valid visa for the trip.

In late 2003 several south Texas congressmen signed a letter to Homeland Security Department Secretary Tom Ridge drawing attention to these inconsistencies and the hardships they cause to both Mexicans and Texas business.

"Hundreds of Mexican nationals cross our southern border each day for business, education, or entertainment, and our local merchants and towns rely on their business to stimulate the economy," wrote the representatives, including Congressional Border Caucus co-chair Solomon Ortiz. "We should not discriminate against Mexican citizens who legally enter the United States. Fairness demands we treat our neighboring countries equally and remove the restriction imposed on Mexican nationals crossing into the United States legally with a laser visa. Fairness further demands we extend the seventy-two-hour stay to parity with the six-month visits allowed for Canadians."

The rules were not changed.

8

ANNEXING HALF

OF MEXICO,

TEMPORARILY . . .

"GEORGE BUSH is a thief," Samir told me. We were driving through the labyrinth of Cairo streets, sweltering in the jammed traffic. Samir is an Egyptian journalist, and there was no question in his mind that the United States had invaded Iraq for oil. That same week the *Economist* agreed in a special report analyzing America and its empire. "America, it is said, is the world's latest imperial power," headlined the *Economist*. "Don't believe it."[1] The article argued that the nineteenth-century policy of Manifest Destiny was the beginning of American empire building that continues today.

In the 1950s, when I was in grammar school, we were taught Manifest Destiny as heroics. I remember studying maps and dreaming of how swell it would be if that fat mass of Canada were part of the good old U.S. of A. Such indoctrination dates from another journalist, John O'Sullivan, editor of the *Democratic Review*, a political journal he co-founded in 1837. O'Sullivan came up with the term Manifest Destiny and used it in an empire-building 1845 *Review* editorial. "The American claim is by the right of our manifest destiny to overspread and possess the whole continent which Providence has given to us. It is in the Future far more than in our past that our True Title is to be found."[2]

More Manifest Destiny propaganda was splashed across an O'Sullivan-founded newspaper, the *New York Morning News*, in an editorial rationalizing the annexation of Texas. "It is surely not necessary to insist that acquisitions of territory in America, even if accomplished by force of arms, are not to be viewed in the same light as the invasions and conquests of the States of the old world," argued the paper, attempting to explain away the double standards of American policy. "Our way lies, not over trampled nations, but through desert wastes, to be brought by our industry and energy within the domain of art and civilization. We are contiguous to a vast portion of the globe, untrodden save by the savage and the beast, and we are conscious of our power to render it tributary to man." The paper made clear just who this "we" was. "The solitudes of America are the property of the immigrant children of Europe and their offspring," it claimed (without the vision to forecast that those immigrant children of Europe would be a minority in California by the twenty-first century). After asserting that Manifest Destiny would halt the expansion of the United States only at the natural border of the Pacific, the editorial concluded, "With the valleys of the Rocky Mountains converted into pastures and sheep-folds, we may with propriety turn to the world and ask, whom have we injured?"[3]

Those calls to conquer echoed the 1845 inaugural address of another president who lost the popular vote, James K. Polk. Polk campaigned on a promise to make Texas a state, despite Mexico's continuing claim to the breakaway republic. The Mexican state of Texas in the 1820s was filling with foreign immigrants, mostly Anglos from the United States and northern and central Europeans. The Anglos, for the most part, were not assimilating into Mexican culture. Many violated Mexican law by bringing slaves across the border into Texas.

Since they were established, both the Mexican and U.S. governments have struggled to secure their national borders. Many of the longtime original residents of North America who lived on the changing line between the two countries were nomadic. Arbitrary borders meant nothing to them. Long before the United States worried about illegal immigration from Mexico, Mexico labored to stop illegal immigration from the north into its state of Texas. By 1824 Mexico decided to combat the border crossers by creating a system to legitimize and control them. The government offered foreigners Texas land if they would agree to farm or raise animals. Spanish was mandated as the official language for business, and immigrants were required to be Catholic.

Soon Texas was swarming with newcomers, most of them from the States. As they settled in, building a permanent life for themselves, they began thinking about making Texas their own, part of the United States. An 1827 rebellion against Mexican rule by a handful of these Anglo settlers was quickly suppressed. But this so-called Fredonia uprising stirred the expansionists in Washington. The U.S. government expressed official interest in buying Texas, an idea Mexico rejected. Charged with studying the growing territorial crisis in Texas, Mexican Gen. Manuel de Mier y Terán arrived at a dire conclusion for his country: "Texas is contiguous to the most avid nation in the world. The North Americans have conquered whatever territory adjoins them. In less than half a century, they have become masters of extensive colonies from which they have disappeared the former owners, Indian tribes. Either the government occupies Texas now or it is lost forever."[4]

Mexican troops moved north, and—just as the frustrated North Americans did about a century later—in 1830 Mexico canceled its liberal immigration law and ordered the Texas border with the United States sealed. And just as it is for the North Americans today, it was an unenforceable policy. The Anglos kept coming south, illegally crossing into Texas and settling. There they joined forces with Hispanics in Texas who were discontent with the Mexican government and in 1836 declared their independence. Almost ten years later, Polk looked to the Republic of Texas as he declared his presidential aspirations: "Since the Union was formed the number of states has increased from thirteen to twenty-eight. Our population has increased from three to twenty million. Multitudes from the Old World are flocking to our shores. Foreign powers do not seem to appreciate the true character of our Government. To enlarge its limits is to extend the dominions of peace over additional territories and increasing millions."[5]

The speech was part of Polk's strategy to grab Texas and more from Mexico. When his administration officially offered statehood to Texas, Mexico severed diplomatic relations with Washington in protest, and the Texans joined the Union on July 4, 1845. Polk further increased tensions between the two countries by offering to buy New Mexico and California, dismissing Mexico's heritage in those states as unimportant compared with the mandates of Manifest Destiny. Meanwhile U.S. troops were on the move. Under the command of future president General Zachary Taylor, the U.S. army advanced to the disputed western Texas border. For Mexico, that border was the Nueces River. But President Polk declared it farther west, agreeing with his new Texan constituents that the Rio Grande (called the Río Bravo by Mexicans) was the real frontier, embracing a borderline created by an act of the Texas Congress in 1836.[6] Polk's interpretation of where the borderline ought to be drawn was not fixed by the U.S. Congress when it resolved to annex the new state. That resolution acknowledged with precise language that the specific frontiers were in dispute, describing the Texas borders as "subject to the adjustment by this government of all questions of boundary that may arise with other governments."[7] Polk decided that if Mexico refused to accept the Rio Grande as the border, the U.S. Army would enforce an "adjustment." Washington ordered four thousand soldiers to duty, assigned to defend a Texas defined as stretching to the Rio Grande. To put this number in perspective, the U.S. Army totaled just over twice that many troops at the time. Polk was looking at the contested border as an excuse for war with Mexico.

Contemporary critics tried to rally public opinion against Polk's empire building. "Occupation," the opposition newspaper *National Intelligencer* said about U.S. troop movements into the territory between the Nueces and the Rio Grande, "is nothing short (as everybody knows) of an invasion of Mexico. It is offensive war, and not the necessary defense of Texas. And should prove, as we think it will, that the President has gone this additional length, then the President will be MAKING WAR, in the full sense of the word, on his own authority and beyond all the plea of need, and even without any thought of asking legislative leave."[8]

An anonymous critic of the war wrote a dramatic and colorful rant to the *Cambridge Chronicle* newspaper, making it completely clear why he intended to reject recruitment efforts of the Massachusetts Volunteer Regiment, solicitations posted after the shooting began that included promises of pay up to ten dollars a month and a mustering out bounty of more cash and land. "Neither have I the least idea of 'joining' you, or in any way assisting the unjust war against Mexico," he wrote. "I have no wish to participate in such 'glorious' butcheries of women and children as were displayed in the capture of Monterey. No siree! As long as I can work, beg, or go to the poorhouse, I won't go to Mexico, to be lodged on the damp ground, half starved, half roasted, bitten by mosquitoes and centipedes, stung by scorpions and tarantulas—marched, drilled, and flogged, and then stuck up to be shot at, for eight dollars a month and putrid rations. . . .

"As for yourself," the refusenik addressed the recruiting officer, "you are employed at an intensely mean trade. Human butchery has had its day. The time is rapidly approaching when the professional soldier will be placed on the same level as a bandit, the Bedouin, and the Thug. You had better quit the business: and in return for your offer and information, if you wish to engage in the woolen manufacture (which is my trade), I will give you all the information and assistance in my power. I am satisfied with my condition. I think a man is more nobly employed, drawing a spinning jack, assisting to clothe his fellow 'humans,' than even leading an army to slaughter them."[9]

Mexican Gen. Mariano Paredes marched to Mexico City and forced President José Joaquín de Herrera from office. Herrera had been unsuccessful in seeking a peaceful negotiated solution to Polk's expansionism, a policy direction unpopular in Mexico. Paredes installed himself as president and announced that reclaiming Texas would be his priority. Polk reacted by ordering U.S. troops past the Nueces River and on to the Rio Grande. "Hostilities have been begun by the United States of America,"[10] responded President Paredes. His commander on the scene, Pedro de Ampudia, demanded in a letter to General Taylor that the U.S. troops depart.

"Your government has not only insulted but exasperated the Mexican nation, bearing its conquering banner to the left bank of the Río Bravo. I require you to break up your camp and retire to the other bank of the Nueces River."[11] Ampudia gave Taylor twenty-four hours. Instead Taylor ordered a blockade of the mouth of the Rio Grande. Paredes ordered his army to "attack the army that is attacking us."[12] They did just that. First shots were fired at U.S. scouts on April 25, 1846, killing fourteen American soldiers.

The attack served well the long-term goals of President Polk and his desire to obtain not only Texas but also New Mexico and California for the Union. Notes to his diary, May 9, 1846, the day he received news of the attack, make clear his choice for war. "Before I had finished reading the despatch, the Secretary of War called. I immediately summoned the Cabinet to meet at half past seven o'clock this evening. The Cabinet accordingly assembled at that hour; all the members present. The subject of the despatch received this evening from General Taylor, as well as the state of our relations with Mexico, were fully considered. The Cabinet were unanimously of opinion, and it was so agreed, that a message should be sent to Congress on Monday laying out all the information in my possession before them and recommending vigorous and prompt measures to enable the executive to prosecute the war."[13]

Polk made his war cry public a few days later, announcing, "After repeated menaces, Mexico has passed the boundary of the United States, and shed American blood upon the American soil. As war exists, notwithstanding all our efforts to avoid it, and exists by act of Mexico herself, we are called upon by every consideration of duty and patriotism to vindicate the honor, the rights, and the interest of our country."[14]

The expansionist Polk found his excuse to start a popular war with the attack on U.S. troops, but it was the United States that sent its soldiers into what could at best be called disputed territory occupied by Mexico. Polk had already made clear his intention to take territory from Mexico by force if it would not submit to inflated American financial claims and sell territory desired by the United States. Mexico did little to work toward a negotiated settlement of the disputes, perhaps understandably: the

Polk administration offered nothing but demands, and war if those demands were rejected.

Once General Taylor crossed the Nueces River, Mexican President Paredes understandably concluded that the nations were at war. He announced that "hostilities therefore have been begun by the United States of America, who have undertaken new conquests in the territory lying within the line of the Departments of Tamaulipas and Nuevo León while troops of the United States are threatening Monterey in Upper California."[15]

Days after Polk's speech asking Congress to declare war on Mexico, and after brief debate, it did. In addition to the fight along the Texas border, Polk dispatched troops to seize Mexico's northwest—the land from New Mexico out to California. It was policy that editor O'Sullivan had long predicted in one of his Manifest Destiny editorials with the cry, "Texas, we repeat, is secure; and now, as the Razor Strop Man says, 'Who's the next customer?' Shall it be California or Canada?"[16]

There was no question in Polk's mind what should be next. In his diary he records a strategy meeting with advisers shortly after the start of the war. "I brought distinctly to the consideration of the Cabinet the question of ordering an expedition of mounted men to California. I stated that if the war should be protected for any considerable time, it would in my judgment be very important that the United States should hold military possession of California at the time peace was made, and I declared my purpose to be to acquire for the United States, California, New Mexico, and perhaps some others of the Northern Provinces of Mexico whenever a peace was made."

Polk flirted with the All Mexico movement, a drive to annex all of Mexico, promoted by expansionist newspapers. Typical was the language used by the *New York Sun*'s editor Moses Beach, in an editorial reminding his readers that the Mexican "race is perfectly accustomed to being conquered, and the only new lesson we shall teach is that our victories will give liberty, safety, and prosperity to the vanquished, if they know enough to profit by the appearance of our stars. To liberate and ennoble—not to enslave and debase—is our mission. Well may the Mexican nation, whose great masses have never yet tasted liberty, prattle over their lost phantom of nationality. If they have not—in the profound darkness of their vassal existence—the intelligence and manhood to accept the ranks and rights of freeman at our hands, we must bear with their ignorance."[17]

Meanwhile, in the Mexican territory of California, Anglo immigrants followed a path much like that of their fellow settlers in Texas. In revolt against Mexican authority, a handful declared California independent. The U.S. Navy landed in Monterey as troops marching west overland arrived at the Pacific. When Polk announced California as Union territory, the California independence movement evaporated. Polk rationalized to his diary, "Although we had not gone to war for conquest, yet it was clear that in making peace we would if practicable obtain California and such other portion of the Mexican territory as would be sufficient to indemnify our claimants on Mexico, and to defray the expenses of war."[18]

President Polk's California dream was accomplished at Monterey under the command of Adm. John Drake Sloat, who claimed the land from north of Santa Barbara to the Oregon border with Washington. He told Mexican Californians that the United States was not their "enemy"[19] and that they were free to stay in an American California or return to Mexico compensated with dollars for their trouble. By the end of the summer, American forces seized southern California while Col. Stephen Kearny marched his troops west to claim New Mexico with virtually no opposition. Kearny joined his fellow empire builders in insisting that they were not conquerors, as this excerpt from his speech to the townsfolk in Las Vegas, New Mexico, makes plain: "People of New Mexico," he announced. "I have come amongst you to take possession of your country, and extend over it the laws of the United States. We come amongst you as friends, not enemies, as protectors, not conquerors. Henceforth I absolve you of all allegiance to the Mexican government."[20] Colonel Kearny continued on to California, leaving rebellious New Mexicans who fought against the occupying Americans until a massacre of rebels at Taos ended their struggle. Many of those defenders of their own country not killed in battle suffered in court, where they were tried (and hanged) for treason against the invading U.S. government.

Californios, Hispanics born in California, revolted against their occupiers with greater initial success. They took back Los Angeles and held it for several months before the Americans returned in adequate force to control southern California. Unlike the fate of their New Mexican countrymen, the surviving Californios were left free after the battle, welcomed to remain as full citizens.

It was a war "unnecessarily and unconstitutionally begun by the President of the United States" according to a House resolution passed eighty-five to eighty-one just before the Treaty of Guadalupe Hidalgo was signed in 1848, ceding half of Mexico to the United States.

Mexicans agreed to the bad deal and remember it well.

In the Veracruz *zócalo*, the town square, Mexican national pride is on prominent display as September 16—Mexican independence day—approaches. The façade of one of the colonial-style buildings is covered with Christmas tree–type lights, strung up in the image of the Mexican flag. The words "¡Viva México!" are spelled out in lights. The stand of palm trees in the square are patriotically lit too: lights creating the Mexican tricolor surround their trunks.

The steamy port is up early. From my balcony at the Hotel Emporio I watch the roll-on, roll-off transport ship *Blue Hawk* fill up with brand-new cars, fresh from a Mexican factory. Across the harbor are the remains of the colonial Spanish fortifications. Tour boats, the *Niño* and the *Isla de Sacrificios* and the *Pirata* bob against their lines along the pier, their crews swabbing them clean. Early lovers stroll and hug. Vendors raise the shutters on their shops peddling T-shirts and straw hats, coffee and postcards.

This is the harbor bombarded by the Americans during their siege of Veracruz, during the U.S. war of conquest, a battle chronicled by one of the invaders in a most amoral description of war. "It is a beautiful siege, not a man here that is not in high hopes," wrote Lt. Col. Francis Belton, who was commanding mortar batteries and studied his handiwork at close range. "The lines and trenches are very safe," he said about his own positions, reporting that all of the firing the day before had done no damage "but to their own beautiful gem of a church in the cemetery. I was in it yesterday afternoon. A beautiful chaste altar stands in the center under the dome—which was shelled thro' and thro'. The splendid crucifix on the altar seems a high work of art. I could see it imperfectly by the mortar and lime falling down, the crown of thorns was displaced and fell below. The candles in the sticks were broken, four shot holes thro' the doors and other ruin around. Every wall has traces of shot and also the magnificent entrance." Belton continues with this paean to the wreckage he wrought, adding, "We are in high spirits."[21]

On the other side of Belton's lines, an unidentified Mexican correspondent cried out in a report first published in Xalapa and reprinted in U.S. newspapers. "How horrible is the scene we are attempting briefly to describe! What sympathizing heart can behold it without his eyes filling with the bitterest tears of grief?" The reporter assailed the United States for its "barbarous manner of assassinating the unoffending and defenceless citizens." The number of civilian casualties was enormous, "women and children, followed by whole families perishing from the effects of the explosion, or under the ruins of their dwellings."[22]

Veracruz offers an English-language guide for tourists. "The city of Veracruz," it explains, "borned on april 22, 1519, founded by the spaniors and headed by Hernán Cortés, which arrived on the Chalchihuecan beaches where is located the City and the porto of Veracruz actually." The brochure identifies Veracruz as the oldest Spanish city in Mexico and site of the first stage of the country's colonization.

A plaque is mounted on the lemon-yellow wall outside the tourist office. It was placed as a reminder in December 1998, honoring those who defended Mexico against *la invasión norteamericana* in April 1914. American meddling in the Mexican Revolution and its aftermath included an invasion of Veracruz that year. Four thousand troops landed on April 22 with the murky mission of confiscating weapons at the customs house. In addition to costing the lives of seventeen U.S. soldiers and more than a hundred Mexicans, the landing united Mexicans against a common enemy they remembered well as the thief of the northern half of their country. With romantic bombast, Emiliano Zapata announced, "If the Americans send a million soldiers, we will fight them, one man against hundred. We may have no army or no ammunition, but we have men who will face their bullets."[23]

The next year U.S. soldiers crossed the border again, chasing Pancho Villa after he raided the New Mexico crossroads called Columbus. The Villa raid was designed to incite a U.S. invasion and a Mexican government counterstrike, creating a confused atmosphere during which Villa could prevail as Mexico's savior. Instead U.S. troops stayed in Chihuahua until 1917, periodically engaging Villa who ultimately was unable to overthrow the Mexico City regime. By February 1917 the American soldiers were back on their own side of the border, Washington now preoccupied with the war in Europe.

Two blocks around the corner in Veracruz from the plaque commemorating the 1914 invasion, where Avenida 16 de Septiembre meets a traffic circle, is another monument. It pays homage to Sebastián Holtzinger, Manuel Busio Cruz, Ignacio Platas, Félix Valdez, Ambrosio Alcalde, Antonio García, and José María Villasanta, identified as heroes who gave their lives in the defense of their country during *la invasión norteamericana de 1847.* Another side of the traffic circle monument lists those heroes, known and unknown, who died during the 1914 attack. This monument is another recent addition to Veracruz. It's dated September 1998.

Citing these memorials is not intended to suggest that Mexico today is revanchistic about its territorial losses to the United States. But these attacks and defeats at the hands of its neighbor to the north are a continuing memory in the common consciousness of the Mexican nation. At the same time few Gringos think of their lands from Texas to California as conquered territory. Such selective memory allowed President Clinton to declare in his Memorial Day speech in 2000, "Americans never fought for empire, for territory, for dominance."[24] In fact that's exactly what Americans fought for when they invaded Mexico in 1846. In his book *The Annexation of Mexico,* the American journalist John Ross, who has been reporting from Mexico for over a generation, suggests that Walt Whitman's commentary in the *Brooklyn Eagle* summed up American public opinion at the time: "Miserable, inefficient Mexico. What has she to do with the great mission of peopling the New World with a noble race? Be it ours to achieve this mission!"

The Treaty of Guadalupe Hidalgo, forced on Mexico in 1848, recognized the artificiality of the border. Article VIII states: "Mexicans now in territories previously belonging to Mexico . . . shall be free to continue where they now reside, or to remove at any time to the Mexican Republic." Those Mexicans living north of today's border were given a year to decide if they wished to retain their Mexican citizenship or become Gringos.

Corridos are a form of Mexican folk news reporting; they are ballads sung about specific events. The writer Elijah Wald calls them a newspaper of the people. In his book *Narcocorrido*, Wald cites several *corridos* that lament in detail the plight of Mexican migrants and their relationship with *El Norte*. The Mexican *norteño* band—also extremely popular in the United States—Los Tigres del Norte has recorded many *corridos* that tell the stories of border crossers. One of them, "La Tumba del Mojado," The Wetback's Grave, was written by *corridista* Paulino Vargas, who says the song reflects reality on the border. "I don't like to invent things, it has to be true. The public knows the difference, it can tell what isn't real and what is."[25] The narrator in the song calls himself a *mojado*, a wetback.

I didn't have a Green Card when I worked in Louisiana,
I lived in a basement because I was a wetback.
I had to bow my head to collect my week's wages.[26]

The *mojado* identifies the border as the "tortilla curtain" and then cries,

Mexicali Rose and the blood in the Rio Grande
Are two different things, but in color they are brothers,
And the dividing line is the grave of the wetback.

Corridos dealing with the border are not a recent phenomenon. The song "El Deportado" was recorded by the band Los Hermanos Bañuelos in Los Angeles, probably, according to Wald, in 1929. The lyrics sound contemporary.

The white-skinned men are very wicked, they take advantage of the
    occasion,
and all of the Mexicans are treated without compassion.

There comes a large cloud of dust,
With no consideration.
Women, children and old ones are being driven to the border.
We are being kicked out of this country.

Goodbye, beloved countrymen, we are being deported,
But we are not bandits, we came to work.[27]

Other *corridos de mojados* deal with the social issues of immigration, such as the intergenerational problems of undocumented workers who establish families in the United States and raise children who are American citizens by birth and speak English. "El Otro México" is a Los Tigres del Norte *corrido* in the voice of a *mojado* who sings about his experiences and new home in the United States, calling it that "other Mexico which we have constructed on this soil that was once national territory."

John Ross likes to tell a story to illustrate how important *corridos* are to cross-border culture. "An old friend of mine in San Antonio, Texas, Salomé Gutiérrez, has written ten thousand *corridos*," Ross told me one evening in Mexico City at his favorite haunt, the bright fluorescent-lit Café La Blanca. "Salomé was in the studio recording a *corrido* band. I think it was '72, maybe '74, and a famous border narco, Fred Carrasco, breaks out of jail downtown. There's a gunfight, three people are killed, Carrasco was killed, and one of Salomé's neighbors sees this, comes running out to the studio. Salomé's got the band. He sits down and he writes a *corrido*. They cut the *corrido*. In San Antonio there are three stations that play *corridos* from dawn to dusk. They ran it over to one of these stations, and for most of the people in west San Antonio, Salomé's *corrido* brought them the news of Fred Carrasco's escape from prison."

Another example of a *corrido* reporting news is the late-1970s border analysis by Vicente Fernández, "Los Mandados." "I call it the Illegal Alien Anthem," wrote columnist Agustin Gurza in the *Los Angeles Times*. "In the *norteño* tune, Fernández brags about hopping back and forth across the border despite repeated deportation. In one attempt he even dyes his hair blond to disguise himself as a *gabacho*, slang for white American. But the ruse fails because he can't speak English." Gurza calls the song "a defiant challenge to the U.S. Border Patrol," the story of "an immigrant who takes revenge on Americans for abuse suffered at the hands of La Migra."

La Migra caught me three hundred times, let's say,
But it never tamed me.
The beatings they gave me,
I took out on their countrymen.[28]

Typical of a lack of Mexican and borderlands cultural literacy on the Gringo side of the line is the fact that the Republican party invited Vicente Fernández to sing at their convention in Philadelphia where they nominated George W. Bush as their presidential candidate—not knowing, according to columnist Gurza, that he is "Mexico's working-class hero."

That the border today is porous, that Mexicans and their culture range far north, should surprise no one. The Gringos arrived after the Mexicans, and the Mexicans never left.

Some Mexicans may dream of reconquering their lost north. Others simply enjoy watching demographic changes begin to reverse the Gringo domination of the southwestern United States. Not only is Spanish becoming a de facto second language in much of the United States, tortillas are threatening white sliced sandwich bread as the most popular vehicle for American sandwich stuffings.[29] Since the early 1990s more salsa has been sold in American grocery stores than ketchup.[30] The border town of McAllen, Texas, is 90 percent Latino, and home to a growing number of wealthy Mexicans. "You get the ease of a manageable American city where almost everyone speaks Spanish," is how the businessman Rubén de León explained his decision to relocate from Monterrey to McAllen. "Essentially you're in Mexico and the United States at the same time."[31]

If there is any irredentist undercurrent among Mexicans and Mexican Americans living and working in the United States, it is not motivated by any desire to be reunited with the Mexican national government. Rather it is to empower the Latino population within the United States, especially in the former Mexican territory of the Southwest, to take political and social advantage of the demographic change in the early twenty-first century that has made Latinos the largest minority in the United States.

One prominent Latino activist group is the Movimento Estudiantil de Chícanos de Aztlán, known by its acronym MEChA. Aztlán is a mythical land of the Aztecs, their place of origin. Some Latinos use the name Aztlán to identify the territory lost to the United States. MEChA was founded in 1969 at the University of California in Santa Barbara, organized in part around a document titled El Plan Espiritual de Aztlán. Its preamble is written in prose typical of 1960s political activism: "In the spirit of a new people that is conscious not only of its proud historical heritage but also of the brutal 'gringo' invasion of our territories, we, the Chicano inhabitants and civilizers of the northern land of Aztlán from whence came our forefathers, reclaiming the land of their birth and consecrating the determination of our people of the sun, declare that the call of our blood is our power, our responsibility, and our inevitable destiny." Whites fearful of the growing Latino population in the United States often point to El Plan Espiritual de Aztlán preamble as proof that the organization is trying to return the Southwest to Mexican rule. Preamble lines such as "Aztlán belongs to those who plant the seeds, water the fields, and gather the crops and not to the foreign Europeans" particularly upset the critics, as does the logical "We do not recognize capricious frontiers on the bronze continent."

MEChA alumni and activists, or *mechistas* as they are commonly known, more or less patiently point out that the language is not a call for territorial independence or reunification with Mexico, but for liberation. Most Mexicans and Mexican Americans in the United States are intent on sharing the American Dream: a better job, a nicer house, fluency in English, sending the kids to college so the next generation flourishes—just like the waves of immigrants before them since Jamestown and the *Mayflower*.

9

EARLY CONTROL
OF THE BORDER

ATTEMPTS BY the United States to control traffic across the Mexico border can be traced to the mid-1800s. Once the United States secured the northern territory of Mexico for its own, laborers were encouraged to come to underpopulated California from China. These Chinese migrants worked for low wages, most of them initially employed as manual labor building the transcontinental railroads. As the number of Chinese in California increased, the migration drew racist opposition and fears of cheap Chinese labor competing with European immigrants and their descendants traveling west for work. Anti-Chinese riots in San Francisco were followed by efforts to prohibit further immigration from China. Congress finally responded and in 1882 passed the Chinese Exclusion Act. It and further similar laws banned Chinese labor from entering the U.S. labor market. In 1924 a general immigration law extended the ban across Asia, a prohibition that stood until 1943 when a quota system based on national origin was first established and very limited immigration from Asia was again permitted.

Not long after the Chinese Exclusion Act took effect, Chinese who wanted to enter the United States found the southern border a convenient and unregulated portal. Europeans who were denied access at Ellis Island and other East Coast ports of entry had already discovered the Mexico route to the American dream. In 1914 the U.S. government reacted by hiring a unit of border guards and assigning them horses, automobiles, and boats to patrol the southern border. These guards supplemented a minimal corps that had been watching the border ineffectively since just after 1900.

Regular army troops patrolled the border during World War I and managed to curtail illegal immigration. After the war, in an effort to combat an increasing number of unauthorized border crossings, the commissioner general of the Bureau of Immigration began attempts to close the border between official ports of entry. It was an impossible effort then, just as it is today.

The first time Mexicans (and Canadians) were subjected to control at U.S. borders came with the 1917 passage of the Immigration Act. Mexicans were charged eight dollars to cross the border and were required to pass a literacy test. The result: a marked increase in illegal crossings, according to authorities at the time. The institution of the national quota system for visas to the United States in 1924 added to the lure of illegal crossings. The quota system was a failed attempt to design and control immigration along racial and ethnic lines. Congress responded to the press of migrants crossing into the United States from Mexico without papers by creating the Border Patrol, today the largest uniformed federal law-enforcement agency in the United States. In addition to the horses, boats, and cars their predecessors used, today's Border Patrol chases migrants with airplanes and helicopters, bicycles and canoes.[1]

Immigration quotas based on national origin were linked to Census figures from the early 1900s, a time when most of the American population traced its roots to northern Europe. The quota system held the number of immigrants from southern Europe, Asia, and Latin America to a minimum. Mexicans were exempt from the quota system; there was no limit on the number of native Mexicans who could enter the United States. These racist and ethnically discriminatory rules were tossed out during the reformations of the civil rights era, in 1965. President Lyndon B. Johnson signed new rules into law calling the old quota system "un-American." Under the reformed immigration laws, a certain number of immigrants were allowed into the United States each year from all over the world. Mexico lost the numerical exemption it enjoyed under the quota system and, like the rest of the world, became subject to a limited number for legal migration into the United States.

But before the establishment of the numerical limits, immigration into the United States from Mexico was consequential, fueled by jobs and by escape from the violence and turmoil of the Mexican Revolution. When the U.S. economy collapsed in the Great Depression, the flow reversed. Mexicans, and Mexican-American citizens of the United States, went south in huge numbers, many against their will. During the 1930s more than a quarter-million people were shipped south.[2] The motivations for the removal are familiar to the twenty-first century: the people were charged with illegally taking jobs and using social services. At the time the exodus south was labeled "repatriation." But contemporary news reports and later studies make clear that legal, permanent residents of the United States, temporary workers with legal status, and U.S. citizens who appeared to be Mexican were forced out of the country along with illegal aliens. The methods used to rid the United States of these workers during the severe unemployment of the depression included "deportation, persuasion, coaxing, incentive, and unauthorized coercion."[3]

Even before the depression, anti-Mexican fervor was again building in official America. Texas Congressman Eugene Black told the House Committee on Immigration and Naturalization in 1928 that Mexicans were not desirable in the United States because they are "germ-carriers, inassimilable, a people who are with us but not of us, and not for us."[4]

One of the leaders of the offensive against Mexicans during the depression was Secretary of Labor William Doak. Doak estimated that in 1931 about 400,000 illegal aliens were living in the United States. But, just as is the case today, Secretary Doak acknowledged that he could not cite an accurate figure. "It is obviously impossible," he wrote Congress, "to arrive at any concrete figures as to the number of aliens unlawfully in the United States." He deftly added national security fears to his mission, telling lawmakers in his pitch for direct power to orchestrate assaults on the immigrant population, "There is a need for strengthening the law relative to the deportation of those aliens who are affiliated with organizations which advocate the overthrow of the Government of the United States."[5]

President Herbert Hoover backed Doak's maneuvers. The secretary ridiculed objections from the American Civil Liberties Union, saying, "The civil liberties crowd always objects, and the worse the aliens are the louder the crowd shouts." In the midst of his crusade to rid the United States of anyone unable to prove legal status, Doak was confronted with a reminder that America was founded as a refuge for immigrants. "Yes," he agreed, "and we've been reaping the harvest ever since."[6]

Doak's deportation raids were carried out with heavy-handed police tactics. They were designed not only to round up Mexicans and Mexican Americans and send them south, but also to scare Mexicans who heard about them, in the hope they would leave the United States on their own. It worked. By the close of the 1930s the number of Mexicans in the United States had dropped over 40 percent, according to official Census Bureau numbers.[7] And that's only counting those who were counted by the Census takers.

Other ethnic groups too were caught in the dragnets. The deportations caused stress on the Mexican economy as it tried to accommodate the resettlers and new settlers.

The mood up north changed radically as the war economy took hold in the early 1940s. Labor was again needed, desperately. Congress enacted a series of laws to bring workers across the border, all created in partnership with the Mexican government: the so-called Bracero program. Bracero comes from the Spanish word for arm and means laborer and fieldworker, referring to the manual labor done with their arms. The Bracero program was supposed to provide needed labor for the United States and a fair deal for Mexican workers. But it was abused from the start, and its repercussions continue into the current era. Workers were often denied adequate housing and working conditions; wages paid were often below guaranteed standards. The result was that many Braceros left the temporary employment that granted them legal status and disappeared into the underground American economy where they sold their labor competitively and worked "black."

The songwriter Phil Ochs memorialized these conditions in his work "Bracero" with the lines, "When the weary night embraces, sleep in shacks that could be cages. They will take it from your wages, Bracero."

After several years of watching its citizens suffer while working in the United States, the Mexican government quit the Bracero agreement and stopped shipping workers north. Ranchers and farmers panicked at the loss of needed labor and lobbied Washington for help. The U.S. Immigration Service—forerunner of the Homeland Security Department—responded along the Texas border by throwing open the gates to the United States and encouraging thousands of Mexicans to enter the country illegally. Once across the border they were arrested and taken into custody by the Texas Employment Commission, which offered them to ranches and farms.[8] Wages slumped as massive numbers of workers came north, unaware of the Immigration Service scheme. The two governments then renegotiated the Bracero program, and authorized migrations resumed. But, of course, workers without papers stayed.

Official reaction to illegal migration came in 1954. Robert May Swing, commissioner of the Immigration and Naturalization Service, created Operation Wetback. Mexicans were seized in the United States and pushed back south. Railroads and ships were used to send the deportees far into Mexico, in a false hope it would discourage them from trying their luck again in *El Norte*. The Immigration and Naturalization Service claimed that more than a million Mexicans crossed the border south during Operation Wetback. That number is much higher than official INS records for deportations, a discrepancy rationalized by the INS which says many more Mexicans were scared south than were officially deported.

It was Operation Wetback that popularized the use of "wetback" as a pejorative word for Mexicans. The folklorist John West calls the word "a gently derogatory term."[9] The Mexican band Los Norteños de Ojinaga was singing about it as the twenty-first century opened: "We will always be the same, even if you become a citizen. In the gringo's eyes, we will always be wetbacks."[10] Slurs were thrown back and forth. Mexicans called deportees returning to Mexico after lengthy stays in the United States

"Gringos" (or *agringados*, meaning Yankeefied) for the attitudes and customs they had acquired up in the north.[11]

The origin of the term "wetback" is obvious. Mexicans who swam across the Rio Grande or jumped off boats along the Pacific Coast came ashore wet. The origin of the word "Gringo" is in dispute. An often-told story is that U.S. soldiers invading Mexico in the Mexican-American War during 1846–1848 marched south singing, "Green Grow the Rushes, Oh!" Mexicans condensed what they heard to just "green grow," which came out as the word "gringo." Another theory is that the Spanish word *"gringo,"* which means "gibberish," became slang to describe those who could not speak Spanish, and most of those who fit that description in Mexico were from the United States.[12] In one of the Spanish-language dictionaries I use, published in Spain, "gringo" is listed as an offensive term. But from personal experience in California and Mexico, I'd suggest that it too could better be characterized as gently derogatory, at worst.

Over the twenty-two years it was up and running, through 1964, the Bracero program shipped about five million Mexicans north. At the border they were stripped and checked for diseases, washed, and deloused.[13] They were also promised life insurance and pensions. Aging Braceros and their relatives are still trying to collect. Ten percent of many Bracero laborers' wages were withheld as part of the labor contract they signed. The money was transferred into a state-owned Mexican bank, since incorporated into the bank called Banrural. Advocates for surviving Braceros claim as many as 98 percent of the workers never saw a peso of their pension money.[14]

"It was humiliating," remembered the Bracero Manuel Herrera at the age of seventy-five. "They rented us, got our work, then sent us back when they had no more use for us."[15]

In 2001 a group of Braceros sued in U.S. federal court, seeking their lost savings. The Mexican government and Banrural say they're investigating. The court case is unresolved.

Attention to the smuggling of Mexicans across the now fortified border was paid in the noir fifties film *Wetbacks*, starring Lloyd Bridges and

Nancy Gates. The picture opens with automobile headlights shining out into the night across water. A smuggler is standing by his car, waving at a handful of Mexicans who are struggling toward the shore, sopping wet.

"Come on!" he yells, "come on!"

In the background we see a fishing boat, and one after another more passengers jump off into the water, swim, and stumble toward the beach.

"Why the devil did you bring him out here?" the smuggler asks his partner, who has come off the boat with a gun trained on the captain.

"My friend," says the partner sarcastically, "was getting ideas."

The captain looks confused. Apparently he had second thoughts about the mission.

"How many you got out there?" asks the smuggler with the car.

"Thirty," says the wet partner, as sombrero-wearing Mexicans run past the two of them. "And let's get them out of here."

A truck is waiting to haul the Mexicans north, but suddenly a siren sounds and from a loudspeaker comes an order.

"Stay where you are! This is the United States Coast Guard. You are under arrest. You are under arrest. Do not board the fishing boat! Hold your position. Do not board the fishing boat! Stay where you are."

The Mexicans panic and run back into the water toward the boat. The captain runs along the shore, and the wet partner fires at him. He falls. The smuggler jumps into the waiting truck and it speeds off. He fires again and the boat captain falls face first into the water.

The theme music surges and resolves. The harsh title explodes on the screen, WETBACKS.

The plot quickly is made obvious. Good-guy cops battle ruthless smugglers preying on poor Mexicans. Our hero is another hapless, down-on-his-luck fishing boat captain who struggles with his conscience and smugglers, helped to a happy ending by a Mexican village filled with sympathetic supporting heroes.

The next scene is a meeting in the offices of the U.S. Immigration Bureau.

"That was nasty on the beach last night," says the Immigration Bureau chief. He learns from the Coast Guard and the Highway Patrol that all the Mexicans were arrested and that the fishing boat captain died. But he's told the smugglers and their truck were lost in the chase, that it was probably a "souped-up, high-powered job."

"I wouldn't doubt it," says the intense chief with staccato authority. "Running wetbacks across the border is a big business these days."

"Big business?" asks a Coast Guardsman. "How much can those poor Mexicans pay, a couple of dollars a head?"

"Sometimes, yes," acknowledges the chief, and then he lectures the group. "Sometimes a family's life savings. There's plenty of work on the big ranches up here picking cotton and lettuce."

"But how much can these smugglers take in?" he's asked.

"Four, five thousand a week," he reports.

The Coast Guard officer lets out a low whistle.

"They've really made it a big business," the chief continues. "They hire the Mexicans out to the ranches as farm labor. Truck 'em from one farm to another."

"Yeah," protests one in his audience, "but how much can they net after they pay off the Mexicans?"

The disgusted chief jumps out of his chair and barks, "They don't pay off! They keep the money and run out on 'em." He points to a map of the border. "Gentlemen, they can bring the wetbacks across the border from Texas clear out there to ten miles in the Pacific, and they can cross by land, by air, and by water. Maybe even underground for all we know." He says he needs a couple thousand more men to secure the border. "This is a war, a war against the most vicious kind of human scavengers."

Hollywood fifty years ago.[16]

Those were the days when Tijuana-born Alfredo Santos was busy smuggling Mexicans into the United States. He used trucks and boats to bring workers north, and was paid $200 for every delivery to Los Angeles and $400 for those he escorted to San Francisco. He was caught and served time in U.S. prison. Later in life, after a career as an artist and gallery owner, Santos looked back at his smuggling days without regret. "To me, I didn't see anything immoral. I was sort of a Robin Hood, I thought."[17]

1 0

BEFORE THE

BORDER CONTROL

GOT TOUGH

THE CHOKE POINT came in the 1980s, and it changed the border completely.

The influx of Mexicans across the border at major urban crossings such as Tijuana and Juárez and Nuevo Laredo increased dramatically while Washington policymakers watched helplessly. Failed attempts by the overwhelmed Border Patrol to curtail the migration at that time set the stage for the disastrous failures the Patrol found itself facing along the rural border two decades later. Those days in the eighties, when waves of Mexicans advanced nightly from Tijuana into San Diego, are a critical moment in the history of the border wars, and the precursor of the contemporary crisis. That endless surge of desperate Mexicans north through shocked U.S. cities precipitated the building of the walls designed to keep them out.

In the early 1980s, I went to see for myself how the immigrant flow had begun to swell. I crossed into Tijuana and stopped for a few minutes to listen to a *mariachi* band playing along the Avenida de Revolución. Then I joined Chief Border Patrol Officer Alan Eliason in his squad car for a tour of the scrubby desert no-man's-land separating Tijuana and San Diego. Operation Gatekeeper and the severe wall built to separate the two cities were not yet reality. Eventually the wall would send migrants east to look for more easily accessible points along the border. As dusk arrived, we looked down on hundreds of people massing in an open field.

"They are about three-quarters of a mile into the United States at this point," Eliason told me as we looked at a veritable crowd moving north.

"What's going to happen?" I asked this veteran of the border wars.

"Right now, they're just going to run on back to the south." Eliason saw the same ebb and flow every evening. His arrival merely moved the crowd until his squad car passed. "If we have a unit behind us, we can maybe cut them off, otherwise we'll probably be running into this same bunch a little farther north after dark."

As Eliason and I talked along the border, Congress wrangled with the bill that ultimately became the 1986 immigration law, the compromise that tried to appease citizens fearful of immigrants, documented and undocumented, and at the same time tried to acknowledge the infusion of needed energy that immigrants traditionally bring to societies, especially America. While debate continued in Washington, we bounced along the rutted dirt trail toward a man already illegally in U.S. territory.

"We're seeing groups of from fifteen to about forty," Officer Eliason said "marching northward. Usually there is a guide accompanying these people, and the guide knows exactly where he is going to take his group."

Across the scrubby desert was a slow and steady flow of people from the Mexican side, people carrying knapsacks, chatting with each other—people on the march.

The border was a clear delineation. A relatively neat row of houses, in line on an east-west axis, ended and the scrub began, desert scarred with the trails used by the immigrants and crisscrossed by the tracks and ruts made by the Border Patrol's four-wheel-drive patrol jeeps. The equation was easy to see from our vantage point: there simply were more people moving north than Eliason and his men could physically apprehend.

"That's the border," he said again, "and these people are on their trek northward right now."

The odds of successfully infiltrating the spotty control were so in favor of the crush north that the sight of our lone squad car did virtually nothing to impede the progress of the evening's movement. We could reach out and touch Officer Eliason's adversaries. They glanced at us fleetingly to check us out, then looked away. Eliason called out to a few men:

"*¡Hola, señores! No quiero molestar. Este señor,*" he pointed to me and my tape recorder, "*quiere no más que hablar con ustedes.*" I don't want to bother you. This man just wants to talk with you.

Unless Eliason stopped his squad car and got out, most of the people heading north illegally didn't even bother moving off the dirt road. The desert wind blew hot and hard, and one brave or fearless fellow responded to our call and stopped to talk, explaining that he had tried first to get into the United States legally and was rejected.

"They didn't want to give me permission." He looked to be in his twenties, dressed in international casual clothes: running shoes, jeans, and a T-shirt—ideal for running across the desert and running from the authorities, natural camouflage for disappearing into suburban southern California.

"Why do you think the authorities refused you permission?" I asked.

"Because you have to have some money in the bank in order to get in," was his reply. And of course he had no money in the bank. His primary reason for coming north was to earn money.

"What do you want to do in Los Angeles?"

"Work," he said. His answer was immediate, without hesitation, obviously honest.

"What kind of work do you want?" My question came from the luxury of a First World perspective—wondering about preference—but he answered politely.

"I am a mechanic," he said, "but I'll do whatever work I can find."

Later that evening Eliason and his colleagues moved against the crush of immigrants pushing north toward the American dream, those hundreds of Mexican nationals waiting for an opportune moment to move past the border. I watched as suddenly an agent jumped out of his four-wheel-drive truck and ran along the Tijuana River where it separated the two countries. The river runs from Mexico into the United States, dry during the summer but an open sewer when it flows, and it creates a break in the fencing between the two countries. The agent chased off a forward group of the Mexicans who had inched into U.S. territory. Another patrol truck raced down the dry river bed, siren screaming, while a helicopter joined the charge, its twin spotlights playing off the surreal ballet below: a mass of immigrants waiting for what they believed would be an ideal time to sprint north, trying to evade the police and disappear into the brush and eventually the urban sprawl of San Diego. In the face of the agents' offensive, the swarm of humanity surged back to the sanctuary of Mexican territory. Newcomers to this nightly life-and-death border dance ran south to safety; the regulars ambled. Vendors with ice chests milled around in the throng, selling burritos and beer. The atmosphere was almost festive.

Like dogs trying to keep errant sheep in place, the agents scurried around the fringes of the mass of people, looking for stragglers to arrest, hoping to keep the crowd in check. They kept in touch over radio.

"There's one right in the middle of Tijuana Road." The officer coming over the squawk box spoke with a thick Mexican accent.

"Is that me you're looking at?" asked his compatriot. "Let me give you a light."

"Ah, ten-four."

"Yeah, okay, you saw me going up the side of the levee."

The guards were equipped with the latest technology. The night was pitch-black now, and I was about a mile east of the frenzied chases under spotlights in the Tijuana riverbed. I was on the north side of the ten-foot-high iron curtain the United States had erected between Tijuana and San Diego, a steel wall jumped over, ripped apart, and tunneled under by motivated migrants. I was at a solitary Border Patrol truck perched high on a bluff overlooking a canyon known as Smugglers Gulch. A starlight camera was mounted on a tower above the truck, and inside an agent—one hand on his walkie-talkie—studied a TV monitor. On the monitor the brush of Smugglers Gulch was clearly visible, as were the roads and the trails. The agent stared at the screen, saw a group of about half a dozen figures scrambling along a path, and picked up his radio.

"I've got a group coming up toward the S-curve," he told agents in the Gulch.

We watched a Border Patrol truck roar into sight on the screen and lock its brakes to a stop. The band of immigrants scattered, but they didn't stand much of a chance. The screen was equipped with a compass, and the agent on the hill was back on the radio.

"Go south fifty yards," he told his colleagues, "they're in the brush."

Moments later the immigrants were surrounded and arrested.

"I'm not frustrated," said veteran Border Patrol agent John Krupa as an immigrating crowd scattered just south of us. "The system works, but the system is overloaded." He looked south and shook his head as he tried to come to terms with his role in these border wars. "We get people who come down here and tour the border and they're shocked." His voice included a hint of a drawl, and with his moustache, easy smile, and militaristic uniform, Krupa came across like an actor in a television Western.

Later that same evening, he proudly showed off the latest in Border Patrol surveillance equipment and shared some Border Patrol humor (Question: Why isn't the border fence electrified? Answer: Because the Mexicans would tap into it to run their refrigerators.) At the San Ysidro Border Patrol station where Krupa was headquartered, the driveway was marked with a huge model of a cartoon-looking chicken. Mexicans who crossed the frontier illegally were known by *coyotes* and the Border Patrol alike as *pollos*, chickens.

Already there were tears in the new border fence made of surplus military landing mats. The barrier was ripped apart in some places and tunneled under in others. Designed to run fourteen miles from the Pacific east into the desert along this, the most heavily traveled international border in the world, the new barrier was not yet finished and was routinely violated. A decade later the Operation Gatekeeper would end the daily dance I watched at Tijuana that night.

"We've got to keep that border closed," insisted Barbara McCarthy to me at the time. She was one of those shocked citizens who toured the border at the invitation of the Border Patrol. An elegant-looking woman with time on her hands ("The kids are gone, and what am I going to do? Play bridge?"), she sat in her opulent San Diego living room, chain-smoking Parliaments and glancing occasionally out of her picture windows at the sweeping California-perfect view of Mission Bay. McCarthy was an organizer at the Stamp Out Crime Council, one of several ad hoc organizations that had sprung up along the border to lobby for a tougher response to illegal immigration.

"If we were honest with ourselves," she readily admitted, "and we were in the position of those Mexicans, we'd do the same thing." But in the next breath she dismissed the people she wanted stopped as "Mexico's problems. When people say we should open the borders I ask, 'How many are you going to take home with you?'" McCarthy saw the immigrants heading in her direction as responsible for much of the crime in San Diego County as well as a drain on local social services, such as the public schools. She wanted to rescind the law that guarantees citizenship for everyone born in the United States. She wanted a law against providing a ride in a car to anyone illegally living in America.

Stamp Out Crime published a newsletter and organized field trips to the border to rally support for its cause. Despite McCarthy's strident attitude toward illegal immigration, she tried to distance her group from the incidences of violent vigilante activity at the border. "You do have to look out for the cuckoo birds," she said, "and they're out there. They give others a bad name." But McCarthy was adamant that groups like Stamp Out Crime did not encourage freelance attacks on border crossers.

Observers at the American Friends Service Committee office in San Diego in the early 1980s agreed that vigilante border violence was a relatively minor problem, especially compared with the attacks perpetrated by bandits and the mistreatment that undocumented immigrants too often received at the hands of Border Patrol agents. "They're not violent,"

Roberto Martinez said about Barbara McCarthy and her ilk, "but they incite violence." Martinez was director of an ongoing Friends project to study border violence. He said he was dumbfounded by the xenophobia he encountered in groups like Stamp Out Crime. "They want me to go back to Mexico," he shook his head, "and I'm fifth generation." His downtown San Diego office was littered with reports and photographs documenting attacks by the Border Patrol on foreign nationals. Martinez and the Friends wanted the Border Patrol to be subject to a civilian review board. "More humane treatment is needed by the Border Patrol," he said. "They have a total disregard for human life."

The human rights organization Americas Watch agreed that the Border Patrol then was more of a threat than the vigilantes. In a report it charged agents with killing and abusing immigrants. "They're naive," said Barbara McCarthy about the Americas Watch investigators, "because they believe Roberto Martinez."

Border Patrol agents didn't deny that Mexicans were injured and killed during the free-for-all encounters that occurred along the border. But from the Patrol's point of view, the violence was a result of illegal incursions into U.S. territory. No one would be hurt, they maintained, if no one was breaking the law. And agents felt slighted that they were so rarely acknowledged for the good that they perceived the Patrol accomplished, from regular drug busts to sometimes rescuing immigrants from the bandits that preyed on them in the no-man's-land.

Pert and bubbly Muriel Watson was another high-profile Border Patrol booster. Her late husband had been a career agent, and she honored his memory with her group, Light Up the Border. Her agenda was direct action. She organized protests by lining up cars and shining headlights south, into the dark fields used as cover by those crossing into the United States illegally. "These were no vigilantes," she says of her compatriots. "You could go from car to car and they were grandmothers, whole families. They'd be sitting with their take-out food and turning on the lights. They understood that something must be done."

Watson saw a direct connection between her protests and the new anti-crime lights along the border, the new access roads for patrolling agents, and especially the new border fence. Her answer to the problem of illegal immigration was simple: "The only safe passage is for them to come through the port of entry and get on the trolley. They should do it legally." Of course, most of those who tried to cross illegally could not qualify for legal entrance into the United States.

While one group of immigrants was identified by the starlight scope, and another was being chased off the Tijuana River levee, hundreds more immigrants were making their way past the Border Patrol, past marauding vigilantes, safely into the United States. "We have to stimulate the Mexican economy," said agent John Krupa. "We've got to get business down there to provide a job base." On this point Roberto Martinez and Krupa agreed, "In the final analysis," said Martinez, "it has to be understood that 99 percent of the people crossing are just poor working-class people."

Just a few feet from the San Ysidro border crossing, the border fence began its path west. At the crossing station U.S. customs guards studied the never-ending train of cars coming into California. Some drivers were diverted to a special inspection lane where more thorough searches were conducted. A stream of pedestrians came north through the border station too. A Border Patrol truck was parked on a knoll east of the official crossing. But there could never be enough trucks and agents.

There one day (and it happens every day, all day long), in broad daylight within sight of dozens of the guards, first one head and then another appeared at the top of the new fence. Experienced eyes looked quickly at the road and saw no Border Patrol. There was a yelp of "Come on!" The bodies connected to the heads appeared, and two young men quickly let themselves down into the United States. In seconds they were followed by a half-dozen more men flying over the fence, all dressed in that usual uniform of border crossers: jeans, a T-shirt, and running shoes.

"Nothing will stop them," agent Krupa said. "These people are going to keep coming as long as the jobs are here."

The group ran north, across I-5, and disappeared into the brush under the Camino de la Plaza overpass. From there they could easily vanish into the teeming neighborhoods of San Ysidro.

The Southwest Border Strategy moved those dramatic encounters I witnessed in the 1980s out of sight of urban San Diego, into the empty deserts of the Southwest. In his Washington office, Congressman Silvestre Reyes—who takes credit for the strategy—talks about the border he tried to enforce during his long career with the Border Patrol. "I was born, raised, worked on the border all my life." He knows the two extremes in the border debate: some Americans want to eliminate all border restrictions while others want to seal the border by using the U.S. military. He rejects either as an agenda "that doesn't take into account those of us who know, understand, and love the border." The border, says Reyes, is a necessity. He points to national security, the economy, public health, and crime as reasons to restrict access to the United States.

In Congressman Reyes's crowded office is a replica of the Statue of Liberty, along with military mementos of his work on the Armed Services Committee. His grandparents emigrated from Mexico and he's a product of the American Dream, a fact he considered as part of his routine while working his Border Patrol beat, chasing Mexicans. "You recognize that there but for fate, you might be going. You have a full understanding of the implications of what you're doing." Reyes is a stout man, grey showing in his neatly combed and clean-parted hair. His military posture reflects his years wearing a badge. No other member of Congress served on the borderline, patrolling the U.S. frontier. "One of the things that always frustrates those of us who wear the Border Patrol uniform is the fact that depending on the political climate and the economic climate, we're expected to have what we describe as 'spigot enforcement.' You either turn it on or shut it off. We cannot work under those circumstances with any degree of success."

Advocates of sealing the border do not understand the "cultural mixing, the economic diversity and vitality that the border region represents to the two countries," says Reyes. He patiently explains that his years of experience taught him that controlling traffic on a border such as the one separating the United States and Mexico is a matter of compromise, and that 85 percent control is about the best the United States should expect. "If we learned anything from the Berlin Wall, it's that you can't build a wall to keep people in or out. We need to recognize that." But he is convinced the government must make a 100 percent effort to achieve that 85 percent control.

Reyes talks passionately about the human costs he's seen on the job. He's lost Border Patrolmen under his command to attacks from smugglers, seen close-up the violence of border bandits who cross into the United States and rob, witnessed the heartlessness of *coyotes* who abandon their clients when a crossing goes wrong. "I investigated a case where a train caught eighteen undocumented people in the middle of a trestle. They had to jump off—it was a calamity of major proportions. Some of them died and some were mangled. Those kinds of things really tear at your gut."

Yet Reyes does not think that opening the border is a viable solution to the heartbreak he's experienced in the field. Instead, he says, resources must be allocated to control it—and from his perspective, that's not happening. "Now that I'm in this position, I'm frustrated because I can't influence policy fast enough to make a difference for those [who die] in the boxcars and the eighteen wheelers. Not only has that happened way too many times in my lifetime, but unless we get serious about managing the border the way it ought to be managed, and with the cooperation of Mexico, people are going to continue to die in those kinds of circumstances." Managing the border, he says, includes freedom of movement for those with proper documentation who want to cross back and forth to shop and visit friends and relatives—but it does not include opening the border for all the Mexicans who want to come north to work or join their families. "We cannot afford a willy-nilly, chaotic border as long as the economies are so disparate, as long as we have a First World economy butting right up against a Third World economy."

If and when Mexico develops an economy and a society equivalent to those of the United States, Congressman Reyes speculates that the southern border could eventually become as free a passage as the U.S.-Canadian frontier. "There isn't a trick to it, it's just the economy of the country. Mexico is a very rich country. They've got oil; they've got natural resources. The only thing they don't have is the ability to manage it in a way that benefits the Mexican people. I think it's unfair to put the burden on this country for the well-being of Mexicans." So Congressman Silvestre Reyes works the halls of Congress, soliciting votes from his colleagues to bolster the Border Patrol.

11

AN UNWELCOMING
PROPOSITION

CONSIDER Rick Oltman's passion as he insists that there must be a tightly controlled border between California and Mexico. Oltman was one of the creators of Proposition 187, arguing up and down the state that he, a pale white man, had a right to the bounty of California, land won from Mexico in war, but that Mexicans did not. This state filled with Spanish place names, tortillas, and *mariachi* bands is now a place, according to his logic, into which Mexicans should not be allowed to wander north at will. An open border with Mexico would be, he told me, a disaster for the United States. "The United States would become another Third World country. Who in the world wouldn't want to come here if everybody could come? At any one time there are a hundred million refugees on the move in this world. I think somebody did a poll in Mexico where they found that 60 percent of the people in Mexico, if they were allowed to come here, would come here. If I lived someplace else, I'd want to come here too."

I've met plenty of Mexicans who do not wish to move north. One particularly sticks in my mind, a Mexico City taxi driver who expressed no interest in even visiting. He said he'd heard about the prejudice against Mexicans in the United States, and that it could be dangerous for Mexicans there. He wanted no part of *El Norte*.

Proposition 187, which was passed by California voters in November 1994, required schools to refuse admission to undocumented students and report them to the state's attorney general and the INS. It was the responsibility of the schools to check the immigration status of all incoming students.

Oltman and his ilk sounded quite unbelievably cruel and selfish when pressed about the inhumane specifics of Proposition 187. The law also denied all but emergency public health care to those in the United States without proper documents: "If they're bleeding," he spits out, "I say stop the bleeding and stabilize 'em and ship 'em out."

Oltman and I spoke during a televised debate about 187. Another pro-187 worker was Ruth Coffey, who fired missives through the group she founded called Stop Immigration Now. "I have no intention of being the object of conquest," she wrote and was widely quoted in California newspapers, "peaceful or otherwise, by Latinos, Asians, blacks, Arabs, or any other group of individuals who have claimed my country." Before finally being fired, a radio talk show host in San Francisco used the airwaves to suggest a cash bounty for every immigrant shot who entered the United States illegally.

Most opponents of Proposition 187 were convinced that, no matter what new laws were passed, the border could never be sealed. They feared that if the new regulations of Proposition 187 were enforced, immigrants in California with questionable legal status would avoid doctors and hospitals, teachers and schools. The result, they pointed out, would be an underclass filled with undereducated sick people often resorting to crime for survival.

The ballot argument in favor of Proposition 187 included bombastic language. "California can strike a blow for the taxpayer that will be heard across America!" it insisted. "Proposition 187 will go down in history as the voice of the people against an arrogant bureaucracy." Actually it's gone down in history as anti-immigrant baiting by California's governor at the time, Pete Wilson. Wilson became a chief strategist for the election campaign of Arnold Schwarzenegger, who immediately upon election as governor fulfilled his campaign promise to repeal the law that allowed illegal immigrants to obtain California driver's licenses.

"WE CAN STOP ILLEGAL ALIENS," screamed the ballot argument, a text peppered with upper-case typography. "If the citizens and the taxpayers of our state wait for the politicians in Washington and Sacramento to stop the incredible flow of ILLEGAL ALIENS, California will be in economic and social bankruptcy. We have to act and ACT NOW! On our ballot, Proposition 187 will be the first giant stride in ultimately ending the ILLEGAL ALIEN invasion. While our own citizens and legal residents go wanting, those who choose to enter our country ILLEGALLY get royal treatment at the expense of the California taxpayer. IT IS TIME THIS STOPS!"

"This is war," said Lynn Rolston, a California political activist with long experience working against U.S. policies in Central America in the 1980s. Rolston and I talked at a grassroots strategy meeting for opponents of 187 shortly after the proposition qualified for the California ballot. "We've got to combat the madness that is happening in this country," one of his colleagues replied to Rolston's war cry. Rolston's sentiments were shared by many opponents of the initiative as the campaign grew nastier. "Governor Wilson is playing with our fears and playing with our frustrations," accused Kathleen Brown, his Democratic opponent for governor (Wilson won the election).[1]

Proposition 187 was called the Save Our State initiative by its supporters, and became known simply as SOS. "You can pass two hundred SOS's," said Professor José Cuellar, chairman of the Department of La Raza Studies at San Francisco State University, during the campaign, "but you're not going to get rid of us. We're here. Get used to it." But Professor Cuellar was not just strident as he worked against Proposition 187, he was also practical, appealing to the voters' pragmatic side. "As the white population of this state ages," he told the Rick Oltmans of California, "it's going to become dependent on the young, multi-ethnic, Latino-dominated workforce to pay taxes and keep the economy cooking."[2]

Lalo Alcarez wrote and illustrated a comic strip called "L.A. Cucaracha" during the debate over Proposition 187. He changed its name from the Save Our State initiative to the "Ship Out Spicks" initiative and renamed Governor Wilson "Auntie Immigration." Another southern California comic, Rene Sandoval, who was appearing on the HBO weekly comedy "Loco Slam" at the time, feigned confusion regarding those who were fighting to deny education and health care to migrants. "They love our food, our music and our culture," Sandoval said. "They love everything about us—except us!"[3]

The opponents of Proposition 187 tried to make clear to the voters two essential arguments against it: denying children public education promotes juvenile delinquency, and denying health care to illegal immigrants produces disease-ridden farm and restaurant workers, tainting the food supply. Finally they pointed out the inconsistency of penalizing the migrants while the employers who draw them across the border and violate the law by hiring them are rarely prosecuted. Nonetheless Proposition 187 passed, and passed overwhelmingly, 59 to 41 percent.

Since Proposition 187 was later struck down by the courts, Rick Oltman and his colleagues seek other methods of restricting opportunities for immigrants as they lobby for a more secure U.S. border with Mexico. Oltman is an executive with an organization called Federation for American Immigration Reform. ("FAIR seeks to improve border security, to stop illegal immigration, and to promote immigration levels consistent with the national interest," according to its mission statement.) During a field trip to Arizona in 2004 he was horrified by the wide-open border he observed in the desert. Mexicans, he said, know that the odds are on their side as long as they get past the border, over the desert, and find a major highway. "If you can hit the pavement," Oltman bemoaned, "you're home free."[4] Of course he didn't intend us to interpret his use of the word "home" literally. Home for Mexicans crossing the border without papers, according to Rick Oltman, is back in Mexico.

12

AMONG THE
VIGILANTES

WITH INCREASING REGULARITY in twenty-first-century Germany, neo-Nazis attack foreigners who do not appear "German" enough. Police blame more than a hundred murders there in the last decade on right-wing, anti-foreigner attacks. Politicians encourage the thugs, saying Germany is not an immigrant country. In Dolgenbrodt, Germany, for one particularly nasty example, prominent citizens hired an arsonist to firebomb a hostel for immigrants. Mayor Karl Pfannenschwarz rationalized the attack by saying, "Look, we are a small village of three hundred inhabitants that lives off tourists visiting our lake. How are we supposed to react when the state tells us to find rooms for eighty-six Gypsies or Africans?"[1]

Walk the back streets of Algeciras in Spain, just across the Strait of Gibraltar from North Africa, and listen to the voices condoning violent attacks against Moroccans who immigrate illegally looking for work. Such attacks are known locally as *La Guerra*, The War. Head over to Italy where Prime Minister Silvio Berlusconi aligns himself with policy proposals giving Italian police authority to shoot at illegal immigrants in boats coming across the Adriatic Sea from Albania.[2] Remember the surprise showing of immigrant-basher Jean Le Pen in the first round of the 2002 French presidential elections, and that Jörg Haider and his far-right Austrian Freedom party enjoyed success at the polls with a strident anti-immigrant policy. Haider made his name condemning *Üeberfremdung*, overforeignerization. Pia Kjaersgaard, the leader of the far-right Danish People's party, gained votes with the cry, "It's a problem in a Christian country to have too many Muslims."

The push of cheap undocumented labor from the poor South into the rich North is creating new battlegrounds worldwide.

At the southwestern border of the United States, Mexicans surge north illegally to fill jobs as distant as Washington and Maine. Americans in border states such as Arizona bear the pain of this illegal migration. They're angry that the federal government is not controlling the border; they fear drugs, disease, and violence from the foreigners pushing across the frontier. The mood of many Americans on the Mexican border often seems similar to that of their anti-foreigner European cousins. Despite rising waves of desperation and frustration in the United States, anti-foreigner behavior here has yet to approach the lawless terror of Germany's neo-Nazis.

Still, a long list of grassroots organizations is lobbying, propagandizing, and agitating to seal the U.S. border with Mexico. Glenn Spencer and his American Border Patrol operate a flashy internet site. Click on "report illegals" on the home page and Spencer offers detailed advice on how to turn in your neighbors. "These are the numbers to call to report employers you suspect are employing illegal immigrants. You may also report immigrants themselves if you believe they are in the country illegally, whether they are working or not. You should have the address of each suspected violator at a minimum, and as much additional information as you can obtain."[3]

Spencer sends model airplanes with cameras mounted on them along the border, transmitting the pictures over the internet. His group operates fixed cameras along the border that also try to document migrants moving north. When his operatives spot what they consider suspects, they say they call the Border Patrol. The continuing worry is that these freelance border guards add to the danger on the border.

The local law is disgusted with Spencer and his antics. Santa Cruz County Sheriff Tony Estrada sees American Border Patrol as thrill seekers. "If you've got five hundred Border Patrol agents in an area, and they have a daunting task, what are five people going to do?" He answers his own question immediately. "Nothing. The only thing they're hunting is publicity."[4]

Websites of other organizations trying to circle the wagons include deportaliens.com, secureamerica.info, and ranchrescue.com. "Private property, first, foremost, and always," is the Ranch Rescue motto. Its material offers not-so-subtle encouragement for attacks against migrants.

Ranch Rescue advertises "operations," inviting volunteers to come join them in Arizona for Operation Thunderbird, in Colorado for Operation Foxbat, and in New Mexico for Operation Jaguar. They say their volunteers stop trespassers, most of whom they suspect of being illegal aliens. "All trespassers were given food and water, examined for injuries by a certified EMT, and evicted off the property by our volunteers. These trespassers were told not to return, and to spread the word among the rest of their criminal element not to come onto to our property. Return to the property by these individuals will result in Citizen's Arrest for Criminal Trespass."

Ranch Rescue claims that late in 2003 volunteers on the Arizona border were shot at by Mexican army troops. "None of our volunteers were injured. These terrorist acts will go unanswered by our own Federal and state governments. It is up to our Citizen volunteers to stand against this very real terrorist threat."

The Ranch Rescue website is illustrated with dramatic photographs of volunteers in military-looking fatigues on patrol with their automatic rifles. Their faces are covered with camouflage paint, their hats festooned with shrubbery.

Volunteers are offered special incentives. "Any volunteer who brings their aircraft (any type, including lighter-than-air craft), motor home (free hookups), or 'retired' military-style vehicle (wheeled or tracked) to Operation Thunderbird will receive a FREE Life Membership. Horse riders, with mounts, are needed to conduct mounted patrols. Those volunteers willing to bring their mounts will receive a FREE Annual Membership. Horse facilities on-site." Regular membership costs $30 a year or $150 for a lifetime.

As do most of the organizations advocating civilian involvement in patrolling the Mexican border, Ranch Rescue brags about its efforts to offer food, water, and first aid to any trespassers they encounter who are suffering from their trek north. And it warns potential volunteers about what the group expects of them.

> Our entire border area suffers from a very real physical danger of confrontations with terrorists, alien smugglers, drug smugglers, and other violent criminals. Since this danger exists, we encourage all volunteers to take the appropriate precautions regarding their physical safety. That danger of confrontation is being faced by private landowners in the border counties every day. Security volunteers are asked to carry firearms, and all members of Ranch Rescue will be allowed to carry their personally-owned firearms if they so choose. Security volunteers will be expected to become full members of Ranch Rescue. Our landowner hosts grant us permission to carry firearms while we are guests on the property. Arizona is an "open carry" state. Arizona state law allows Citizens to openly carry sidearms on private property, public highways, and public places other than government buildings and establishments where alcohol is served. If you do not feel capable of the more physically demanding tasks, we still need people to help with the organization and coordination of this effort. We also need Support volunteers to drive the vehicles, operate video cameras, monitor radio traffic, secure our base camp, and pass info along to our landowner hosts.

The names sound official: Civil Homeland Defense Corps, Ranch Rescue, American Border Patrol. But they are not part of any government agency. Instead they are independent groups composed of angry and frustrated Arizonans who say that, since the federal government has failed to secure the U.S. border with Mexico, they're going to do what they can to keep immigrants without valid papers out of Arizona.

American Border Patrol founder Glen Spencer says he wants to send all Mexicans in the United States without proper official authorization back home. "They're able to outsmart us all the time," Spencer says about his nemeses. "It's about telling the American people what's going on at the border," he says about the publicity he generates with the patrols he organizes. Roger Barnett created Ranch Rescue and watches the border with his gun handy. "If you go out there and you're not armed, you're a fool. Who's going to protect you out there?" Barnett and his colleagues detain Mexicans they assume are in the United States illegally and hold them for the Border Patrol. He calls the border "out of control" and blames Washington. "The government has left us alone out here—they forgot about us. They got one hell of a problem here with these invasions from Mexico."[5]

From the Mexican perspective on the south side of the border, these are vigilante groups. Mexican legislator Efren Leyva calls them time bombs, potentially destructive to the U.S.-Mexican relationship.[6] He and other Mexican officials want their American counterparts to disband the citizen patrols. Not a chance, say the vigilantes, who deny their intentions are to use violence against illegal migrants.

Meanwhile, migrants are being killed along the trails from Mexico into Arizona. Three men who Maricopa County Sheriff Joe Arpaio assumed were illegal were discovered tied up and shot late in 2003. His office reported nine similar murders in the county's wild desert. The sheriff theorized that the men were killed because of a conflict with smugglers or drug dealers. "We think they throw them right off the roadway to send a message."[7] Reports of unsolved shootings along the border are commonplace. Border Patrol agents are targets; migrants are targets. Who is doing the shooting? *Coyotes?* Bandits? Drug traffickers? Vigilantes?

Many of the cases remain unsolved.

Tombstone, Arizona, is a typical Western tourist mecca. In the late nineteenth century the mining boomtown's saloons really were a haven for outlaw gunslingers. Today busloads of tourists come to Tombstone looking for the warm Southwest sun and to cheer the actors who recreate the famous gunfight between Wyatt Earp and the Clanton Gang at the O.K. Corral.

But underneath the veneer of simple, friendly locals catering to out-of-town visitors, Tombstone is a simmering cauldron of conflict. The

Mexican border is just a few miles south. Tombstone lies directly in the path of undocumented migrants heading to Tucson, Phoenix, and points farther north.

Several months before my first trip to Tombstone in February 2003, an out-of-work California schoolteacher drifted into that town and took a job washing dishes in the O.K. Café. Before long, Chris Simcox hung up his dishtowel and went to work as assistant editor at the weekly newspaper, the *Tombstone Tumbleweed.*

"The owner had basically given up on this paper," Simcox told me. Soon after he went to work for the paper, he bought it. Local gossip says the capital came from his new girlfriend, the owner of the O.K. Café. "The paper was failing horribly. We were barely selling—maybe four hundred copies a week. It wasn't making it. You know, no advertising." The previous owner put the paper up for sale shortly after Simcox joined the staff of three.

His takeover of the *Tombstone Tumbleweed* is a story Chris Simcox tells often. His office phone rings incessantly. Reporters worldwide want to hear him complain about illegal immigration into Cochise County, and about how he founded the vigilante group he calls the Civil Homeland Defense Corps. Since he bought the paper, Simcox has turned the weekly into a propaganda sheet for his group's border activities. It's a change he's proud to report. "It's been nonstop. I mean I've done hundreds and hundreds of interviews. It's working."

What's working? I ask him. What are you accomplishing?

"Getting everyone across this country to understand what's going on down here in this border. We've been at war since 9/11, basically. We were attacked by people who came in, and then you watch what goes on in this border and you think, my God, it's a free-for-all. There is no real national security when you have an open border like this one here. Our government will not protect our borders. That's my number one concern."

This concern fills the sixteen-page paper each week. The January 30, 2003, issue of the *Tumbleweed* is typical. The editorial complains that a couple of tourists from Oregon were unable to get the county sheriff or the Border Patrol to respond when they called after they "spotted a group of eight suspected illegals walking just off the road. . . ." Frustrated, reports Simcox, the couple came to the newspaper's office because they had heard about the Civil Homeland Defense Corps. "There are so many illegals everywhere we go," he quotes them as telling him. "We can't even take a hike anymore without running into a group. We think this will be the last time we winter here in the south near the border. Our government had better do something!"

Simcox ends his editorial with his call to action. "Sounds like it is up to us, friends, the citizens. If you don't like it or it scares you. You can hide, or run, or you can join us as the eyes and ears of the citizens who can make a difference. Civil Homeland Defense is the only immediate solution." In a following editorial he charges that five thousand "illegals" came through Cochise County while Border Patrol officers watched the Super Bowl. "*Hasta la vista*," he writes, "welcome to the United States. Hope you enjoyed the game."

Forty-two years old when we talk in 2003, Chris Simcox looks much younger. His office is cluttered, dominated by his computer terminal and his electronic drum set. He wears the Tombstone uniform: work shirt, blue jeans, cowboy boots.

"I want America to know that they're not getting the real story," he says about his newspaper's perpetual lead story. "I've created a group of volunteers. And we go down [to the border] and we actually help do the job. That's the Civil Homeland Defense Corps. We are aiding and assisting the Border Patrol and plugging the holes on the border."

Simcox is wide-eyed and excited. "I mean, granted it's, you know, the little boy with his thumb in the dike, basically. But we go down to the border when we can and with however many numbers we can put together, and we help patrol that border. Using the same tactics and the same procedures and the same humane interaction that the Border Patrol uses. We work shoulder to shoulder with Border Patrol. We're on Border Road, which you'll see when you go out with us. We're in our vehicles. We drive back and forth. We create a presence that says, 'There's activity here, don't come across.'

"They're human beings. I mean, there's a reason why they're coming across, and that's because Mexico's not taking care of their needs, their own government. I've seen people out there in bad shape. But I've also been shot at by, you know, drug dealers. There's been so many drug busts, it's incredible. Something's not right."

Soon after Chris Simcox bought the *Tombstone Tumbleweed* he slapped an editorial across the front page of the paper that screamed: "Enough is enough! A public call to arms! Citizens Border Patrol Militia Now Forming!"

It's impossible to determine if Simcox has slowed migration from Mexico, but he has certainly managed to disrupt life in Tombstone. At Curley Bill's Bed & Breakfast ("The Best and the BADDEST in Tombstone! Wyatt Earp Slept Here—You Can Too!!!"), a few blocks across town from the *Tumbleweed* offices, Larry "Curley Bill" Alves is disgusted with Simcox's talk about guns and shooting. "His military training was in the Boy Scouts," he says. "I'm a conservative Republican, but I'm an ex-senior noncom in Vietnam. He's a little kid who never got to play soldier." Alves sees a direct relationship between his bed-and-breakfast business and Simcox's ability to draw national news coverage. "This militia stuff hurts tourism. People in this town don't like this at all."

Alves's wife, Sally, continues the assault on the new guy in town. "Local people are sick of listening to all that crap," she says about Simcox's tirades in his newspaper. "If you could still run people out of town on a rail, he'd be run out of town on a rail."

But Simcox insists that Sally and Larry Alves are wrong.

"The business owners certainly are unsure because this town survives on tourism. They don't want to do anything that's going to rock the boat or potentially hurt tourism." But he's convinced that cancellations at Curley Bill's are not his fault. "This does not hurt tourism," he says about his Civil Homeland Defense Corps. "This has not changed this town at all. In fact, with the amount of people that come in that door wanting to meet me, from other places, we're *attracting* tourists."

No question Simcox is generating attention. The day he and I talk, a reporter from *Newsday* is in town looking for him. And Simcox is waiting anxiously for a camera crew from HBO that he's expecting wants to film him for a documentary about the border.

"We do nothing but identify where they're coming across," Simcox explains. Days before, he and one of his troopers were arrested by a National Park Ranger for straying onto federal land at the border. The specific charges were carrying a loaded weapon inside a National Park and interfering with law enforcement. Rangers confiscated Simcox's patrolling gear: a pistol, two-way radios, a police radio scanner, a mobile telephone, and a camera.

"Why were you armed?" I ask him.

"I'm always armed. It's my Second Amendment right. The U.S. Constitution and the Arizona state constitution give us rights to keep and bear arms. I have a concealed-weapons permit. I refuse to be a victim. I've had now eight death threats since I've started this."

He says all the volunteers carrying weapons along the border pass a proper gun safety class and hold a concealed-weapons permit. "They know the law. They're responsible citizens. We're not out there threatening people, which is why we conceal our weapons. We're not out there looking for trouble.

"If we see any crossings, we let the Border Patrol know right away. We just do nothing but report the crossings and the illegal activity, at the encouragement of President Bush. That's all we do. We're neighborhood watch volunteers." The Border Patrol is less enthusiastic. "As long as they don't impede our duties in the field, we don't really deal with them," is the official response from the U.S. Border Patrol's Tucson sector spokesman, Frank Amarillas.[8]

Simcox is worried not only about Mexicans. He fears that terrorists know how easy it is to cross the desert into the wilds of Arizona, and are sophisticated enough to blend into the transient community of international tourists that frequent Tombstone and nearby Bisbee.

"I'm the only male in my family that never served in the military." Curley Bill is correct: Chris Simcox has no military experience and no police background. It's a lapse he regrets. "I do come from a family that always gave its service to its country, okay? We love our country, we're willing to fight for it. I've lived in New York most of my adult life. I have seen so much crime and so many people who come here from other parts of the world who commit crimes." As he quickly skips through his biography, Simcox highlights an event that may explain his fixation about Mexicans coming across the border.

"I've been a victim of crime by a guy who didn't speak English in New York City. I was mugged."

I point out that just because the guy didn't speak English doesn't mean he wasn't born in Manhattan.

"True. True. It's just a crime. But crime is out of control. Drugs are out of control." Simcox quickly changes his target and blames the federal government for failing to secure the borders, "so it's just my basic patriotic duty to do what's necessary."

Not that Simcox and his followers believe they can secure the border with Mexico, not even just the Cochise County border with Mexico. They hope their efforts force Washington to militarize the border.

"Troops on our border," is the solution, he says. Troops would create "a true sense of national security. When you talk to the folks out there, that's the only thing that will deter them from coming across. They're not afraid of us. They're not afraid of the Border Patrol. They're not afraid of anything. They're going to come in to America because we leave it wide open, and it's so easy. Troops on the border would force Mexico to deal with their own people, to start spending some of their money to support the citizens of that country. Build infrastructure. Improve their cities, improve their schools, improve their education. That's why they come here, because they admire our system. Well, if they admire it why the hell aren't they doing it themselves?"

"Chris Simcox's principal malady is that he is an incurable racist," writes Miroslava Flores on the website La Voz de Aztlán.[9] Another La Voz de Aztlán writer identifies Simcox as a "vigilante thug calling for anti-Mexican armed militia."

Not so, Simcox protests. "Since when do your nationalistic views and your patriotism and your wanting to provide security for your neighbors and fighting crime make you a racist?"

He insists he's not a vigilante. "A vigilante is someone who is judge, jury, and executioner. Someone who certainly takes the law into his own hands. We don't. We report illegal activity, that's it. That's all we do. And we create a deterrent to anyone who would break the laws of coming across that border."

Despite his protestations, when I first called his office to arrange a meeting with Simcox, his assistant said he couldn't come to the phone because he was holding Mexicans he suspected of being in the United States illegally in place under a Tombstone tree while a colleague tried to summon the Border Patrol.

"We do not apprehend." It's obviously a matter of definition. "We locate. We don't hold 'em. We just follow 'em. We give the Border Patrol the coordinates of where these people are, whoever they may be." He insists he doesn't discriminate against Mexicans. "We have turned in people from Poland, from Germany, from Spain, from China, from all over the world. I don't care who's on the other side of that border, if they're coming in to America illegally. Okay? That's dangerous. Since 9/11, that's dangerous. It's not about racism, this is about national security."

Chris Simcox tells me he knows what to look for when he patrols the border. "People who've entered this country illegally—it's quite obvious, most of the time." Of course, even trained Border Patrol agents make identification mistakes. The mayor of a Los Angeles suburb—Latino, but a native U.S. citizen—was famously picked up in an INS raid, and Cheech Marin starred in a tragicomedy about such a false arrest, *Born in East L.A.* Doesn't Simcox risk making an embarrassing mistake: tracking a U.S. citizen—perhaps even a loyal *Tombstone Tumbleweed* subscriber— and calling the Border Patrol to deport him or her?

"So what? They get their feelings hurt, they can go see their therapist. We're in a time of war."

It's a Friday. Chris Simcox invites me to hang around with him and his group all weekend. The plan, he says, is to meet at the newspaper office at 5:30 Saturday morning and drive south to patrol the border. Dawn is a prime time for illegal crossings, he tells me. The weekend days are scheduled to be filled with classes for his posse provided by a former

Delta Force Special Ops trainer. Another border patrol outing is planned for Saturday at dusk.

A half-hour south of Tombstone is the dusty border town of Douglas. The two-lane blacktop from Tombstone to Douglas is tumbleweed and sagebrush studded, punctuated with billboards addressed to President George W. Bush. They sport the international "no" sign, a red slash through the word "invasion."

"Mr. President," reads one, "Mexican Federales and Soldiers Are Shooting at Our Border Patrol. Order Your Friends to Stop!" Another refers to September 11th. "Mr President: Homeland Security Starts Here, Cochise County, AR, USA," and adds a sardonic "Maps Available." The map offer is used on another sign that says, "If This Were Crawford, TX, the Marines Would Be Here."

Cross-border traffic became a crisis for Arizona when the U.S. government reinforced patrols at San Diego, El Paso, and other urban crossing points. When the wilds of the Arizona desert became a favored crossing point for migrants without proper papers, it wasn't only the migrants who suffered. Arizona became overrun with desperate trespassers. The Border Patrol increased its manpower on the Arizona line exponentially in an effort to try to combat the sudden flow of huge numbers of migrants moving north through the state.

"I was born and raised here." I'm in the modern Douglas ("The premier Southwestern border community") city hall, a block from its fading Main Street, talking with Mayor Ray Borane. "I've seen illegal immigration all my life. I remember when I was a kid, there wasn't any fence there." Mayor Borane is disgusted with the likes of newcomer Chris Simcox. "I am part Hispanic. My mother is half Mexican. I was raised in this town, and I was raised with her side of the family, the Mexican side. All through my life I have been very sympathetic, very compassionate towards the plight of Mexican people."

When the harsh Arizona desert corridor turned into a highway of death for many of the migrants, Mayor Borane says he felt compelled to respond. He complained to his congressional representatives, the president, the attorney general. He wrote an op-ed piece for the *New York Times* addressed to "those who live in the nation's more wealthy places." Borane lectured New Yorkers. "Do you have any idea what havoc you cause in our area and in other border towns, all because you hire illegal immigrants to make your beds, mow your lawns and cook your food?"[10]

The mayor paraded statistics for New Yorkers. He cited the more than 200,000 Mexicans and other migrants deported by the Border Patrol in just over six months. He told the story of 28 migrants suffering from heat exhaustion rescued the week before he wrote to the *Times*, all evacuated by helicopter to local hospitals where one died. He recounted a shootout between *coyotes* and their clients, a highway wreck that injured 33 people jammed into an old van.

Don't blame the migrants, Borane insisted. "Can you even begin to fathom the arduous, debasing journey people endure to serve you comfortably in the luxury you are so accustomed to?" He cited the armed vigilante groups that responded to the crisis, calling their actions wrong and adding, "But it is what your demand for cheap and unregulated services has driven them to."

As we chat near the American flag in the mayor's office, Borane is agitated, calling the technology and manpower assembled on the U.S. side of the border a charade. "The only thing it lacked was a fucking idiot like that guy Simcox up the road. Excuse me, but it gets me really frustrated when I talk about this. Simcox writes that idiotic call to arms, and they make him a media idol. It's so outlandish—reminiscent of the Old West."

Mayor Borane is disgusted that the Border Patrol puts up with the meddling of Simcox and other vigilante groups. "What other agency in this country would? Our local police wouldn't let somebody come in and say we're going to help you run down felons. The army certainly wouldn't. The FBI wouldn't. The CIA."

One of the reasons Ray Borane expresses such disgust with Simcox and the other vigilantes is that their patrols add to the problems faced by the migrants without preventing illegal cross-border traffic. "People think I'm a bleeding heart for the illegals. I am in a way. They're being used and abused by their own people. They're robbing them on that side. They're being abused over here. And they're on their way to work. They're going to jobs that are given to them by Americans. Jobs that Americans don't want. And they're risking their lives to do it, to support their families. You know why Simcox is a problem? Because while those people are lying there having to wait for him to play his little game—his childish game— they won't go across the border because they don't know what to expect from him. They're suffering in the weather. They have no money. They're just sitting there waiting him out."

In Mayor Borane's *New York Times* piece he cites a little-known group of victims found along the border. "Children," he writes, "are often separated from their parents in Border Patrol roundups and end up in shelters." I walked across the border from Douglas to Agua Prieta to learn more. Borane had sketchy information for me: the children are taken to a shelter called Casa Pepito, he told me, run by a woman named Sylvia—he could not remember her last name.

I found Sylvia Villalobos with little difficulty. Along one of sprawling Agua Prieta's main streets is the storefront office of a local legislator. I asked the two men on duty for directions to Casa Pepito. "You want a ride?" one of them offered me a lift in his truck. I had planned to walk, assuming that Agua Prieta was a sleepy crossroads like its across-the-border neighbor, Douglas. On the contrary, Agua Prieta is bustling and stretches miles south into the Sonoran desert, with a population approaching ten times the fifteen thousand living on the U.S. side. As is the case for so many of Mexico's northern border cities, Agua Prieta is booming as a jumping-off place for Mexicans heading north and a center for border trade and industry.

The U.S. Border Patrol sometimes picks up children who become separated along the border from their parents during a family crossing. But often children are entrusted to *coyotes* by parents already living in the United States who wish to reunite their families. If these smugglers are caught, American authorities send the children back to Mexico. The

Border Patrol also finds children wandering the border area alone. Some have decided to attempt the crossing alone, others have been abandoned by *coyotes* who feared capture.

"Sometimes the children cross separately," Sylvia Villalobos is explaining to me how children end up at Casa Pepito. If they're found by the Border Patrol, they're turned over to the Mexican consular officials in Douglas who send them over the line to Casa Pepito. "We look for the mother or any relatives." During the search "they stay in Casa Pepito. We give them medical services, we feed them. We try to help them with psychological help too, so they don't feel so bad. It's like a home. They live as a family."

On Villalobos's desk is a fat binder filled with forms and pictures. For each child processed there are before and after photographs: when they first arrive at the shelter and when they are reunited with their family. "When we talk to them we ask, 'Where is your mother? Do you have a phone? Where do you live?'" Local social services in the hometown are then engaged to help. The success rate in finding the children's families is an extraordinary 100 percent. "Sometimes we have hard times. We have had two children who spent six months here. Sometimes the families cannot come and get them, and we have to travel all the way to Mexico City or Guadalajara to return them to their families. But usually they stay one day or two."

Of course, not all the children can offer their phone number and other critical information. On one page of the binder I spot the photograph of case number 114, who arrived at Casa Pepito December 1, 2002, from Chihuahua, age seventeen days. Others are five months, a year or two old. Such little children are either traced by the birth certificates they carry for identification, or are reunited with their families when the parents send word to the Mexican authorities that they have lost track of them. "Sometimes the parents cross through the desert while the children go by water." The parents go without the children, worried that "the crying of the baby is an alert for the immigration people," and turn their children over to *coyotes* who take the children across—for a fee. "Sometimes they are so intent to cross the border, I think they don't care who does the work as long as they get their children across." She shows me the picture of a teenage boy, turns the page of the binder, and there he is again, with his father.

The number of suffering children is staggering. According to the Mexican Foreign Ministry, 9,800 unaccompanied minors were repatriated from the border where they were caught crossing illegally in the first nine months of 2003 alone.

I walk back over to the U.S. side. When the immigration officer asks me what I was doing in Mexico, I tell him about my visit to Casa Pepito. He nods. "It's a continuing problem. It breaks my heart to see kids suffer. See these grey hairs? I'm only forty."

"That asshole!" says the bartender with disgust. I'm in St. Elmo, a rowdy saloon in Bisbee, an old copper-mining town between Douglas and Tombstone. Buzz Pearson is tending bar, talking about Chris Simcox. "The guy has no idea what's going on." Buzz sports a shaved head and greying goatee, a big silver earring in one lobe. Powerful arms tattooed, arms that won him the power lifting championship of Arizona. His band plays at St. Elmo: Buzz and the Soul Senders. "I've 86'ed him from St. Elmo," says Buzz about Simcox. "I'm not down with his thing.

"It's too complicated," Buzz says about the border, "to have a bunch of yahoos patrolling on their own. I'm sure it'll cause problems. Somebody will get shot. A lot of them are looking for excitement," he says about Simcox and the other vigilantes. "I think it's going to blow up in his face. Something bad is going to happen or people are going to realize he's in it for his ego."

Susan Nunn knows Tombstone from a vantage point few enjoy. She was the night manager at the Tombstone Best Western motel, the Lookout Lodge. "Quiet and peaceful," offers the Lookout Lodge's advertisements. "Rooms with views. Walk to town." Views, yes. Quiet, not very. Walk to town, walk from Mexico.

The Border Patrol was hustling in the late 1990s to find additional agents to assign to the border around Tombstone. "They brought a bunch of guys down from Washington State," Nunn remembers, and these out-of-state agents needed temporary housing. They took rooms at hotels along the Arizona border. "I had a bunch of them at the Best Western. They slept all day. In the evening they'd go out and they'd be all over the hills all night long. While they were gone, all the illegal immigrant traffic was coming by the motel with their problems."

At ten o'clock each night Susan Nunn locked the Best Western's front door. A telephone just outside the door was available for late arrivals to call the motel office; it also rang in Nunn's bedroom.

"The immigrants would pick up this telephone because they needed help, they needed a room," Nunn tells me. "All night long they would be on the phone—'We're in trouble. Our people are wet, our people are cold. Please come help us.' I'd ask them if they were illegal, and if they said yes I'd figure they were honest enough that I could help them. If they'd lie to me, I say, 'Walk on downtown, it's another mile.'"

If the migrants admitted to Nunn that they were in the United States illegally, she'd check the register for vacancies. "If I had a room, I'd put them in it. I didn't care how many people. They're wet. They're cold. They're crying. They're old. They're young. They're babies. I mean, my God! They were coming at us from all directions.

"My theory at that motel was, I am not the law. I have no right to discriminate. If someone comes up here and they have the money and they have an ID, I do not have the right to say you are not allowed to have a room."

The travelers paid.

"They would always have the money in a plastic bag so it wouldn't get ruined if they got wet." The Best Western rooms typically contained two beds, "and they would put maybe fifteen people in that room." Nunn says she made it clear that she didn't mind the crowds and that she had no intention of calling the authorities by holding her index finger up to her lips to indicate their secret was safe with her. She brought food to the rooms and never needed to warn her guests from south of the border that Border

Patrol agents were their neighbors. After resting, the migrants were back on the road. "In the middle of the night they'd be gone. As soon as they got dry and warm they would move on."

The morning after I met Chris Simcox, I crawled out of bed at Curley Bill's into a frigid sunrise, warmed up the car, and headed across Tombstone to the newspaper's office. Simcox said his posse would convene at 5:30. Southern Arizona heat is murderous in the summer, but winter cold and rain and snow also abuse the migrants. Tombstone is 4,500 feet above sea level. I sat in the car with the heater on listening to radio stations from Dallas and Salt Lake. I waited. I read the *New York Times* I bought the day before in Douglas at the Gadsden Hotel, the architectural star of Douglas's struggling main street. I waited. It got light. I waited. Chris Simcox was a no-show.

I drove the few blocks over to the O.K. Café and nursed a cup of tea. While I was deciding what to do next, I started to overhear bursts of conversation from the table next to me. "Twit . . . ego-driven . . . underqualified." A man was talking to a woman. "It was terrible, I was pulling my hair out." And I started paying close attention when he said, "Chris can't shoot for shit." This was the day Chris Simcox told me his troops would be trained by an ex-military expert marksman. The fellow at the next table looked the part, with his trimmed moustache and Airborne baseball cap. "He's so enamored of all the attention . . ." I got up and introduced myself to James Garrett, who was only too happy to talk about his client, Chris Simcox.

"This is such a complex issue that is being so grossly oversimplified," he began. "Normally I run under a code name down here, for obvious reasons, because this is going to get ugly at some point," Garrett told me. But he says he decided to identify himself to me and speak on the record because of his concerns. "At the highest level it's a political problem," he says of the border, "because it's about sovereignty. I think sometimes we all slip into clichés because they fit, not because we're intellectually suffering from a deficit but because they simply are able to capture in a pithy way a conceptual issue." It's six in the morning, but he's fired with emotion and energy. "A nation without borders is not a nation. And we have lost control of our borders. At the more immediate level, we have an abrogation by state, certainly federal—and I would also suggest local—law enforcement of the responsibilities for protecting the citizens who live along this border. When citizens cannot leave their home without a radio and a gun, when they escort their children to the bus stop under arms . . . ," he pauses with disgust. "As a Vietnam combat special ops veteran, I did not fight for this. For me it's a very personal issue. I have to be somewhat careful at times not to let that personal focus cloud my strategic judgment."

Garrett tells me he is "tactical officer" for the Civil Homeland Defense Corps. It is a "very uneasy" relationship, he says. His job this day is to provide concealed-weapons permit training to the group. On other occasions he offers other kinds of training. But he's rethinking his role after working closely with Simcox. "He mentioned to me the other day that he wants to start doing night ops, and he has no clue. At night the rules change big time. During the day I think it's a great idea to have citizens taking an active part. And if that deters them, good."

But Simcox, worries Garrett, is not the man to lead such a movement. "He's made an absolute fool of himself. He lacks the intellectual basis for the issue. At some point it's going to turn into a tactical issue," Garrett says about the border. "I think it's going to turn into a shooting issue. But right now it's a political issue, and it has to be handled with a serious degree of sophistication. It has to be packaged very carefully."

Then why would Garrett want to get involved with Simcox?

"Because I think the model we're working up has the potential to be the most effective and the least offensive—as opposed to Ranch Rescue, which is running around in camouflage. That's just a wreck waiting to happen. Or like the American Border Patrol which takes photographs and, okay, so what? Simcox is the only game there is because he has that newspaper. It's a voice. Without that, you have no voice."

We head back to the newspaper office to collect the students where a sheepish Simcox apologizes for standing me up. "I forgot to tell you. If it's raining we don't go out."

Our motorcade of border watchers heads south out of Tombstone. We get off the blacktop and speed along dirt roads, past a scattering of homes, finally turning into Ray Bouton's driveway. Two nooses hang from trees. Three flags fly from his big red Ford pickup: Old Glory, the Marines flag, and the Revolutionary War's Don't-Tread-On-Me banner. Bouton has offered an outbuilding on his land for the concealed weapons training class. We're less than a mile from the border.

Ray Bouton wears blue jeans and boots, a work shirt with snaps, and a black cowboy hat. A loaded automatic pistol is shoved into his belt. He offers to show me his personal war zone.

"These trees out front here," we're walking past the nooses, "which are probably sixty, seventy feet from my house, I've come out and found—the politically correct phrase for it is illegal aliens, but I call 'em wetbacks. They actually camped out in front of my house in those trees. My daughter's bedroom is over here." He makes clear the proximity between the ad hoc campground and his girl's room. "They come through from the border. They walk through here, cut my fences. I find 'em out here, trash all over the place." And as we walk he shows me the trash, piles of it. Liter water bottles with Spanish-language labels, soiled diapers and baby wipes, bottles of electrolyte supplements. And pair after pair of women's underwear. Ray Bouton's theory is that the discarded underclothing suggests rape victims.

Bouton regularly encounters the trespassing migrants. "Sometimes they ask for water. None of them are violent or aggressive. I don't consider them a real threat. But they don't come with signs stating that their intentions are good. I happen to think their intentions are to look for work. But when I find bottles of tequila, empty cans of Tecate beer, pornographic magazines and pornographic comic books, I do have a concern for my daughter and the children around the area.

"What I usually do is grab a pistol, if there's only several in a group. If there's a large group—thirteen, fifteen, twenty, I usually go out with a rifle. I've got a rifle that holds thirty rounds in a clip. I walk out with that because these people are desperate. I don't know what a desperate person's going to do. My . . . our only line of defense right here is me. We don't rely on the Border Patrol or police at all."

Bouton's place is remote. A call to the authorities, even if they were to respond, would mean a long wait for a patrol car. "They couldn't get here to do anything to protect you in time." Not that he would expect the cops to care. "Most of the Border Patrol and the police have become so apathetic with the numbers of illegals that come through this area, they don't bother. It's just another day in the office for them. They can put in their eight-hour day and go home. They don't have to think about it. I have to live here, with the fear of it, twenty-four hours a day. I live by the weapon here."

Once he has the trespassers under control, if he senses no threat, Bouton just wants to get rid of them. "They're usually trying to get north. I just direct them, tell 'em, 'Vamos! Andale!' and point. Then I go in and call the Border Patrol and keep an eye out. I don't go out and hold a gun. I don't hold 'em on the ground or threaten in any way. But I do want them to see that I have a firearm, a defensive firearm with me."

Bouton says he just wants them off his property. "They have more rights in this country than you or I. I can't hold 'em. If I hold 'em at gunpoint, I'm detaining these poor or pathetic migrants that are just coming up here . . ." He trails off in disgust. I find it hard to believe he'd face any difficulty from the authorities if he detained a trespasser on his own property. But he tells me I'm wrong. "Even if they do come through and cut the fence—and they've cut my fences—it's not worth what would happen to me. These wetbacks that have come through from another country—criminal trespassers as far as I'm concerned—have filed lawsuits against ranchers and other people in the area who have come out and detained them. I have seen, with my own eyes, down on the border, Mexican civil rights groups handing them water, food, and pamphlets telling them where to go in the United States for help, how to get north. Maps and phone numbers of civil rights organizations. If they're in any way detained by any of us legal American citizens, we're the ones at fault. We're the ones in the wrong."

How often does this happen? Does this happen once in a while, does it happen every day? Is it something that you're thinking about all the time? Is it just part of your routine?

"Pete," he addresses me with the informality that comes fast in the rural West, "this is something I think about all the time. How many Americans do you know who live with a gun? I sit with my family at night and watch TV with a pistol by my side. When I go to bed at night there's a pistol by my bed, there's a rifle in the corner loaded, ready to defend my home."

So you're living scared on your own ranch, I suggest.

"I'm not scared," he rejects the characterization. "But I'm apprehensive. I'm on edge all the time."

I ask him again how frequently he encounters trespassers.

"It's every night of the week."

"Every night of the week?"

"It's every night."

Bouton says migrants use his hoses to secure water, sleep in his hay or the beds of his pickup trucks. Sometimes the bolder or most desperate of the intruders ask for provisions.

"I will give them water. There's no person in this world that I could refuse a drink of water unless it was a child molester or a rapist or murderer.

"I happened to be sitting right on this porch here one day this summer, and of all things I was doing, I happened to be cleaning a rifle. And this wetback walks around the corner. It was in the summer, it was in the high nineties, and this guy was just completely done. I could see the signs of heat stroke, heat exhaustion. I work in the Grand Canyon, I'm familiar with the signs. I ran a hose over him. Then I went in the house and got a tortilla and loaded it up with grape jelly and sugar to revive him. Then I called the Border Patrol. I eventually got out of him that he was going to Wilcox. He had a brother in Wilcox and he was going there to look for work. But he was lost. He didn't know where Wilcox was or how to get there. When the Border Patrol came he got up and went toward the Border Patrol vehicle looking to get in it because of the air conditioning."

"It's a human tragedy," I say. "Aside from whatever problems you have with your fence and your concerns for your safety, it's a human tragedy."

"Oh, it is," Bouton agrees. "I have no hatred for these people. I know the Mexican people. I've lived here with the Mexican people for I don't know how long. I have friends that are Mexicans who don't like what's going on here." I don't blame these people at all for wanting to better themselves. I do blame the Mexican government for not doing more for their people. I think the Mexican government condones what's going on here.

"I've been in Mexico, three hundred miles south of the border to the beaches, back into the interior, in the mountains. It's a beautiful country. That country supposedly has as many resources as the United States. Plenty of oil. These people are our neighbors, next door, but we don't seem to want to do anything for them. I don't think that's our job, but I think the Mexican government is just a cash system for the super rich. To me Vicente Fox is the biggest pimp in the world. He prostitutes his people to the United States so he can live in a lap of luxury. As long as they can come up here and bring back the $8 billion every year to Mexico, to put into his economy, he doesn't have to do anything."

Ray Bouton's analysis is a little rough around the edges, but it's filled with reality. I ask him why he doesn't just move—sell the ranch and find a place in say, Montana, hundreds of miles from these daily crises.

"Pete, I'll tell you what. I once lived six hundred yards from the Mexican border. I was still in the United States. Six hundred yards from the Mexican border or six hundred miles, I'm still an American citizen, and I shouldn't have to run in fear because of criminals from another country.

"I've got too much pride to turn around and run. Americans are known for standing and fighting. We as Americans don't turn our backs and run because Mexicans are going to come up here and run us out of this country. You hear Hispanic pride, Mexican pride, we're proud to be Mexicans. Well, if you're proud to be Mexicans, stay in your country and make some type of change in your country. We did it in our country. Do it in your country."

In an outbuilding on Ray Bouton's border land, the motley bunch of about a dozen unofficial border patrol volunteers gathered by Chris Simcox assemble for class. Country music plays. A sign on the wall proclaims, "Hunters, fishermen, and other liars gather here." The decor includes guns and knives, cell phones and walkie-talkies. Stacks of *American Rifle-man* magazine are scattered about the room.

"My name is Storm," James Garrett introduces himself only with his *nom de guerre*. He makes no mention of being "tactical officer" for Simcox and his Civil Homeland Defense bunch. Instead he specifically announces that he is not formally connected with them and is on the scene only to teach what the state of Arizona requires a citizen to know in order to obtain a concealed-weapons permit. And he introduces himself to the group.

"I spent ten years in Special Ops, United States Army Special Forces. I spent combat tours in Vietnam and Central and South America. I was an instructor at the commando school for U.S. Army Special Forces at the Special Warfare Center. I did almost ten years in law enforcement beginning with the LAPD, and my last tour of duty was as a Border Strike Force Ranger in New Mexico on the drug deals over there, one of the dreaded 'Men in Black.' I've been teaching weapons and tactics for about thirty-seven years. I don't know it all. But I've had to learn a few things because I'm alive and some other people aren't. Last year I retired as a professor of criminology and forensics. I could no longer teach in the current higher education environment of political correctness. You will find out from some of the remarks I make in here that I am anything but politically correct."

"That's okay," interrupts one of the eager students. "Neither are we." The group laughs.

Storm tells his students to introduce themselves and explain why they want to be licensed to carry a gun. One more thing: if they were to be reincarnated as a wild animal, which animal would they choose to be?

"My name is Chris," says Simcox. "I want to learn how to avoid park rangers." His bunch laughs. He gets serious and says he wants to learn more about the law "and come back as a bear."

Ray Bouton introduces himself and says he's pleased to be the host of the event. He's already taken the course, he tells Storm, so he'll skip the class. But first he wants to explain why he chose not to apply for a permit after he took the course. "I thought that communist-slash-socialist Gore was going to be president. I figured getting the permit would be just an open door for him to come down with the storm troopers and bust through the door. That's what I think of the government."

"Right on!" says someone.

Ray says he'd like to come back as a poodle with free run of Hugh Hefner's mansion. Around the room the responses are more predictable.

"I want to come back as a lion."

"Alligator."

"Eagle."

"A fly on the wall."

"I want to carry a gun to protect myself, my wife and family from nuts."

Another eagle.

A coyote (!).

"I want more confidence handling confrontation situations."

Still another eagle.

"What I want you to notice," says Storm, "is all the predators. Being a predator is better than being prey."

Storm refers repeatedly to his work toward a Ph.D. as he warms up the class for the two days ahead of them. "I can teach a chimpanzee to shoot. I can't teach a chimpanzee judgment." His automatic pistol is strapped to his belt. "I've done my share of killing, and I do not take any pleasure or pride in it. If you do, leave." About controlling suspects, he teaches, "If you don't intend to shoot him that instant, keep your finger off that trigger."

"We need a revolution," Storm tells me after the class, frustrated that "my government precludes me from fighting the Mexicans." One of the places where those Mexicans Storm wants to fight come across the border is at Naco on the Arizona Sonora border. I'm in the Gay 90's Bar. You can't get any closer to Mexico: the parking lot is right on the border. The owner of the bar and dance hall, Lionel Urcadez, was born and raised in Naco, on the U.S. side.

The wall of corrugated metal on the far side of the Gay 90's parking lot is not dressed up to hide its utilitarian purpose. It's a nasty-looking slab of a barrier, lined with lights and cameras. It is impossible not to compare it with the harshness of the Berlin Wall. Except, of course, that the U.S. wall is designed to keep them out, not keep us in. Just as was the case in Berlin, though, it doesn't work. Lionel Urcadez sees the failure every night from his bar's south-side doors.

"The border wall hasn't stopped anything," Urcadez tells me. "It doesn't do any good at all. They just jump the wall." The migrants put steps on the Mexican side to climb up the wall, then use ropes to lower themselves into the United States. "It's a complete waste of money, the Border Patrol. I've never heard someone from Mexico say, 'It's too rough. I can't get across.' They get across. I've seen people who get caught ten times. But still they keep trying, keep trying until they get across."

Directly across the street from Lionel's saloon is the official port of entry for the United States. But the proximity of the government office does little to deter migration. "Right there at the border station is where most of the people come through. Every night. There's not one night when we're closing up that they're not jumping the fence. You can watch them. Sometimes the Border Patrol is right there in the middle of the street and they're just running past them. They chase them but they get away. Every night. Every single night."

Lionel Urcadez appreciates the frustrations of ranchers and other property owners along the border. "I get mad when they come through here. They come in my bar. Then the Border Patrol comes in and disrupts my business. It's harassment." With all their cameras and manpower, Lionel figures the Border Patrol should be able to do their job without busting into his bar.

More work visas for Mexicans is the obvious solution, says Lionel. "I can't get anybody to work," he says about finding legal local labor. "People don't want to work. These people come to work. They'll work twelve hours a day and seven days a week. They want to make money so they can go back home. It's hard to get good help to work."

The migrants he sees are passive, scared, and no threat. They tell him stories of borrowing from banks for seed and equipment but not reaping enough from their farms to pay back the loans. To Lionel these are tragic, desperate people being taken advantage of on both sides of the border.

Despite the missteps of Chris Simcox and other vigilantes working the border, the official federal response suggests little worry. "I've seen a lot more concern expressed about what these groups could do or might do as opposed to anything they actually have done," Russell Ahr, special assistant to the director of the Citizen and Immigration Services Phoenix District, tells me. Ahr all but endorses the private patrols. "My understanding is that these groups engage in patrol activity. They drive around and attempt to spot groups entering. They try to communicate with the Border Patrol to alert them about groups they might otherwise not be aware of." Nothing illegal about that, says Ahr. If they go on private property, they must have permission. Ahr suggests Simcox and others study regulations carefully when they patrol public lands while armed because of the varying rules regarding firearms. But he understands the concern for self-defense. His officers, he says, are finding more and more people-smugglers resorting to the practice common among drug smugglers of protecting their illicit businesses with potent firearms.

"If I'm understanding you correctly," I suggest to Ahr, "you guys don't mind and maybe you're even glad these private patrols are there."

"I didn't say that," he protested. "We don't support anyone undertaking any activity that is illegal. But by the same token we don't oppose anyone engaging in any activity that is legal."

"Are you glad they're there?"

"I'm afraid they may encounter some circumstances they're not prepared to deal with. I'm a little concerned if they end up encountering an armed group of narcotics traffickers or alien-smugglers. The Border Patrol will tell you there have been occasions when they run into groups that may have a firepower advantage over the agents themselves. That's a real potential for tragedy. These groups haven't shown much reluctance to fire at federal agents, so I'd really be amazed if they'd show reluctance to firing at people who are not in uniform."

The day before I talked with Lionel Urcadez, the Homeland Security Department raised the threat color to Orange, next to highest. I walked over to Naco, Sonora, and wandered around the dusty border town, once a Pancho Villa haunt. A statue of the revolutionary priest Miguel Hidalgo y Costilla dominates the main drag—Hidalgo breaking a chain, one broken link in his outstretched right clenched fist, the rest of the chain far from the broken link in his lowered left hand.

I crossed back through the elegant adobe-style U.S. Border Station where the bored solitary customs agent on duty looked up from his supermarket tabloid to ask, "You an American citizen?"

"Yup."

"Okay."

So much for Code Orange. This marked the first time I had ever crossed a U.S. frontier without showing identification. I looked at his newspaper.

"Studying for the lieutenant's exam?" I asked, pointing to the paper.

He laughed.

A look at the Police Beat column in the *Bisbee Observer* is a reminder of how easy it is to get across the border, and that illegal migrants can't let their guard down until they are far from the line. "February 6—Bisbee police reported undocumented aliens on Mill Road and turned them over to the Border Patrol. February 8—Bisbee police reported four undocumented aliens on Warren Cutoff Road and turned them over to the Border Patrol. Bisbee police reported 20 undocumented aliens near the Bisbee overlook and turned them over to the Border Patrol. Their vehicle was impounded. February 9—Bisbee police reported three undocumented aliens in front of the Anniversary Home and turned them over to the Border Patrol. February 10—Bisbee police reported two undocumented aliens on Mill Road and turned them over to the Border Patrol."[11]

If the lawlessness along our southern border is breeding the beginnings of a homegrown American-style fascism among some border dwellers, at least for now it's a lot less ugly than the murderous border wars roiling Old Europe. But Washington ignores its responsibilities to maintain order on the border at great peril. Valid arguments can be made for militarizing the border and tightly controlling all movement across it. Valid arguments also can be made for legalizing the cross-border trips of Mexicans who wish to come north and take the jobs that American employers urgently need filled. But there is no good argument for maintaining the status quo: a lawless and dangerous frontier attracting desperate migrants, lined with frustrated residents tempted to take the law into their own hands.

The champion for those who want the U.S. military to close and patrol the border with Mexico is Colorado Representative Tom Tancredo. "Our borders are porous and we need to do something about that," is his common theme, one he reiterated in a late 2003 speech to the House.[12] "Many millions of Americans understand that there is a problem, but perhaps they do not know why and they ask me all of the time. I get I do not know how many letters and e-mails and calls to my office. Over and over again the question is, why can't we do something about this? There are countless news reports about the fact that we cannot control our own borders, about the fact that people are coming across and we choose to do little or nothing about it. People say to me, why is this happening, Congressman?"

To his colleagues Tancredo explained that the answer is simple: the U.S. government does not have the political will to seal its southern border. "I assure you, Mr. Speaker, we have the technical ability to do so. We have the resources. We have the technical attributes necessary, combined with human resources to secure our borders. We can do it."

In speech after speech, Tancredo calls for securing the border, declaring—correctly—that current policy makes it easier for drug smugglers to cross with their products, results in ranches and park land being ruined by trespassing migrants leaving their garbage on makeshift trails, and creates the opportunity for terrorists to hide among the throngs of Mexicans coming north.

"It is an invasion," says the Colorado congressman.[13] "It is an invasion, but we do not intend to address it. We are fearful of actually trying to stop it for fear that there will be a political backlash here." Republican lawmakers, he insists, worry that their big-business campaign donors don't want to disturb the status quo because they seek cheap labor. And Democrats, he claims, don't want to alienate the Latino vote.

During the debate in Congress before the Iraq war, Congressman Tancredo told his colleagues that the United States was already fighting a war. "Our borders are war zones," he told them.[14] "There is a war going on on our borders. People are being killed on our borders. Troops are needed on our borders. Our homeland needs to be defended."

13

TWO-WAY

TRAFFIC

MEET MY FRIEND BOBBY. "I'm a disc jockey," he spits the words out with disgust and repeats them through his teeth, "a disc jockey." He complains about how little creativity is needed for the work. "Less talk, more music," he says with irritation, mocking the lines that were written out on index cards for him to read at one radio station where he worked. If he deviated from these short scripts, he would be chastised by the program director. Bobby is a Californian who plays in Mexico.

On the volatile California border with Mexico, the heavy traffic goes both directions. Mexicans struggle north for jobs, desperately searching for survival work—usually underpaid and often taken advantage of, they labor for food and shelter and a few extra dollars to send home to extended families. At the same time wealthy Californians hurl themselves south, seeking recreation, renewal, and fulfillment—a spiritual and leisure regeneration too often elusive for them during their driven routines at home.

Bobby is just back from a three-day quickie cruise to Mexico with his most recent date. "I needed to escape," he says. He bought it through a cut-rate tour broker—$300 for three days on the Norwegian ship *Southward*. They sailed from Los Angeles to Catalina Island and on to Ensenada. "It had everything, all the amenities. Casino, swimming pools, bars all over the place. As much as you can eat, as much as you can drink. You've got to pay for the drinks, but that's standard. We're already talking about going back to Mexico again, to take advantage of diving, because it's really terrific diving."

Bobby has been to Mexico several times, he can't remember exactly how many, probably five, he thinks. On this last short trip, he and his date spent their few hours of Ensenada shore time walking around. "You couldn't go more than a block before some kid or old person would hit you up for Chiclets."

Bobby shakes his head. He sips coffee, eats some chocolate chip cookie, squints against the bright California sunshine. We're talking at a sidewalk café. He's wearing a freshly laundered blue work shirt. His blue jeans, too, look professionally washed. On his feet are white socks and white running shoes. There's a gold Rolex on his left wrist, traces of grey in his closely trimmed beard and hair, and a bright blue earring in his left earlobe. "I could tell you it's a sapphire, but it's not. It's glass."

As do most tourists, Bobby and his date stopped in at Hussong's bar in Ensenada. He describes the *mariachis*—"wrinkled guys with Kmart suits and traditional polyester ties. Wrinkled faces with gold teeth smiling out. You could tell they were proud of those gold teeth. And Nancy's saying, 'Play this, play that.' And the guy says, 'By the way, it's three bucks a song.'"

A photographer took their picture together in Hussong's. "That was four bucks and we gladly paid. I expected to see a Spectra, you know? A state-of-the-art Polaroid. But this guy had an old Polaroid, one of those with the film that you pull the paper off." He tells the story as if it were an archaeological discovery, saying the lines slowly and emphasizing each word: "One of those with the film that you pull-the-paper-off. The photographer," he isn't quite finished with him, "the photographer had a proud, old noble look. Like a gentleman. And he took pride in his work."

Is he the Ugly American? I ask Bobby, who puzzles over the question.

"It was all the cruise crowd," he says about Hussong's. "It was all white faces. The only faces that were not white were the photographer and the musicians. It seemed funny to go to Hussong's and say, 'Let's capture the flavor of Mexico,' when everybody is from Dallas, L.A., and Hayward. And everybody is speaking English."

Such insulated and isolated travel is the norm for Bobby and a great many Americans. Two of his earlier Mexico excursions were Club Med vacations, once to Cancun, a resort famous for the chain link fence that keeps the locals from getting too close to the vacationers. "Cancun is the one I enjoyed most," says Bobby, "because I actually went out to the Mayan ruins. They gave me more of an insight into the culture and history than just looking at an adobe church. You really got a sense of the grandeur of the past."

Club Med took him and some of his curious colleagues out of their enclave and off to the ruins one day in a minibus. Bobby recalls the free bar in the bus on the trip back from the Mayan remains with a silly smile. "Vodka, beer. Everybody got blitzed, really drunk. That's the way this American finished up his day of culture. Getting down and partying."

At about the same time Bobby was playing cards in the *Southward's* casino ("I really got energized on the boat playing cards. I started with six dollars and by the end of the evening I made sixty!"), Manuel was making his third trip north—illegally—across the Mexican border and into the United States.

Manuel is in his late thirties when we first meet. He is a round-looking man, still boyish, with an open, ready grin under a moustache that looks stereotypically Mexican. We sit and talk in the kitchen of one of his employers as he eats a burrito lunch. He works as a day laborer, traveling between his adopted work home of Marin County, California, and his family home in Sinaloa, Mexico.

This day he's cleaning out a backyard, loading old fence posts into a truck, preparing a garden. His yellow T-shirt is dirty, so are his running shoes and his jeans. He's earning ten dollars an hour for the work, more than most of the laboring jobs he finds. In Mexico, Manuel earned his money performing stoop labor on local farms. The most he could manage to make was about five dollars a day. The simple economics of the job market drive him north.

On this trip he chose Nogales as a crossing point "because there are so many Latinos living on the Arizona side." This time, for the first time, he didn't need to pay a *coyote* to help him cross the frontier. He's an old hand now himself; he knows the ropes. "I must be watching all the time," he says in Spanish between bites of tortilla, "so I'm not grabbed by the *Migra*." At the Nogales crossing "it was cold and raining. I just walked across in the middle of town. No one stopped me."

He was on his way to a telephone to call a friend when a man stopped his car and offered Manuel a ride up to Phoenix. He took it, explaining, "I am somebody who has studied how people behave. I could tell the guy was no risk because of the way he talked." Once in Phoenix, Manuel hopped on a plane to San Francisco. His total elapsed illegal travel time from Mexico to Marin County was about five hours.

His two earlier trips were not as easy. For the first Manuel paid a *coyote* $55 to hide him in a van that passed through the Tijuana checkpoint, its dozen or so illegal passengers undetected by overworked U.S. border guards. The passengers jumped out near San Clemente, where the Border Patrol maintains a secondary checkpoint. "We ran into the brush and put a dark blanket over ourselves. When we felt it was safe we started walking north." A car stopped and a woman offered Manuel a ride into Los Angeles for $30. He grabbed at the chance, spent the night at her house, and started working the next day.

"We were making fiberglass molds for ceiling tiles," he says. A friend from Sinoloa found him the job. It was piecework. He made five dollars for each mold he finished. But he could crank out as many as a dozen a day. From there he made his way to better working conditions at a factory producing fiberglass pipe. Eventually he quit that work and headed up to the San Francisco Bay Area where friends and relatives already lived. He found work painting apartments for eight dollars an hour.

After several months he saved almost $2,000 and sent most of it home to Sinaloa so his six brothers and sisters could join him in California. At Christmastime Manuel went home for a visit, stayed a week, and paid another *coyote* $300 to help him back across the border. "Again we were in a packed van." They crossed at Tijuana. "When the border agents are changing shift, they are not paying as much attention."

Why did he rush back to California after only a week? "There was no work at home." And home it continues to be for Manuel, even though he's spent most of the last three years in California. "I am a Mexican, but I am in the north. I don't feel like a *pocho*"—a Mexican who has lost his sense of being a Mexican.

Manuel hoped to study at a university in his earlier years. He finished secondary school and two years of college preparatory work but then lacked enough money to continue. "I feel I lost a chance at a better-paying profession," he now says. During his last trip south, his father died. "It's all my responsibility now," he says of his mother and the house his father left behind.

The Sinoloa house still suffers from a dirt floor kitchen, is equipped with just an outhouse, and needs plenty of other work. So Manuel labors in California and sends money south, money known in Mexico by the Spanglish word *migradollars*. The brothers and sisters are back home, the illegal life in California not to their liking.

Some half-dozen years after that conversation with Manuel, my phone rings. It's Christmas 2003, and an excited Manuel is on the line. He's celebrating in California with his wife and their two children. "It is the best Christmas present!" he tells me. The three of them managed to get visas to the United States, and joined him the night before Christmas Eve. A few days later we all met at a local Starbucks. Manuel is rounder—he pats his belly and laughs—but retains his baby-faced look. He beams as he introduces his eight-year-old daughter and nine-year-old son, both of them shy and equipped with barely a word of English. They sit quietly while we talk, eating sweets and looking angelic.

While his wife and the children are in the United States legally, Manuel is still without papers. He all but shouts, "*¡Soy el Ilegal Fuerte!*" I am the Strong Illegal! We agree to meet again in a few days to talk about the changes in his life. This time it will be at the local Chevys, the pseudo-Mexican restaurant chain that used to be owned by Pepsico.

Mexican music is blaring when we get together after the New Year at Chevys, and we find a booth in a far corner of the dining room, searching for a place where we can hear each other talk. The place is filled with both

Latino and Anglo families, the waiters and waitresses easily slipping back and forth between English and Spanish, as needed. We're hundreds of miles north of the border. Manuel has been back and forth three or four times in the last several years. "It was terrible," he says. "I was caught by Immigration two or three times. I was in jail until the next day when they kicked me out. The first time was in Agua Prieta, the second time was in Nogales, Sonora." His travel route was dictated by the Southwest Border Strategy, when the border controls were reinforced in California and Texas, choking much of the illegal trafficking of Mexicans north to the Arizona-Sonora desert frontier. There the self-appointed vigilantes patrol the north side, combining with harsh weather and the Border Patrol as a barrier to entry into the United States.

"We crossed during the afternoon," Manuel says about the Agua Prieta escapade. "Later, when the sun was going down, we walked the whole night, until dawn, about five or six in the morning—more than twenty miles."

"You climbed over the fence?"

"That's right, we climbed over the fence and then walked through the *Cañón del Diablo*. In the morning, at the rising of the sun, is when we were caught by the Immigration. We were really tired." The migrants were bruised raw by the chafing of their clothes against their legs; their feet were blistered. When the Border Patrol appeared, Manuel says he and the group of about a dozen fellow travelers from his hometown weren't afraid. They were so tired they were relieved. "There were a lot of poisonous animals. Snakes. During the night it was really cold. We had to walk in order to keep our bodies warm. The guy told us, 'You guys sit down!' And we said, '*Gracias.* Thank you very much!'"

The Border Patrol officers took Manuel and his compatriots back to the border where, he told me, they were forced to agree to so-called voluntary deportation. Manuel signed the required paperwork; he was photographed and fingerprinted. And then he jumped the border again. "Of course," he says—a necessary part of doing business. He was caught and deported a second time before successfully running the gauntlet and returning to his work in northern California.

"Finally, the third time I got here. This time it was harder," he says. He and his colleagues headed north without a guide, confident that their own experience would serve them as well as a *coyote*. "We had to walk the whole night, and then all the next day we walked through rivers and streams. The whole night, the whole day. We arrived really tired in the evening, and we slept." Where they arrived was still in the middle of nowhere: the Arizona desert, but far enough north that they felt safe to rest. "We were so tired we simply collapsed without eating. We woke up because the sun was so hot. We were hungry, thirsty." Help came from the Papago Indians, who gave them water and offered them a ride out of the desert. "They drove us to the Phoenix airport. Just to be driven from Papago territory to Phoenix we had to pay $400 or $500 each."

Manuel was making this arduous commute in order to visit his wife and children in Sinaloa, but he's had enough. "Now I don't want to go back." The hardened border has turned him into a permanent U.S. resident. When his family arrived two days before Christmas, they had been separated for the two years following the September 11th attacks. His wife and two children arrived in the United States, on six-month tourist visas, arranged by one of Manuel's employers. Manuel smiles. "But I don't think they're going back. The kids are in school."

Manuel's immigration status, of course, remains that of an illegal alien. But he acts fearless. "No, I don't have papers. But if the INS kicks me out, I can always find my way back here. Not my family. That's different. I don't want my wife and my kids to do that because it is very, very dangerous. There are rapes. There are a lot of bad people all around. There are people who take wives from husbands when they are crossing, just to rape them. That's the reason they separate the wives from the husbands when they are crossing the border. It's terrible. They take your money. But I can do it myself. I don't have a passport. But I am here. What do I need a passport for? I am the one who has to work. And I work here."

"Give us a work permit," is Manuel's answer to the border wars. Manuel says the powerful drug and immigrant traffickers do not want that solution because an end to the chaos on the border would be bad for their business. "We found forty pounds of packed marijuana along our path. One of my friends hid it and marked the place. He and his father went back to get the stash and moved it over to Phoenix to do the business." That forty pounds of marijuana was worth much more than the price of the two-hour ride in the Papagos' car. "On the border you get a lot of corruption. And things are getting worse. That's why I don't want to go back. I want to stay at least five years here without going back home."

But Manuel's mother is still in Sinaloa, and he expects he'll make more clandestine trips south, insisting he's *el Ilegal Fuerte* and unafraid. "If they kick me out, I'll get back here. I know how. I have to do it. I have to work." His hourly rate is up to $25, and he's complaining about new immigrants from Mexico and Central America working for far less money, endangering his flush pay scale.

So what are you now, I ask him, a Mexican or a Gringo?

"Both. Because I have to spend part of my life down there and part of my life up here. I like it here, and I like it down there. I have friends here, and I have friends down there. Part of my family is down there, and I have family up here. I want them to study here now, so they realize what life is all about. I want them to know what it means to be here, so they are not being told stories about what the United States is like. I want them to know what life is here and also down there. Then they will have an opportunity to figure out for themselves where they want to live. They can take more advantage of what's available here than I can, because I am older." We're speaking Spanish; Manuel speaks minimal English. "They're going to speak two languages, so they can figure out both sides."

So Manuel has one foot in Mexico and the other up here. "That's right," he agrees, "with the border right between my legs. But it's not going to change. Who is going to change it? These presidents, Fox and Bush? When Fox comes here he comes just to wander around and have a good time. When Fox took office he said he was going to fix the problem. How many years have already passed! He cannot even fix the problems in Mexico. How can he fix the problems up here?"

We move to the table with Manuel's family, order quesadillas and burritos, wine and tequila. A waitress brings ice cream for the children, and Manuel's little boy tells me in school this day he's learned how to say "yellow" and "blue" in English.

14

THE POROUS,

SHIFTING BORDER

I WELL REMEMBER making an illegal left turn in Ensenada and quickly
settling the problem with the cop who pulled me over by paying a few pesos in cash. Mexican police are notorious for the bribes they extort from
citizens. That was almost thirty years ago. Despite many publicized anti-
corruption campaigns, little has changed. Corruption in uniform remains
an epidemic with no cure in sight.

Periodic attempts are made to clean up the corrupt police forces of
Mexico. Late in 1999 the new police chief in Mexico City, Alejandro Gertz
Manero, decided that one route toward reducing graft was to swap his
force of male traffic cops for a new corps made up of supposedly untainted
women. In a setup that seemed doomed to fail—especially in macho
Mexico—the chief designed new teams of traffic enforcers made up of two
men and four women. Only the women were authorized to write tickets;
the men were their bodyguards.

Police Chief Gertz explained his philosophy with misplaced hope.
"You very seldom have any corruption problems with women in Mexico.
We are trying to regain the confidence of the people. I think it will be easier for women to get closer to the people. In Mexico we see women as more
gentile, more polite. If a group of men has been perceived for so many years
as being corrupt, and you don't have the perception of corruption among
women in the police force, why not give them a chance? I trust them"[1]

It didn't work. I know from personal experience.

Mexico City traffic police in their familiar green uniforms—both men—pulled me over in early 2004. I was in a brand-new black Neon rented from Hertz, driving just past the airport on my way to the downtown Holiday Inn. I needed to turn left, and I distinctly remember switching on the left-turn signal.

"*Joven! Joven!*" the first cop called out to me, motioning for me to pull over where he had already stopped another car. I would have kept going, but the light was red for me and traffic blocked my path. My initial reflex was to act as if I could not understand him and spoke only English, asking him why he pulled me over. But he tired of that game quickly and called over his partner who demanded my license in clear Spanglish.

"You didn't signal left," he announced. I told him I knew that I had. He ignored me, pulled out his ticket book, and gave me a quick lesson in bribery.

"You want to take care of this right now?" he asked, after writing "1500 pesos" on the back of a ticket blank.

"I don't have that much," I told him, and I didn't—in Mexican cash.

"How much do you have?"

I asked my wife to look for some money knowing that she kept her pesos in a separate purse and that she was carrying only a few hundred. She pulled out two hundred—about twenty dollars' worth—and I passed it to the cop.

"More," he said.

My wife fished deeper in her purse and came up with another fifty.

"That's all we have," I told him as he relieved me of the money.

"Put your seat belt on," he ordered as he handed back my license and waved us off, pocketing our money.

Later, Mexican friends insisted we had bargained well, that the fine for not signaling *is* fifteen hundred pesos, and that the routine payoff to avoid the complications of a formal ticket is about twenty-five dollars.

The traffic cops who took our 250 pesos count on such bribes to augment their meager salaries. Workers throughout Mexico rely on bribes for survival. Corruption pervades the government, where it is used to obtain and maintain power. Drug traffickers exacerbate the crisis with their access to phenomenal amounts of bribe money. In April 2004, for example, more than 550 police officers were suspended in Morelos state, charged with providing protection for cocaine traffickers. "The corruption [in Mexico] is so endemic, so overwhelming," wrote *Washington Post* correspondent Mary Jordan when she reported the news, "that it holds the country back and destroys initiative."[2]

The dysfunctional Mexican economy is the prime force that drives immigrants north. As a journalist, I've seen in detail how this systemic bribery infiltrates and infects news reporting south of the border. Colleagues have shared their stories with me, a few of which I recount here to show how pervasive the corruption is, and therefore how difficult it will be to root out. These are the examples I was privy to; they are, alas, replicated in all industries and professions.

Cruising south on Interstate 5 in San Diego in the silver Chevy Malibu I rented from Avis at the airport, my immediate destination was Tijuana, just south of the border, across the busiest frontier in the world. Tijuana brags about itself as "The World's Most Visited City."

The U.S.-Mexico border is the only place in the world where the First World meets the Third World face-to-face across an artificial boundary. This man-made marker remains so porous that, even after the events of September 11, 2001, most clever and determined Mexicans (or other non-U.S. citizens) can make their way illegally over the line and into the United States. The result of this continuing migration is a border that exhibits a variety of forms far north of the actual international boundary.

The car rental experience is one example. Few U.S. companies allow their cars south of the border. Avis allows such travel for an additional $24 a day in insurance charges. The insurance comes with a booklet titled "How to Handle an Accident in Mexico."[3] Except that this brochure fails to report some critical news. "If there are injuries in any vehicle involved [in an accident]," it instructs, "you and the adjuster may be asked to accompany the police to the precinct house."

As a matter of fact, in the event of injuries, all drivers involved in the accident likely will be arrested and kept locked in jail until the cause of the accident is determined.

The booklet continues, "The adjuster will handle all details with the police." Well, he or she may well do that. But note that the booklet does not suggest how long it may take to handle those details. Meanwhile the drivers languish in jail.

Avis also provides renters with a handy bilingual booklet called "Tourist Guide Tijuana," published by the Tijuana Tourism Board.[4] On a page headlined "Recommendations for Visitors," it advises, "No police officer is authorized to receive money." Of course not. That could be considered a bribe and would be against the law. But most motorists who have experience traveling in Mexico would probably agree that it is naive to consider—even since the reforms of the Fox administration—that a deftly placed peso note no longer alleviates problems with the law.

A more useful source is Carl Franz's classic *The People's Guide to Mexico*. Franz offers this advice: "Even though Mexicans claim that the *mordida* (the bite) no longer exists or that it is unnecessary, we have found it alive and working quite well in all parts of the country. I have given 'considerations' to everyone from post office workers who couldn't seem to remember my name to border officials who didn't like my looks."[5]

Franz offers a practical guide to the *mordida*:

"You don't bribe someone by stuffing a wad of bills in his pocket and saying, 'Here ya go baby, a little something for the wife and kids!' There are more subtle and respectable techniques used to feel out the other person on their attitude and price. The easiest of these for the inexperienced person to adopt is the, 'Gee whiz, I sure wish you'd tell me what to do' angle. Other effective openers to the payoff are: 'Is there any way this can be worked out?', 'Will there be an extra charge?', and the national favorite, 'Is there any other way of arranging the matter?'"

News you can use, despite the posters in Mexico City that feature an apple and the legend: *Por un México íntegro, ya no más mordidas*. For a Mexico with integrity, now no more bribes.

I pull off Interstate 5 and park the rented Chevy on the U.S. side. I want to walk into Tijuana again. There is no apparent immigration control for those of us heading south by foot at the world's busiest international border crossing, just the incessant click, click, clatter of the one-way turnstile rattling against the mechanical device that makes walking through it northbound impossible. The foot traffic continues past the Mexican customs office and the sign indicating a required stop for those traveling with taxable goods. Ha! A lone customs officer sits out front sipping a soda, watching without expression the constant flow of people past customs. No one is stopping to declare "taxable goods," and he's inspecting no one. Just before the business district, a couple of border guards with machine guns strapped over their shoulders chat with each other. The sun is setting through the golden smog.

The first sign I see is huge: "CIPRO," it yells, offering what the drug store claims is a generic version of the anti-anthrax drug for cut-rate prices.

I walk on toward Avenida de la Revolución, Tijuana's main street, past Club Fetish.

"Hey, *amigo*," calls out the barker. "Hey, professor!" (It must be my beard.) "Check it out. Nice-looking girls. Naked."

I've been in Tijuana only a few minutes and I've already received some basic news about drugs and sex: both easily available. It reminds me of the popular Manu Chao song lyrics: "Welcome to Tijuana: tequila, *sexo*, marijuana." It's a catchy tune that ends with a blast of machine-gun fire and the sound of an eerie empty wind.

In response to this image problem, the Tijuana city fathers are trying to influence the media with a positive propaganda campaign. The *Comité de Imagen*, the Image Committee, was organized to clean up the dirty streets, install public art, and urge police authorities to stop referring to narcotics traffickers headquartered in Tijuana as the Tijuana Cartel.

Another clean-up-Tijuana campaign is a fascinating experiment in web-based direct and unedited news available to the public (and an intriguing resource for reporters). The city government announced in mid-2002 that it had installed a closed-circuit TV system in police stations, with cameras trained on the station house and jail cells. The system, they said, was designed to reassure the public that the police were not taking bribes or torturing suspects and prisoners. Images from the cameras are broadcast on a public website. A click on the website allows complaining Mexicans to register their problems with the police over the internet.

"The objective is to be accountable for everything we do," announced Antonio Martínez, the Baja California attorney general. Cynics may suggest that a clever cop could bribe and torture out of camera range. Nonetheless, if past experience with video surveillance is a guide, at least some crooked cops may well forget the cameras, providing news reporters and human rights workers with unprecedented proof of the official corruption so famous in Mexico.

Try as they might in Tijuana, the border town can't lose its reputation as a sin city.

"I've got the camera ready, señor!" says the photographer working with Pepe, the Zebra-stripe-painted donkey on Avenida Revolución in Tijuana. Nearby is a sign in English: "Welcome to Tijuana. You can be arrested for immoral conduct. For more information visit or call us." It's signed, Baja California Secretary of Tourism.

Sometimes it's the Tijuana police who are arrested for immoral conduct, perpetrated against naive or unlucky Gringos. During 2003 at least a dozen U.S. tourists formally complained about abuses they suffered at the hands of the Tijuana police, from theft to assault to rape.

"I feel lucky to be alive," Ron Terwilliger told *San Diego Union* reporter Sandra Dibble after he made a shopping trip across the border. He said he was handcuffed by police, threatened with a gun, and forced to withdraw money from his bank at a Tijuana ATM before finally being released from custody. Tijuana officials acknowledge that corruption continues among some police, and they insist they will prosecute officers who take advantage of Americans if the U.S. citizens will cross back to Mexico and testify against them.[6]

Dianna Murray came forward and announced herself as a victim of the Tijuana police after reading that she was not the only American to suffer at their hands. She says she was raped by two Tijuana policemen after a minor traffic accident, raped "right on the street," within sight of the U.S.

border, and left on the curb bleeding. "They laughed a lot," she said of her assailants. Another woman reported to California officers that after she and her boyfriend complained about a restaurant bill, a waiter called police. She says she was taken to a hotel, handcuffed to a bed, and raped by four officers. Still another woman was stopped after using a script from the United States to buy a prescription drug at a Tijuana pharmacy. She says she was raped by four policemen, one of them a supervisor in a division of Tijuana's police department that specializes in providing help for tourists. He was arrested, jailed, and charged with rape.[7]

Just as border-created problems are not confined to the borderlands but reach throughout the fifty states, so do they stretch south throughout Mexico. Crooked cops and institutionalized bribery remained endemic well into the Fox administration's six years of power, despite the promises of reforms. The corruption is especially problematic regarding the media in a Mexican society in transition, a society trying to redefine itself as at least an emerging democracy. As long as the media are targets of intimidation, abuse, and bribery, the economic crises that drive migrants north will likely persist.

My first Tijuana appointment this trip is scheduled with the co-founder and co-director of the crusading weekly *Zeta* (slogan: "Free like the wind."), J. Jesús Blancornelas. In 1997, Blancornelas was the victim of a vicious assassination attempt that killed his bodyguard and left him permanently injured. As he tells the story, his car was cut off in Tijuana traffic by gunmen who pumped over one hundred rounds into it. Seeking cover as soon as the shooting started, Blancornelas managed to avoid all but four of the shots, one of which just missed his spine. He spent a month hospitalized, more time recovering at his home, and finally returned to work.

But the attack on Jesús Blancornelas was not the first attempt to silence *Zeta*. His partner, the paper's co-founder, Héctor Félix Miranda, was murdered in 1988. Neither shooting slowed down the reporting that *Zeta* is now famous for. On the contrary, the paper and Blancornelas became examples of a new type of Mexican journalism: investigative and courageous. He and the paper continue to win international press freedom awards.

Zeta's offices are south of the Tijuana tourist strip, in a residential neighborhood. A tiny sign identifies it, but the building is easy to spot: a long Mexican military SUV, with smoked windows and a telltale communications antenna on the roof, is parked out front. Across the street sit two old Ford sedans, plainclothes guards waiting and watching inside.

In the compact courtyard of the house that's been converted in *Zeta*'s headquarters, two plainclothes "greeters" confront me with a casual, "*Buenos días.*" One of them makes a practiced parting of his jacket front to display the automatic pistol stuffed into the waistband of his trousers.

"You here to see Blancornelas?" one asks. They seem to know of my appointment, and let me pass.

In the small waiting room I sit by a photograph labeled "Luis L. Valero E. 1959–1997," the murdered bodyguard. I'm told Blancornelas is delayed.

Zeta was founded in 1980 and quickly gained a reputation for disclosing Mexican government corruption and reporting on the activities of drug traffickers. These investigative stories were a surprise for Tijuana readers, accustomed to government corruption and drug trafficking being glossed over in most papers. Cash payoffs to publishers and their reporters—in the form of so-called government subsidies or outright bribes—long kept most Mexican papers filled with celebrity gossip, violent street-crime news, and bland political coverage that was little more than the official ruling-party line.

The sprawl of Tijuana—from the tourist traps downtown to the *maquiladoras*, assembly plants, luring factory workers up from the interior to the squalor of its slums—makes for a vibrant news town. *Zeta* made its pages come alive with the details inside that sprawl, providing a tribune for politicians who were working to overthrow the long-ruling Institutional Revolutionary Party (PRI) and covering the illegal drug scene infesting the borderlands.

After a long wait I'm told my meeting with Blancornelas must be postponed. He's still behind closed doors and won't be available as scheduled. I find out why a few days later when the next issue of *Zeta* hits the streets. Blancornelas's byline is trumpeted throughout the paper over articles about the presumed shooting death of one of Tijuana's most feared drug smugglers, Ramón Arellano Félix. Blancornelas had been working the story in meetings with Mexican and U.S. authorities and other sources while I was waiting for our delayed interview. The photographs in the paper of a cadaver reputed to be Ramón are gory, reminiscent of the New York tabloids in the thirties and forties, a drool of blood flowing from his open mouth. This is big news along the border, where prominently placed WANTED posters on both sides offer a $2 million reward from the U.S. government for each of the notorious Arellano brothers. At about the same time Ramón was killed, the other brother, Benjamín, finally was arrested. Blancornelas believes it was the Arellano brothers who hired the gunmen who attacked him in 1997.

A few weeks later I return to Tijuana and am warmly received at *Zeta* by Jesús Blancornelas. Dressed in a black leather jacket, white slacks, and a sports shirt, he has a closely trimmed grey beard and grey hair. His black frame glasses add a professorial touch to his appearance.

Blancornelas says that much of what is reported about narcotics trafficking in the Mexican press remains fantasy, yellow journalism. "The only case that I know of a journalist being attacked by narcotics traffickers is our case," he says about himself, "after we published three articles which we know made Ramón Arellano really mad. But journalists are not in as much danger of being attacked as people claim as long as we tell the truth. When a journalist crosses the line and starts taking money from narcotraffickers, that's when danger starts. Because after that, if the day comes when something is written that they don't like, the journalist could be killed."

Blancornelas says his paper's troubles with the Arellanos began when *Zeta* published a letter from the mother of a trafficker allegedly killed by Ramón Arellano. In the letter the mother called Ramón Arellano a coward. "We published the whole letter, publicly telling him he was a coward. He got mad and came against us."

Zeta is now essentially an armed camp. Blancornelas says his notoriety works to his paper's benefit because it attracts important sources. "The protection came after the attack. But many people were informing me about narcotrafficking. The fact that I am in this office without the freedom to go out in the field results in more people coming to me with information. So, under these circumstances, with more information, it is important for the Mexican government to protect me. I make the information public."

Does that make *Zeta* and him a one-story paper and reporter?

"No, not at all," he says. "Now we are writing a lot about it because of Ramón Arellano's recent death and the capture of Benjamín. We do not have plans to write about narcotrafficking on our front page this week.

"The only thing the Mexican media needs in order to gain credibility is to tell the truth. Nothing else."

Credibility, maybe. Security, no. For that, the impunity long enjoyed by those who intimidate, assault, and assassinate Mexican journalists must end. In early summer 2004, another *Zeta* editor and investigative reporter was gunned down in a Tijuana street. Francisco Ortiz Franco was murdered as he sat in his car with two of his children. Three months before he was killed, Ortiz had started working with a group of international journalists investigating the murder of *Zeta* founding editor Félix. At a demonstration honoring Ortiz and demanding an end to the attacks, political cartoonist Abraham Dominguez said, "We are always ready to lose our lives, but it shouldn't be that way."

Blancornelas is conscious of the business value of his notoriety and the commercial value of the fact that his paper is different from most others. He shows off the front pages of several Baja California newspapers from the day we meet. All display screaming headlines and pictures featuring a tunnel from Tecate to California that was used by drug smugglers and that police were blocking with fill. But *Zeta* buried the story in its inside pages. The tunnel had been discovered weeks before. Blancornelas considered the fact that the police were finally closing it off a follow-up story of minimal importance.

Blancornelas rejects *gacetillas*, those press releases disguised as news stories that are so common in Mexican papers, press releases not identified as the paid-for advertisements they are, often placed by government agencies. The income from *gacetillas* historically forces newspapers into a compromised position of dependency on the government, which can yank these pricey ads from any paper that fails to fill its news pages with content acceptable to government media manipulators. This policy of rejecting *gacetillas*, says Blancornelas, costs *Zeta* a great deal of lost revenue.

The Fox administration does not pressure *Zeta* in any manner, Blancornelas says, but it is much more difficult for his reporters to get information from the Fox government than was the case during the Zedillo administration, despite the reputation of Fox for creating a more open regime.

Tijuana is crowded with four million residents, I ask if the people are well served by the media. Are they well-informed? "No," Blancornelas complains. "We"—and here he speaks collectively of Mexican media in general—"lack credibility because we have lied too often. We'll pay for that until new generations change it. Luckily the internet now helps disseminate information."

When his partner was killed, Blancornelas tells me, he decided he could not leave the newspaper business, as he had planned. He needed to investigate the murder. "We gave names, and the police did nothing about it. Some of the criminals are now living in the United States." International observers agree that the police work has been inadequate in the Héctor Félix Miranda murder investigation, along with the investigations of the murders of several other Mexican journalists in recent years. Blancornelas keeps Félix's name on the paper's masthead as co-director and runs a full page each week drawing attention to the crime.

As we says our good-byes, I ask Jesús Blancornelas if he is a role model. "No, no, no, no," he insists. "There are no role models except the truth. The truth is the role model."

Carlos Fuentes deals with the fluidity of the border and the exchange of information across it in his novel *The Crystal Frontier*. A character named José Francisco is stopped at the border on his motorcycle.

José Francisco brought Chicano manuscripts to Mexico and Mexican manuscripts to Texas. The bike was the means to carry the written word rapidly from one side to the other, that was José Francisco's contraband, literature from both sides so that everyone would get to know one another better, he said, so that everyone would love one another a little more, so there would be a "we" on both sides of the border.

"What are you carrying in your saddlebags?"

"Writing."

"Political stuff?"

"All writing is political."

"So it's subversive."

"All writing is subversive."

"What are you talking about?"

"About the fact that lack of communication is a bitch. That anyone who can't communicate feels inferior. That keeping silent will screw you up."[8]

Atzimba Romero rushes over between assignments from the TV Azteca studios on the south side of Mexico City to meet me in a glitzy bookstore and coffee shop in the posh southern California-style shopping center Perisur. She's young, intense, and anxious to tell her story.

It was the seventy-eighth anniversary of the founding of the Mexican railroad union, an important event on the Mexico City news calendar. At the ceremony to mark the occasion were the labor minister, the railroad owners, officials from the union. "Lots of reporters were there," Atzimba Romero tells me. "Perhaps they knew it was payoff day."

This is not a memoir of those scandal-ridden days of Mexico's past but a report from early 2002. This is not a report from the impoverished and marginalized provinces but from Mexico City.

After the formal ceremony, reporters had an opportunity to obtain comments from union leaders. The reporters then were invited into a press room at union headquarters. "The cameramen and the cameras were ordered out," Romero says, "and the door was closed. Another door opened. I was nervous. What was going on?"

The railroad union was not Romero's beat. The regular union reporter was ill that day, and the assignment desk sent her to cover the celebration story.

After the second door opened, the reporters lined up.

"I kept asking, 'What the hell is going on?'"

"A man, a Televisa reporter, said, 'Little girl, stop asking. We're going to get our payoffs. It's embarrassing, but we're going to get our *chayo* [a Mexican fruit and the commonly used slang word for bribe in journalism].'

"Then it was my turn," Atzimba Romero continues, "and I came up to a short man who was handing out envelopes. He gave me the stapled envelope and I said, 'What is this?'

"He was very surprised and upset and insisted I take it and leave. I said, 'Don't mess with me!' I threw it in his face.

"I left really upset, and a reporter for *Reforma* came up to me and said, 'We are the only two who did not take the money.'* He told me he was going to run a story about the bribing the next day, but he needed to know how much was in the envelopes."

Romero said she found the Televisa reporter who had suggested she just take the money and approached him with a microphone but no camera.

"I asked, '*Señor*, how much did you receive in that envelope?'

"The only reason he did not beat the crap out of me is because there were so many people there.

"He asked me, 'Why didn't you take it? You could have given it to your crew.'

"I asked, 'Did you take it?'

"He said with a shrug to suggest the answer was obvious. '*¡Sí!*'

"I said, 'You make me sad. I'm embarrassed for you.' And I left."

Reporter Romero got into her company car with her crew and left the union building. About twenty minutes later, she says, while they were on their way back to TV Azteca's studios, the dispatcher called on the mobile phone and told her that the reporter who usually covered the railroad union beat wanted to talk with her cameraman. The dispatcher told her to put the cameraman on the line and she would patch through the call from the beat reporter. The cameraman talked for over twenty minutes, she tells me.

---

*Reforma was founded with a policy that prohibits bribes. Reporters are forbidden to take anything from sources on penalty of being fired. They are required to pay for everything associated with their news gathering work, even a cheap coffee and sandwich during a lunch meeting.

"When we arrived back at the station, the cameraman asked, 'What are you going to do?' He told me it wasn't really the beat reporter on the phone, but someone who told him, 'You don't know me, but I am the person in charge so that everything goes smoothly at the union.'"

Atzimba Romero told me she thinks the cameraman does know whom he was talking with at the union, and that he was threatened or pressured. The cameraman warned her. "If you say anything," he told her, "all the reporters who took the money will be against you and say it's not true." He told her it happens every day in Mexico, and there is nothing she can do about it.

"The cameraman was so insistent that I realized he was scared."

She kept asking him where the money came from. Did it come from the labor minister or from the union? "He told me, 'Please do it for me because I have a labor-related problem and they're helping me at the Labor Department.'

"I told my cameraman, 'Ahah! This is coming from the labor minister!' He said, '¡*No sé, no sé, no sé!*'" I don't know, I don't know, I don't know.

Romero decided to take the matter to her bosses. She approached the vice president for news, identified the incident as a direct threat, and asked what action the company intended to take. She announced that she wanted to do a story on the payoffs.

"He congratulated me and told me the network would back me." But no story was broadcast because she did not actually receive any money.

And she feels the effects of her actions on the job. "When I go to news stories now and run into reporters who took the money, I am shunned."

Atzimba Romero is convinced that poor pay is no excuse for taking bribes. "It's not a matter of having money or not. It's values. It's something you have inside. It was so routine, so natural, so part of the day's work for everyone in that line. It can't be a problem of poor people, you can't justify it as poverty in the DF [Mexico City]."

We leave the exclusive shopping center, walking past the armed guards who protect the upper class in their oasis. I take a taxi back to my hotel, across miles of miserable traffic, air so smoggy you can chew on it, and a cityscape that defies routine maintenance: unfinished, crumbling, paint peeling. I pass the fortresslike American embassy. Hawkers work the cars stopped for red lights, hawkers selling such an odd array of unneeded goods: Spider-Man dolls, inflated plastic rackets equipped with balls tied to them with elastic, steak knives, fly swatters. Who impulsively buys their steak knives from a vendor at a red light?

Another day, en route to a meeting with a colleague, I made my way at dawn to the Observatorio bus station on the north side of Mexico City for my first-class bus ride to Morelia. I was early enough to grab a bite to eat. A cheese sandwich on a fresh roll with onions, avocado, and refried beans looked good. And coffee. The clerk handed me the sandwich and a cup of hot water. *"No, no. Café con leche,"* I protested. She said, yeah, yeah, and pointed me to the adjacent table where the jar of Nescafé sat with a spoon. "Make it yourself," she instructed. Four hours and two Hollywood B English-language subtitled movies on the shrieking video monitors in the bus later, we had climbed out of Mexico City's smog, up and over conifer-covered mountains into Michoacán and down into its capital, colonial Morelia.

"Call me from Café El Centro just after eleven," Francisco Castellanos had told me when I called from Mexico City. I called. No answer. I bought the magazine he writes for, *Proceso*, ordered a coffee and orange juice, waited and read, called again. No answer.

I decided I'd better sit back and relax. I looked at the cathedral. I ordered breakfast. There was nothing else to do yet. Finally the waitress told me I had a phone call. "Sorry I'm late," Castellanos said, "I'll be right there." At a quarter to one, he showed up, all smiles, sat down and said hello to me, and then proceeded to chat up the fellow at the next table until finally our appointment began, some two hours late.

We hailed a cab and started talking. As the taxi barreled along mountain roads, Castellanos regaled me with details of the bribes and payoffs enjoyed by Michoacán reporters, editors, and publishers. These payments are often in a form called *convenios* in Spanish, an agreement by politicians to pay the newspapers for publishing ads or announcements from the government as a device to funnel money to the papers. Control, or at least great influence, is the understood commodity being purchased by the *convenios* and by similar paid news stories, *gacetillas*.

Francisco Castellanos punctuates his tales of corruption with specific ideas of what can be done to change the endemic problem of tainted news reporters. "What we need here is a conscience, because most of my mates are *empíricos*—that is, they are self-taught. They are not professionals. They did not study at the university. They just got a press card and became journalists."

These "journalists" make little money at the papers and hence are susceptible to corruption. "Let's make a comparison. A correspondent for a big newspaper in Mexico City who is working in Michoacán receives about two hundred U.S. dollars a month. But when you add all the money he gets underground, it totals about eight hundred dollars." In addition to payments from the government, he tells me, the reporters may get payments directly from the political party that controls the government. "The new PRD government says it will end all these *convenios*," according to Castellanos. "They say there will be no more corruption. So you can understand why all the journalists are really angry now, because it was their source of income."

Not that every reporter in Michoacán was corrupted by the PRI, says Castellanos. "Only three or four of us who are correspondents here in Michoacán did not take the money, out of more than three hundred journalists in Michoacán who did."

Castellanos says he has been offered bribes and payoffs. "But I haven't accepted them. I have been offered bags full of money, I do not know how much." The blatant and insidious nature of the corrupted relationship between government and media in Mexico is made clear in one of his examples. "On the holiday *El Día de la Libertad de Expresión* [Free Speech Day], one official of the government approached us with a big brown bag, like a bag for bread, filled with packs of five-hundred-peso bills.

"He told me, 'Here. This is a present from the governor.'

"I said, 'No thank you, I don't want to have anything.'

"He said, 'You don't want the governor to be angry with you.'

"I told the guy, 'I don't care.' I said I was sorry he was going to be angry but I couldn't accept money from the government because I was an independent journalist and I had to write whatever I wanted. If I accepted the money, I would be obligated to say and not say certain things. I was with a *compadre* who is a publisher of two newspapers, one in Apatzingán and one in Uruapan, so they broke the advertising agreements [the *convenios*] with him in order to try to pressure me to accept the money. My friend called me later and said, '*Compadre*, if you don't take the money they'll take the *convenios* out of my newspapers." But Castellanos tells me he refused nonetheless.

Later that day we were speeding down the rural mountains of Michoacán back to Morelia in a battered old taxi. Castellanos was in the front seat with the driver, I was in the backseat. Suddenly the car was careening around the two-lane blacktop. The driver brought it under control and to a stop. Flat tire. We got out and waved traffic around us as the driver jacked up the car and attached the spare.

"My sister knows a guy with a tire shop who can give you a good price on a new tire," offered the local journalist.

"That's okay. No thanks," the driver said. "I'll just go to Cosco."

The *mordida*, the bite, is a kind of *ballet folklórico*, engrained in the culture. The writer Tom Miller, who made a coast-to-coast trip along the frontier, saw it repeatedly. "I wasn't sure of the etiquette in a situation like this. If twenty pesos was not enough, he might be insulted. If it was too much, I wanted change. Every Mexican official I have ever seen take a *mordida* uses a graceful and smooth motion for grasping and pocketing money. I flicked a twenty-peso bill toward the Juárez cop. In one sweeping motion the bill disappeared in his right hand while his left hand returned my driver's license."[9]

I found examples of the fluid border during a day of study at a Spanish-language traffic school, where the instructor explained how to avoid police profiling. At the traffic school, hundreds of miles up into California from the border, I was the only Gringo in attendance. I had been stopped for an illegal U turn in downtown Santa Rosa. Since part of my penalty was traffic school, I figured that the Spanish-language version would at least provide me with a day of language lessons. The instructor overtly announced it as a survival school for Latinos facing an often offensive dominant culture. He made it clear he was going to provide important news during the day. "Gringolandia is like baseball," he explained. "If you don't understand the system, you're out."

He was specific, calling Republicans hypocrites for advocating states' rights but trying to use state and local governments to enforce immigration laws. He explained how corruption in the United States takes a different form than the Mexican *mordida*, using special-interest donations to the Bush campaign as an example.

"*Corrupción republicana*," he called it.

"Who makes the laws?" he asked, answering, "Special interests who get the ear of politicians with soft money."

This was scarcely the kind of traffic school the courts expected.

"Whoever has the money gets to sit on the *burro*," he taught us. The lessons came one after another.

"If you don't have medical insurance, they will treat you like a dog in this country. *¡Hasta la vista, chica!*"

But there is a law requiring that emergency medical attention be provided, protested one student.

"Ha," he responded. "They won't give it to you. Try it out!"

More advice: "Watch out in Oakland and L.A. where the cops will go after young men and pretty women for little things."

He explained how the police obtain DMV records when they swipe the computer strip on a driver's license. "So don't lie."

The students, all in the class for the opportunity to remove a violation from their records, paid rapt attention. "Watch out," insisted the lecturer about the propensity of the police to stop Latinos, "they're after you."

This sort of nontraditional news reporting directed at Mexicans far north of the nation's political boundary is an example of the subculture taking care of itself. The traffic school instructor was not out of touch with reality. His classroom was in Novato, California, in Marin County, just north of San Francisco. There, at about the same time, Novato High School senior Andrew Smith was busy on the final draft of an editorial for the school newspaper, an anti-immigrant rant targeting Mexicans.

"The American culture is being disintegrated through this multicultural atmosphere that everyone's trying to push," was Smith's point of view.[10] "If you don't have a country that's strongly based on one type of culture, then there's no glue that will hold it together in a crisis. There are a whole bunch of illegal Mexicans coming over. People come across the border pregnant, have a kid, and now the kid is a burden to the United States because their parents are not able to take care of them. We're just allowing people to take advantage of us. It's going to end up destroying everything that's good here."

Where does Smith learn this argument? He studies at the speakers of his radio, listening to the pantheon of right-wing talk-show hosts. One of his favorites is the hate-mongering immigrant basher Michael Savage.* "It's a good way to get information," Smith said of the Michael Savage show, a barrage of misinformation, opinion, and vitriol. "You don't have to search for it, it's presented to you." Asked if he ever checked on the veracity of what he hears, he responded, "I would if I felt the need to. Usually I just listen to what's been said and think it over and discern what I think is true and what I think is false. It helps me form opinions on topics I wouldn't normally have heard about."

My home in Sonoma is one county farther north from Smith's home. In sleepy Rohnert Park, a tract-house bedroom community, the president of the local high school's Conservative Club, Tim Bueler, created a long-running crisis with an essay in the club's newspaper assailing undocumented immigrants. The motto of Bueler's club is "Protecting Our Borders, Language, and Culture." In his diatribe Bueler identified migrants without proper paperwork as "unsophisticated, poor and unedu-

*Michael Savage broadcasts nationwide. At the time he was based at the Disney-owned radio station KSFO in San Francisco.

cated, who do not in any way hold strong family values." He struck out not only at immigrants but at those who disagreed with him, saying "liberals welcome every Muhammad, Jamul, and Jose who wishes to leave his third world state and come to America—mostly illegally—to rip off our health care system, balkanize our language and destroy our political system."[11]

The assault earned Bueler (who says he also studies the Michael Savage Show) a coveted interview with the right-wing Fox News Network announcer Bill O'Reilly. "I'm going to try to give you some advice," O'Reilly said during the interview. He told Bueler to watch his rhetoric, because it was getting him into trouble and it "clouds the issues you want to talk about." O'Reilly knows. He tries to carefully walk a line between his inflammatory language and the issues he wishes to rant about. In an interview with Texas Congressman Silvestre Reyes, O'Reilly promoted militarizing the border, at one point telling Reyes, "We'd save lives because Mexican wetbacks, whatever you want to call them, the *coyotes*—they're not going to do what they're doing now, so people aren't going to die in the desert. So we save lives, all right, and we seal it down and make it one hundred times harder to come across."[12] During the controversy that resulted from O'Reilly's use of the word "wetback," his employer suggested it was just a "gaffe" and O'Reilly dismissed it as "slang." He told the *New York Times*, "I was groping for a term to describe the industry that brings people in here. It was not meant to disparage people in any way." Congressman Reyes doesn't accept the excuse. He calls O'Reilly's use of "wetback" an insult. "Bill O'Reilly is an entertainer," says Reyes. "Off camera he's actually a nice guy. Turn on that damn camera and he becomes an entertainer, and he likes to be outlandish and he tries to be overbearing." People such as O'Reilly, says the congressman, "are not trying to solve anything. They're trying to exploit people who are well intentioned and who are trying to solve some of the most complex issues and problems that our country faces. That's his livelihood, but he's still accountable."

It wasn't O'Reilly's first use of "wetback" in a public forum. After a speech in Easton, Pennsylvania, the local newspaper reported that O'Reilly talked about the need to secure U.S. borders. "O'Reilly criticized the Immigration and Naturalization Service for not doing its job and not keeping out 'the wetbacks.' He has often blasted the INS for allowing illegal immigration."[13]

A look at the website promoting Michael Savage's book and radio show makes it clear where Conservative Club president Tim Bueler gets his inspiration. "Save America Now," screams a headline on the site that solicits contributions to something Savage founded called the Paul Revere Society, which stands "for the reassertion of our borders, our language, and our culture." That's the same language used by Bueler's high school club to explain its purpose. On his website Savage explains further, "Some say that the borders are arbitrary, English is only one of many languages in our new 'Multicultural America,' and that we share no common history or values. We believe in the Sovereignty of our Nation. That English is our national 'glue.' And that we all do share in the pillars of the Bible, the U.S. Constitution, and the Bill of Rights. These documents and what they stand for are our common cultural heritage."[14] The Tim Buelers out in radioland are obviously listening carefully.

15

CROSSING THE
BORDER THROUGH
THE ETHER

~~~~~~~~~

KBBF IS the type of radio station my friend Juana María tunes in for news and information about the Latino migrant subculture. Its studios are down a chuckhole-filled dirt road in southeast Santa Rosa, California, the Latino side of the city. Housed in a beat-up double-wide mobile home, the signs pointing to KBBF are hand-painted and fading. Operations manager Felipe Ramirez shows me into his tiny office, stacked with CDs, the monitor turned up loud enough for us to hear the talk program in progress live on the air. On the shelves of a bookcase are his trophies and souvenirs, including a doll from Oaxaca and a bottle of mezcal. He's wearing a pinstriped suit with a knit pullover shirt, open at the neck. A trace of grey is creeping into his downturned moustache, adding intensity to his expressions of concern for the migrants from Mexico in his audience.

The news and music and other information broadcast by KBBF and all the other Spanish-language radio stations on both sides of the border provide a critical cultural link for migrants from Mexico. "Besides the telephone, which gives them a direct line to their families and loved ones back there," says Ramirez, "the radio keeps them in touch with their hometowns and their families." KBBF broadcasts programs simultaneously with stations in Mexico, including talk shows with listener participation by telephone.

Some of the KBBF programming is directed only at new immigrants. The show "Bienvenidos a America," for example, deals solely with immigration issues and offers listeners an opportunity to call in and ask specific questions about problems they face in their new land. Lawyers and social workers, police and firefighters, along with other experts, are invited to the studios to share information with callers and the audience.

"We try to be very, very careful not to encourage people to come across the border," Ramirez says, "not to break the laws and smuggle yourself across the border." But for those already here, no matter their immigration status, the station is a problem-solving service. "Many times they are afraid to go to the doctor, for fear of being turned down or having to show documents of their legal status. We try to guide them. Sometimes their fear goes too far and a person dies, especially a child, and all because they were afraid to ask for help."

Hungry and tired migrants on the road, who have been listening to the radio station during their trek, sometimes head for the studio in desperation, convinced that since the station broadcasts information designed to help them, it will also provide food, water, and clothing. They ring the buzzer on the trailer door.

"Sometimes people arrive here and say, 'We are hungry and we need to eat.' They have children. They say, 'We're traveling to Los Angeles,' or 'We're going to Salinas.'" The program director tells me that when such needs exceed the resources at the radio station, he gets help from a variety of social welfare organizations. He tries to provide help to illegal migrants already in the States without encouraging those who are considering a break north.

In some cities along the two-thousand-mile U.S.-Mexico border, U.S.-based border radio is a consequential factor in the Mexican marketplace. More and more border stations in the United States are looking at their audience as a combined one, since their broadcast signals recognize no fence and the borderlands communities on both sides often are interested in similar cultural offerings. Stations are both creating programming and selling advertising with a borderless mentality—and getting premium prices for this approach.

At least one group of television stations, Entravision Communications Corporation of Santa Monica, California, bases its company business strategy on servicing the borderlands. From San Diego–Tijuana to Brownsville-Matamoros, Entravision bought stations in six cross-border communities, choosing TV stations in such relatively small U.S. cities as Yuma, Arizona. Because these cities are small advertising markets, the costs of buying the licenses was minimal. But the broadcast signal of the Yuma station, for example, does not recognize the political border and blasts into Mexicali, a sprawling Mexican city of more than a million. Although the U.S.-based Nielsen Media Research ratings firm surveys only their north-of-the-border viewers, Entravision's chairman Walter Ulloa is not complaining.

"We don't get credit in the rankings for our Mexican viewers," he says, "but we do get dollars from Mexican advertisers who want U.S. viewers, and we get the big U.S. brands looking for viewers in Mexico."[1]

In the last decade of the twentieth century the Mexican border population doubled to more than sixteen million in the six border states. One of the Entravision stations, KINT in El Paso, sells 15 percent of its airtime to Mexican advertisers. In 2001 station manager David Candelaria generated advertising income selling time to candidates in the Ciudad Juárez mayoral election, the first time a U.S. station had sold advertising in a Mexican election campaign.

In 2000, Los Angeles Pacifica station KPFK began getting reports of interference—classical music mixing with their signal. Don Mussell, group chief engineer for Pacifica Radio, went to Los Angeles to investigate and followed the interference south.[2] He discovered XHLNC in Tijuana, licensed for only one thousand watts at the same frequency as KPFK, but broadcasting between forty and fifty thousand watts from its five-hundred-foot tower. He hired engineers to measure signals of that and ultimately several other radio stations across the border, accumulating a raft of data and information that he forwarded to the Federal Communications Commission.

Mussell says all the FM stations in Tijuana are outrageously overpowered, flaunting their compliance with both their licenses and the U.S.-Mexico broadcasting agreement established in a 1992 treaty. He says he has also determined that the AM signal at 690, broadcasting from Rosarita Beach just south of Tijuana and owned by the U.S. radio giant Clear Channel, was broadcasting at about 150,000 watts instead of the 50,000 for which they are licensed.

The Guadalajara husband-and-wife radio team Víctor and Marta Díaz own XHLNC, the station Mussell originally found interfering with KPFK. The Díazes claim they are in compliance with their license and that KPFK is simply jealous that their new Mexican station is filling in the dial at a place where Pacifica's signal formerly drifted.[3] Told of Mussell's claim that his studies prove the Díaz station is broadcasting at greater power than allowed, Víctor Díaz denied the charges.

"That's the first I've heard of it," Díaz told *Los Angeles Times* reporter Susan Carpenter. "Maybe Mexican watts are different."

One of the living experts on both the history and the contemporary role of border broadcasting is Bill Crawford. Crawford is co-author with Gene Fowler of *Border Radio*,[4] the definitive book on the so-called border blasters: stations beaming signals north from Mexico into the United States. Border radio is another example of the porous nature of the U.S.-Mexico line.

"These stations were wonderful," says Crawford. "They were set up in these little towns along the border, tiny, tiny little hamlets. Originally the border radio stations were some of the biggest employers in these towns. Wonderful broadcasting outlaws, such as Dr. Brinkley, set them up. Dr. Brinkley made a fortune with a 1930s version of Viagra, a goat gland transplant operation to cure male impotency. He actually transplanted male goat gonads into a man's personal equipment and was kicked off the U.S. airways, whereupon he moved to Mexico. He set up the first really high-powered border blaster."

Mexico approved licenses for these overpowered stations in retaliation for the U.S. government assigning clear-channel frequencies to U.S.-based radio stations without consulting Mexico. Many of those of us who grew up in California and other border states listened late through the night to Wolfman Jack howling advertisements and playing music, taking advantage of the fact that no border could stop his radio signal.

"Wolfman Jack had his start on the station that was founded by Dr. Brinkley," Crawford says. "Jack was one of the most successful entrepreneurs along the border. In the early sixties he actually made most of his money selling time to preachers who weren't allowed to solicit donations over the air on U.S.-based stations. He sold time to J. Charles Jessup, and Reverend Ike, and all the wonderful preachers. This was where the electronic church was first born, broadcasting in English on super high-powered stations to the American market. Historians don't even know how powerful some of these transmitters were, especially at XCRF. I've heard tapes of air checks of XCRF in Ciudad Acuña recorded in Finland, in Norway, as far away as the South Pacific. People from the military have told me that during and right after World War II, on aircraft carriers in the South Pacific, they could pick up these high-powered border radio stations."

The lore from these stations includes stories Crawford loves to tell about the local effects of their high power. "Yeah, birds flying near the antenna would fall down from the sky, dead. People have told me that if you lived close enough to these transmitters in the evening, you didn't need to buy any electricity because the lightbulbs would light up by themselves. The electrical power was that intense. People could actually hear these stations on barbed wire fences. If you just leaned down close to the barbed wire you could hear it. One person told me that his dad could hear the stations on his dental work."

Contemporary Spanish-language border radio, along with U.S. stations broadcasting in Spanish, seeps into the U.S. interior, often providing a needed public service for Mexicans living north of the border. Their announcers read messages for the Mexican nationals at work in the United States and their friends and relatives left behind. Similar messaging is traveling the internet. Websites keep migrants to the United States connected to their hometowns. Some Mexican *pueblos* have constructed sophisticated sites to keep their emigrants informed about local news and affairs, including family gossip. Extensive e-mail travels through the sites. Some sell advertising to firms in both the United States and Mexico.

One example of a cross-border website was created by José Herrera when he was a computer science student at the Illinois Institute of Technology. He first built the site simply to post information for his friends and family. But he discovered that his personal website was being used by visitors outside his circle of friends and family who were seeking information about Durango state. He added information exchanges for more than fifty Durango towns and cities besides his own, keeping them updated and illustrated with contemporary photographs. "Seems like a lot of people like the idea," Herrera told Sam Quinones, the journalist who first documented the explosive growth of these websites and the critical support they provide migrants.

16

THE DRIVER'S
LICENSE DEBATE

ONE OF THE lasting political changes wrought by California's anti-immigrant Proposition 187 was the amendment to the driver's license law requiring motorists to prove their legal residency in order to obtain a license. Thirty-seven other states enforce such a demand. Statistics make it clear that the sad result of these laws is that undocumented migrants don't take the driver's test and don't buy auto insurance—that requires a driver's license. Instead they just get out on the highway and drive, unlicensed and uninsured, worried about getting stopped for a traffic violation.

In 2003 the California legislature finally passed a bill authorizing driver's licenses to be issued to anyone who passed the test. Some two million undocumented workers in the state were in a position to benefit from the change, along with the rest of us who could look forward to safer highways. California's governor at the time, Gray Davis, fighting to save his job from a recall campaign, signed the bill, hoping to gain Latino votes. The strategy was desperate; he had vetoed a similar bill the year before. Davis then lost the election to Arnold Schwarzenegger, whose first act as governor was to make good on a campaign promise and strongarm lawmakers into repealing the law. If you refuse, he told the Democratic-controlled legislature, I'll take the debate directly to the voters. Polls showed that such a referendum would result in a repeal, so the legislature collapsed in acquiescence rather than suffer another setback.

A couple of months later, proponents of licensing all drivers in California, no matter their immigration status, were still scrambling to figure out what to do next. One of those was the Democratic lieutenant governor Cruz Bustamante.

In his utilitarian office far down the Capitol halls from Schwarzenegger's plush quarters, the lieutenant governor sits behind a heavy dark wooden desk covered with papers, looking somewhat formal in a dark blue shirt with a patterned green tie. He explains why there should be no correlation between immigration status and driver's licenses.

"It's a recognition," he says a couple of months after Schwarzenegger took office, "that people who are here, who are working hard, who are staying out of trouble, paying their taxes, need a way of getting to and from work." He rejects the idea that licensing all drivers on California roads and highways jeopardizes security. "If you look at what took place on 9/11, every single one of those folks was here legally. Every one. They didn't do anything illegal for fear it would bring attention to them. Their driver's licenses, their entry into the United States—everything they did was legal. It's a mischaracterization that giving driver's licenses to the undocumented somehow gives them an umbrella to hide under or a shadow to hide in."

The arguments against licensing undocumented drivers are as hollow as the arguments against providing health care and education to undocumented migrants and their children. These people are forced to drive to navigate our automobile-based culture. They cannot buy insurance without holding a driver's license. By denying them driver's licenses, we fool ourselves if we think that will keep them off the highway. Instead they will drive without insurance and often without knowing the laws and customs of our highways since they are not forced to learn them in order to pass the driver's test that we're not allowing them to take.

This argument is backed up by California Highway Patrol statistics. About one in five of the fatal accidents that occurred in the first four years of this century in my home county, Sonoma, involved unlicensed drivers, and in most of those wrecks the unlicensed drivers were deemed at fault. Over half of those drivers were born in Mexico. Because the California

Highway Patrol does not attempt to ascertain the legal status of residents involved in crashes, it cannot be determined for sure if those Mexican-born drivers were in the United States legally, but it is safe to assume that had they been documented, at least some of them would have made the effort to obtain licenses. Similar statistics are at play nationwide, according to the American Automobile Association. Longtime Sonoma County–based Highway Patrol Lt. Dan Moore is convinced that licensing drivers makes sense. "To obtain a driver's license in California, you have to pass a driving test and a written test," he points out. "I'm not going to say that will make you a safe driver for the rest of your life, but it will ensure minimum standards. That's why we have driver's licenses."[1] And in California the driver's license test is administered in several languages, including Spanish.

Lieutenant Governor Bustamante easily moves from the specifics of the driver's license law to a broad assessment of the value that undocumented workers bring to the California and U.S. economy. "A very large part of California's economy is driven by labor that most people in California don't want to do. By definition, a farm worker works. That work, out in the Central Valley, is very difficult work. I know. I've done it. Anybody who's picked peaches or has loaded boxcars or has done any of the picking, harvesting of any kind out there, knows it is very difficult, backbreaking work under a hot sun and difficult circumstances. This is the work that most people don't want to do. And the pay is not that great." These crucial workers, he says, ought to be licensed when they drive to work. "About 70 percent of the people who work in agriculture, all those people who put food on your table, are not here with permanent residence." He ticks off more numbers—30 percent of the construction industry, 40 percent of the service industry. "Each of those has a huge number of people who are here undocumented. I'm a little befuddled by those who believe that somehow providing an opportunity for working people to go out and get insurance and learn the proper etiquette of driving on the streets of California is wrong."

The foolishness of denying driver's licenses to California drivers is only exacerbated by the fact that just across the state's northern border,

Oregon does not check immigration status before issuing a license to a driver who passes its test. And Oregon licenses are valid in California (and all other states).

The driver's license bill was drafted by California State Senator Gil Cedillo. We meet on a cool Sacramento day in his Capitol office. "I'm from southern California," he explains as he takes off a long winter greatcoat. Senator Cedillo says he expects to figure out a compromise with the new governor, ultimately drafting legislation that Schwarzenegger will sign. Meanwhile he takes a long view of migration from the south, convinced that prejudice against Mexicans without papers will wane with coming generations. "The role that nannies play in this process," he muses, "that gardeners play, that home-care workers play. The nannies are raising people's kids. And when those kids grow up, they're going to be bilingual. They're not going to have a hostility to the language. These kids will grow up and they will relate to the nannies' kids. They're not going to have an English-only attitude, they're not going to fear that."

That's a comforting scenario. But at the same time Cedillo worries about the potency of right-wing talk radio to perpetuate fear and hate against migrants. "In those cars," he says about California's commuter culture, "starting at three o'clock, there's some buffoon who is just blaming every problem they have on immigrants. The white working class is frustrated. We're into this generation where for the first time the children are not going to do better than the parents."

Senator Cedillo calls himself a typical Mexican American. He didn't learn to speak Spanish until he was an adult. He grew up in Los Angeles, rooting for the Dodgers and studying at UCLA. "My only experience as a kid with going to Mexico was going to Tijuana to visit my grandmother. I didn't want to go there." Now he's pleased to find Mexicans in his district. "They're vibrant. They're innovative. They're industrious. I just love driving around L.A. and seeing these guys who grow corn in their backyard. These guys will probably be owning a chain of markets in one or two generations, starting with a little corn stand."

The arguments against allowing undocumented drivers a license include the fact that they broke the law crossing the border, so they should not be afforded the privilege of driving. Of course they drive nonetheless. But the government is inconsistent. Many undocumented workers decide to pay federal and state income tax. The tax authorities don't check to make sure they are working in this country legally before accepting their money. The U.S. Supreme Court has ruled that legal residency in the United States cannot be used as a test to prevent students from studying in public schools.

Another argument against issuing driver's licenses to illegal migrants is that the official government document helps legitimize the residency of people who are in the United States without proper paperwork.

"Yeah, that's valid," Cedillo says. "But it's a good thing. It facilitates the process of immigration for these people. Ten to twelve million people are here, working. They are imbedded in the foundation of our economy. It would be tough for us to prosper in certain sectors without their labor.

"You know there are a significant number of parking valets in California who have no license. We won't let them drive themselves to work, but we'll put the keys of a Porsche or a Hummer or a Jaguar in their hands in a heartbeat."

Cedillo likens the attempts to keep Mexicans out of the United States to prohibition. "We wanted to regulate the consumption of alcohol. So we did that. It didn't work. We changed the law again to recognize reality." Reconcile the border law with reality, he says, and open the U.S. border to Mexicans who wish to come north.

"We have a trade reality. We have a need for human capital. We want security. We want things to be done orderly. These things argue for a different type of border and a different type of understanding of our relationship with Mexico."

17

ILLEGAL

AMERICANS

MEXICO FIGHTS its own illegal immigration on its southern border. Central and South Americans slip into southern Mexico without proper documents. They're seeking a better life in Mexico or, more likely, hope to use Mexico as a bridge to the United States. The Mexican border guards at the Chiapas-Guatemala frontier struggle to identify foreigners. Physically there is nothing to distinguish a Mexican Mayan from a Guatemalan Mayan, and the 620-mile Mexican border with Guatemala and Belize is mostly wild and unguarded jungle. One device the Mexican border patrol agents use is to demand that the travelers sing the Mexican national anthem, and not only the first verse but the second and third. Imagine the scene at San Diego if instead of asking, "Are you an American citizen," border guards demanded that returning tourists sing the second and third verses of "The Star Spangled Banner."

For an American heading south into Mexico, border formalities are minimal. A trip overland to a Mexican border city rarely warrants more than a glance from Mexican officials. A visit farther inland requires a tourist permit, a simple form to complete. Longer stays and business trips demand more complex paperwork. But comparatively Mexico's border is wide open. In 2002, for example, U.S. authorities deported almost a million Mexicans. Mexico sent 642 Americans back across the frontier.

Mexico operates a national immigration detention prison in Mexico City where illegal immigrants are held while their cases are pending. Deported Americans usually spend only a few days locked up and then are bused from the prison to Brownsville or Laredo. Mexican authorities do not go looking for Americans without papers; they stumble on them when the Gringos are stopped by police or seek help.[1]

Americans in Mexico legally can and do end up in Mexican jails and prisons for breaking Mexican laws. Heading south on Interstate 5 from California into Mexico, signs suggest that travelers tune into the radio station broadcasting at 1700 AM. It transmits endless repeats of recorded bilingual border information, advising travelers regarding Mexico's rules on importing automobiles and its prohibitions on guns and ammunition. What it doesn't bother reporting is that Mexican border guards watch the motor and foot traffic with relaxed detachment. As the freeway ends, most cars motor past the sign suggesting that drivers stop if they're carrying something they wish to declare to customs. Northbound, the line of cars waiting to be inspected by U.S. border guards is backed up to the horizon.

But periodically the Mexican authorities do spot-check incoming cars. Drivers who didn't listen to the radio alerts and passed the big signs reading WARNING: ENTRY OF FIREARMS INTO MEXICO PROHIBITED can find themselves in accommodations they did not expect and probably could not imagine. "I made a bad, bad mistake. Ruined my whole damn life, I guess," said Johnny Manuel from prison in Ciudad Juárez. Manuel claims he took a wrong turn and ended up crossing the bridge into Mexico by mistake, with three of his fiancée's guns in his car. Mexico sentenced him to five years behind bars.[2] His is not an uncommon story.

Americans stand out in the crowds on Avenida Revolución in Tijuana. The hustlers bark their wares at the Gringos; the cabs cruise by slowly, cabbies yelling.

"Taxi?" asks still another driver.

"No."

"You want woman?" is the next question. It is especially easy to get into trouble in Tijuana and other Mexican border towns.

South from the tourist strip that hugs the international frontier, the nightclubs and trinket stands give way to upholstery shops, car dealers, and a more residential district. There, miles from the tawdry downtown but still within sight of the hills of San Diego County on the north side of the border, La Mesa Penitenciaría is temporary home for Americans who found trouble in Tijuana and got caught.

"I had a car accident," Keith Prohaska explained. He had been locked up in La Mesa for three weeks when I met with him, charged with drunk driving and destruction of private property: the parked cars he hit.[3] But he talked like a prison veteran, "You learn real quick, Spanish is not the language here. Money is."

We were standing around the noisy open yard inside La Mesa. Word spread that I was looking for Americans to interview. Prohaska, the drunk driver, still sounded dazed about his sudden confinement. "I had several drinks at dinner. I don't know how long I've got here." He was already disgusted with his own government. "The American consul is absolutely useless. All they do is call home collect and give us vitamins."

Alex Hines was a little more than a third of the way through his seven-year sentence for possession of one gram of marijuana and contributing to the delinquency of a minor. "It was just seeds," he complains. "If I had killed somebody I would have been out already." For almost two of his years inside La Mesa, Alex's wife and two small children lived in the prison with him. "Oh yeah, my wife was here. Everyday she'd go out, go to the store, shop, do what she had to do, do laundry, whatever, come back in. We'd walk around the field."

A Marine serving five years for counterfeiting tells me that life isn't so bad for him, considering he is in prison. "There are certain benefits you can't get in the States: women and bottles."

Another Marine agrees. "This is a better jail than jail in the States. Let me put it this way: If you've got the money, you can get anything you want."

"Except out," interrupts Phil Trembley, who says he has been locked up for a year, and then looks at his watch and adds, "and eleven days." The charge was homicide, but Phil had not yet been tried, let alone convicted and sentenced.

"I was in a bar," Phil says. "Somebody slipped me some drugs. They tried to rob me and I killed somebody. Okay?" As is the case with so many people locked up, Phil feels wronged. "Whether I'm guilty or not, there's a lot of extenuating circumstances. I'm not going to say my hand didn't do it, but I'm going to say I feel, personally, that it was self-defense."

Phil's story is a typical border tale. He was picked up by the police after the killing, he says, and then abused. Then he languished in prison, expecting his own government to do more to help him out of his predicament.

"I was beaten and electrocuted and locked in a little room for the first five days I was in Mexico," he says coolly. "The first three days no one knew where I was at, including myself. I didn't even know what part of Mexico I was in. I was cold. My clothes were completely ripped. They had electrocuted me. They tied wires to my testicles. They put soda up my nose. They beat me. You know, they beat me in the eyes and the kidneys where there were no marks."

Phil says it was three days before the Shore Patrol and the U.S. consul showed up with a few blankets. "I got in trouble the last day in January, and you can imagine how cold it was. I was in a little cell with defecation about five inches deep, and I was handcuffed with my hands behind my back for three days solid, day and night. So I slept with handcuffs on, in defecation. In the mornings the Mexicans, when they brought my food, it was two corn tortillas with some beans. They threw it in my cell. I wasn't allowed fresh drinking water. We drank water from the tap. I was so sick. I was throwing up." The U.S. Navy started shipping him bag lunches so he wouldn't be forced to eat jail food. But his stomach was a mess. "I had diarrhea, I was freezing at night, I was cold. I had to fight to get a bed, to get a place to sleep."

After his arraignment, Phil Trembley was moved to La Mesa to face an open-ended period of incarceration while the authorities put together their case against him.

More Americans end up behind bars in Mexico than in any other foreign country, probably because so many Americans travel south of the border naively looking for fun and profit. A substantial number of those American prisoners are physically and psychologically tortured. Many others are arrested and quietly manage to bribe their way out of trouble with the arresting cop before they get downtown and become a statistic.

The high walls of La Mesa didn't keep the outside world away from the convicts, they just kept the inmates away from the outside world. When I visited, guards armed with rifles crouched on top of the walls, looking sinister in their blue jeans, T-shirts, and baseball caps. Their lack of official uniforms seemed especially threatening, a reminder that the authority they represented did not necessarily answer to a government that controls them. They looked like freelance toughs, adding to the mood of whimsical justice that pervades the Mexican legal system.

One guard was on duty at the front gate of the prison, a swinging door in the chain-link fencing, working alone. The gatekeeper casually cradled a machine gun and watched over a steady stream of visitors coming and going, deciding who could come in and who could not, a decision based as much on deals and bribes as on law and order. Searches of visitors were cursory operations. Inmates could buy just about anything they wanted or needed inside the prison.

The warden was expecting me; I called ahead. He looked smart in his suit and tie. Four shotguns in a case scattered with boxes of shells were behind him. He offered me free run of his teeming institution.

Behind his office, in an open alleyway leading to the yard, the warden had collected La Mesa's American inmates: the alleged murderer, the counterfeiters, the drunk driver, a robber, all in their twenties, and a convicted child molester serving a thirty-year sentence, a much older fellow. None of them knew when he was getting out of La Mesa; all agreed they were being treated better than most other inmates because they were Americans, Americans with money.

In the yard—which looks like a stage set for a small, poor Mexican village—the inside of the actual prison wall is difficult to see. In most places it is covered by what the Mexican inmates call their *caracas*, private quarters referred to as "houses" by the Americans. They are tiny but adequate private rooms actually built onto the prison's walls. Furnished with shag rugs and TVs, equipped with padlocks controlled by the inmates, they bring to mind kid's clubhouses more than prison cells.

"I did all of this," one of the counterfeiters proudly shows off his studio apartment, barely larger than his bed. An English-language San Diego television station is coming in loud and clear on the black-and-white set. "I did all of this, even the wiring." Where did he get the wire and the connectors and the electrical outlet? "A hardware store delivered it."

Some of the houses are up on a second floor, complete with balconies, barbecues, and a sweeping view of those close San Diego hills.

"At first it was really scary," Alex Hines, the inmate doing seven years for marijuana possession, says. But soon he learned to deal with his new routine. "I get up, eat, go with a few other Americans who are in here. You know, we just talk. That's about it. Watch TV. Listen to the radio. Walk to different places back and forth in here, to different cells people are living in here. That's about it. Then go eat, go to sleep, and occasionally, like when I have visits here, like when my wife's here and stuff, we go eat and, you know, everything else you could probably do on the outside."

Alex's house includes two bedrooms, a bathroom, and a kitchen. He has room for a couch and apologized for the mess, but the day I visit the Mexican woman prisoner who cleans for him hadn't made it over to his place from the women's side of the prison. With a smile and wink, Alex suggests she performs other services for him too, when his wife isn't visiting or living with him. We run into his maid later over in the women's section of the prison. They hug and hold hands while we talk. The guard escorting us hoots over the handholding, but Alex just smiles. Cooking, cleaning, and prostitution are the most common chores available to the women inmates for making money in the prison economy.

"It's pretty well set up," Alex says proudly about his house. "You'd be surprised, this is like no prison at all. This is like—they just take me off the street and put me in another world, but away from everyone else. And I have to get along with all these people in here." He tells stories of stabbings and killings in La Mesa. "I never thought about death until I came here," he says. But on the high-rent side of the prison where his and the other Americans' *caracas* are scattered, life is relatively quiet. The nasty fights and fires usually occur across the yard in the maximum-security section of the prison, or where the poorest prisoners share unlocked cells.

"Where I live, it's fine. It all depends on how you're set financially. If you've got a lot of money, you can do anything here."

Alex Hines's *caraca* cost him about five hundred American dollars to secure and furnish. For the duration of his sentence, it's his. The prison administration takes time payments for the house. Alex and the other inmates buy what they need from the outside, get it from visiting friends and relatives, buy it through the prison marketplace, or do without. Nothing is free. Even the routine beans and rice from the prison kettle require a payment to the guards.

Mordidas these daily expenses are called, the ubiquitous word in Mexico for bribes, the little bites needed to do business in Mexico. Everything in prison carries a price: blankets, cots or the more comfortable beds, showers, and, of course, illegal recreation like drugs, alcohol, and women. The guards provide the goods, take a cut for themselves, and augment the warden's salary with his percentage. This controlled, market-driven economy keeps prison costs low for the government and makes the job of guard and warden appealing because there is plenty of extra money to be made for warders who know how to work the system.

Radios blare pop music throughout the prison yard, competing with the official announcements coming over the loudspeakers. The prison doesn't appear to be a penal institution as much as a walled city.

The Americans order out to Tijuana restaurants or grocery stores for their food, or eat at one of the inmate-owned-and-operated restaurants in the yard. These are actual private eateries. The open-air restaurants are complete with hand-painted signs, just like those on the streets of Tijuana. *Cantina* announces one restaurant's brightly colored signs. Up on the makeshift wall is a listing of hamburgers, fries, and other menu offerings. The counter, too, is restaurant-issue Formica. Commercial bottles of ketchup are set out with the meals, along with restaurant-style napkin dispensers. Inmate customers and guards sit on red Naugahyde-covered swivel stools. A jukebox pumps tunes out into the yard.

"I'm never going to come back to Mexico again," Alex Hines tells me about his plans after his release from La Mesa. "Never." He goes back to a game of Risk with his friends.

Alfredo Anzaldúa served as the U.S. government's consul for American citizens services in Tijuana. That Americans were packed into La Mesa was no surprise to him. "They come here to do things they would never think of doing in the United States," he said about Americans who cross the border and get into trouble. "They get blind drunk. They buy drugs. Then they try to buy their way out of trouble."[4]

Just before vanishing inside Mexico, the American writer and journalist Ambrose Bierce sent one last dispatch to the States in the form of an October 1, 1913, letter. "Good-bye," wrote Bierce in a message that at least some of the desperate American inmates of Mexican jails ought to be able to appreciate. "If you hear of my being stood up against a Mexican wall and shot to rags, please know that I think that a pretty good way to depart this life. It beats old age, disease, or falling down the cellar steps. To be a Gringo in Mexico—ah, that is euthanasia!"

18

ON THE

KENTUCKY

BORDER

PROFESSOR DAVID COFFEY lives in a revitalized Victorian home on an all-American-looking tree-lined main street in Bowling Green, Kentucky. Coffey is an agricultural sociologist at Western Kentucky University, and he's found plenty to study in his rural home state, where he's watched the Latino population grow at an astounding rate. In the process Coffey has become a strong advocate of the minority. "They're working in tobacco, landscaping, horse farming, poultry processing, fruits and vegetables, and forestry," he tells anyone he can get to listen. "These are the people who roof our houses, mow our lawns, paint our houses, wash our dirty dishes in restaurants, and clean our dirty laundry in hotels." Coffey estimates that only about 15 percent of the Latinos now living in Kentucky enjoy legal immigration status, and he is fascinated by the underground subculture that exists in Bowling Green, invisible to most citizens. He is enthusiastic about the social changes coming to Middle America from its neighbor to the south.

One evening when we share a meal at a Mexican eatery, Coffey introduces me to the employees, many of them relatively fresh from south of the border. "They work for three or four dollars an hour when they first arrive, working ten- and twelve-hour days," he tells me. "They get one day a week off and all they can eat." When the busboy is caught up with his work hustling dishes, Coffey motions him over to the table. He is a newcomer, just arrived in the United States a few weeks earlier but proud and happy to show off the few English phrases he's already learned.

"How are you?" He smiles. "Want more soda?" He smiles again, and then offers, "I love you, baby!"

"They're the slaves of the new century," says Coffey. The busboy will likely be working long hours for low pay until he works off the two thousand or so dollars it cost in *coyote* fees to get across the border. Coffey points out a table where a young white couple are eating, washing down their enchiladas with Mexican beer. They are college age probably, but not necessarily drinking age. "The help asks them for proof of age," Coffey explains. "Then they study the driver's license, give it back, and serve the beer. Of course they can't read," he laughs.

The restaurant manager walked across the border several years before this night. I ask him why he chose to stay in Bowling Green. "Because no problems," he tells me. "In California and New York *hay muchos problemas*." He's speaking Spanglish. "Here there are no problems and lots of work. The Americans of Kentucky," he says, *"are muy amables,"* kind and friendly. "There are no problems because Mexicans work hard." He believes Coffey's estimates are high, and that only about 5 percent of the Latinos in Bowling Green are legal. But he points out that all of them carry papers testifying to their legal status. A set of U.S. identification papers, from a driver's license to a Social Security card, takes about three hours to procure on the Bowling Green black market. The going rate rarely exceeds twenty dollars a card.

The restaurant manager goes by at least a couple of different names, not unusual in the Latino migrant community. He asks me to call him Israel. Israel came to Kentucky from Veracruz where he was friends with the Cabrera brothers—Pioquinto and Guillermo—two of the men who were packed into the death trailer at Victoria, Texas. Israel took Pioquinto's body back to Veracruz.

"I knew him when he was a little boy," Israel says. "I'm older than he was, probably five years. I knew him in Veracruz and when he came to America. He used to work in Oregon, then he moved to Glasgow,

Kentucky, to work in the milk. His daddy was sick. That was the reason he went to Mexico, to see his daddy. And when he was coming back, he died in Texas. They put him in that trailer." Pioquinto had made the cross-border trip successfully about three times, Israel tells me, and he expected no trouble.

"Let me tell you something," Israel leans forward. "He was talking to me probably five days before he died. He was talking to me and he say, 'Hey, *pues cómo no*, are you okay?' And I say, 'Yeah, where are you?' And he say, 'I'm in Texas.'" Pioquinto was checking to see if Israel could help him make the trip back to Kentucky. Getting across the border from Mexico is only half the battle for migrants coming north without proper documentation.

Twenty to fifty miles north along the border, the Border Patrol stops all traffic on northbound routes: trains and trucks, cars and buses. Typical is the Sarita checkpoint blocking US 77 from McAllen and Brownsville to Kansas City and Chicago, Memphis, and Louisville. And Bowling Green. INSPECTION STATION explains the green highway sign bringing traffic to a stop, a wait that can stretch to hours when inspectors decide to make thorough searches. Usually they spot-search the cargo and look under the chassis with mirrors on poles. Police dogs sniff for drugs and explosives and people. Drivers and passengers are asked, "Where are you going? Where do you live? Are you an American citizen?" If the agents don't like the answers they receive, they say, "Prove it!" They demand identification. If they suspect the identification that's presented to them is stolen or faked, they detain the traveler and begin deportation proceedings. The Border Patrol also roams beyond these official checkpoints, conducting raids and random checks wherever they suspect illegal immigration, to the extent that their budget and staff allow. Pioquinto was asking Israel for help getting past those checkpoints.

"I said, 'Absolutely, I can do my best.'" Israel tells me. "But he said, 'I'm not asking you only. I have to see somebody else. If I need you I'll call you.' I said, 'Yeah, no problem. Take care of yourself.' He said, 'Take care of yourself too, buddy.' And that's the last time I heard from him. Later his brother called me from Mexico and said, 'Hey, you know what happened? Pioquinto died.'"

Well established in the United States with a decent job, Israel says he's helping the family, sending money whenever he can afford it to Pioquinto's wife and daughter who moved back to Veracruz after his death. "They need money to live in Mexico. I don't send a lot of money, but like a couple months ago I sent her three hundred dollars. I only make a little money, you know. I don't make very much. I give whatever I can. He got a little boy and he got two little girls. The middle girl is my godchild. I talk to them sometimes on the phone. I ask his wife if they are okay and how is the little girl." Israel shakes his head. "It was really sad, and really hard times."

Israel favors temporary work visas as a solution to the border crisis that killed his boyhood friend. "Whatever money you make, you pay tax to America and keep the rest for your family in Mexico, so you don't have to pay *coyotes*.

But Israel is another immigrant without papers who does not favor an open border between his old and new countries. "The problem in the States is too many peoples, you know? If they open the border, everybody will want to come to this country. This country is number one in the world and it's really nice, and I know that this country is nice to everybody, but, see, look what happened September 11th because they give a chance to anybody coming here. I don't say that everybody is mean. Some people we are nice, but some people, we are stupid. We got shit in our mind. So I think it is a great idea if they make a contract, if the Mexican president talks to the American president and says, 'You know what? I've got a thousand people. Please let me give a job for these people and I promise to you that in six months they'll come back, and they can help you.'"

Most of the Mexicans picked up by the Border Patrol are seized as they cross the border. For many of the migrants, immediate deportation is just part of their commuting routine. The Border Patrol packs them onto buses and escorts them back to the border, and they walk back into Mexico. The process is called "voluntary return" by the *Migra*. It allows the seized migrants to avoid the more serious consequences of a court date and formal deportation.

The "voluntary return" arrangement works like a revolving door. The migrants come north, get picked up by the Border Patrol, and are sent back south. Then the next day, or even the same day, they come north again. Eventually, if they're persistent and stoic, they'll probably make it into the United States. New policies of the federal government are designed to reduce the number of such repeat attempts. "What's happening now," Barbara Hines sees in her immigration law practice, "is that the databases are more sophisticated, so they can tell that someone was picked up just yesterday. A lot of those people are now prosecuted for criminal reentry. It's not just a civil violation to break the immigration laws, it's actually criminal. So some clients have to serve sixty days or ninety days in jail, and then they go into the deportation system."

Another tactic the Department of Homeland Security uses to find illegal migrants in the United States is to knock on the doors of local jails. Along the border, DHS crews look at the sheriff's rosters and interrogate inmates they suspect are outlaw border crossers who got in trouble in a saloon or were picked up for wife beating or drunk driving. Old-fashioned immigration raids still occur. The raids are another source of suspects for agents who go after Mexicans in shopping center parking lots or restaurant kitchens or on factory floors.

The captured Mexicans, along with migrants from Central and South America and the rest of the world, are shipped to a holding pen. The DHS Port Isabelle Processing Center in Texas, or the Corrections Corporation of America facilities in Laredo or Taylor, Texas, are examples. Corrections Corporation of America is a private company that runs detention facilities as a contractor for the federal government. The only undocumented migrants who end up in a federal prison are those who are prosecuted for illegal entry. These are usually migrants who were officially deported and got caught returning, or those who were repeat offenders of the "voluntary return" method. Those caught without prior records are usually held in county jails or in one of the DHS or CCA holding facilities, just long enough to process them for the trip south. Only those being held for violating Texas law are confined at Huntsville and other Texas prisons; the procedure is the same in other states.

The deportees held in Texas and then sent south are not necessarily only those who were picked up along the vast Texas-Mexico border. The Border Patrol is continually inventing new procedures for dealing with the migrants they arrest. One experiment was to fly migrants seized along the Arizona-Mexico border east to Texas, then deport them through Texas ports of entry. The idea was to make it more difficult for the migrants to repeat the crossing. The Texas border is more secure than the Arizona border. Another anticipated benefit of shipping the border crossers hundreds of miles east was to sever any ties they might have with *coyotes* and other logistical support along the Arizona border. The immediate result of these human transshipments was to create a homeless problem in the Mexican border cities of Ciudad Juárez, Nuevo Laredo, Reynosa, and Matamoros, places already teeming with poverty and unemployment, slums and overcrowding.

South of the Rio Grande, city governments complained. "We don't like Juárez being used as a point for massive deportations," was the response from Ricardo Chavez in Ciudad Juárez city hall. "The city is not prepared to deal with this, and there is already a shortage of jobs here. It's a bad situation. People are sleeping in parks and under bridges." One of those deportees complained bitterly about the shackles used to confine the migrants during the plane trips to Texas. "If they have to deport us, they shouldn't treat us like criminals. It's humiliating. We're just working people."[1]

Barbara Hines sees his point, especially when migrants are housed in jails and prisons alongside hardened criminals. "A lot of these people have never been in jail before. Even if you're not commingled, it's a very frightening experience. Because to immigrants it's a labor issue, and for the United States it's a criminal issue." The U.S. government calls the long-distance deportations humane because they deter repeated attempts at crossing the harsh Sonora desert, the wildlands where thousands of migrants have died since the California and Texas borders were fortified.

Bowling Green, Kentucky, suffers from ludicrous city planning. The gracious historic city square and most of the surrounding businesses struggle in competition with endless strip malls along miles of four-lane Scottsville Road, the route from the eviscerated downtown to the interstate highway. At Ford's Furniture along Scottsville, the marquee alternates flashes of 12 MONTHS FREE FINANCING with GOD BLESS AMERICA onto the oversized parking lot. From Ford's eastbound, the blight includes the Montana Grill and Tumbleweed restaurants, the Buick and Chevrolet dealership with its acres of blacktop and cars, the Home Depot and Best Buy, the vast new Kroger supermarket and its adjoining strip mall. Scottsville Road doesn't only draw business from downtown, it consumes itself. The old abandoned Kroger left vacant across from the sparkling new one can't be much more than twenty years old, and it's now just the flagship of a strip-mall ghost town.

Few Bowling Green old-timers are reconciled to the chain-store look of their city and the lack of human scale. No one walks around Scottville Road; the distances from one megastore to the next are huge. Doing business in Bowling Green requires an automobile; there is no scheduled bus service, and taxis are expensive. "I don't want to go to no mall to do my Christmas shopping," one cab driver made clear. "I want to go downtown."

On the other side of the old Louisville and Nashville Railroad tracks from Scottsville Road, from David Coffey's elegant Victorian home, and from the quiet downtown is what was historically the black Bowling Green neighborhood. It looks rough but is changing rapidly. Burned-out and boarded-up houses sit alongside tidy bungalows. This wrong side of the tracks is an entry point to the American Dream, and it's filling up with Latinos. They can shop at the local general stores named *La Mexicana* and *La Perlita*, the *Mercado Hispano* and *Los Camaradas*. Prominent banners on the façades of the stores offer the services of express companies that will ship money to Mexico and other points south. They do a big business in prepaid telephone cards that offer cheap rates for calls to Mexico. The marquee on Teresa's Restaurant urges, PRAY FOR OUR TROOPS OPEN 6 AM. Nearby is *La Luz del Mundo* church. Up the street is Don Chuy's bar and dancehall, its advertising limited to a simple, *BAILE VIE. SAB.*, DANCE FRI. SAT.

In the late 1990s David Coffey managed to get a grant from the U.S. Department of Agriculture to teach a few Spanish words and phrases to

Kentucky farmers and basic English to Latino migrant workers so that some of the mutually dependent strangers could begin to get to know each other. Because the classes were subsidized by the federal government, undocumented workers were not allowed to attend. Coffey's Latino students all held H2A visas, the visas granted to agricultural workers for specific jobs for specific periods of time during the growing season. "Mr. and Mrs. Farmer came in first, workers second, separated. The first night it was quite apparent that the Latinos were scared. They were very subservient to the Gringos. The first night we did body parts. We had them pronouncing each other's names, shaking hands, and naming body parts." They were instructed to touch each other as they named the arms and legs, heads and shoulders. "I'm sure most of our growers had never touched a Mexican. And most of the workers had never had an encounter touching a Gringo. As a result, after they touched each other and started pronouncing names, giving a '¡Mucho gusto!' and the handshakes, everything just melted, and we started laughing with arms around each other and all that, which to me was worth the grant." They walked into the schoolhouse separately, but they walked out arm in arm.

Coffey loved surprising the two groups by bringing them together to socialize—"We had Thanksgiving meals in Mexican restaurants." Most of the workers in the class came from Nayarit, and after the harvest he organized a trip for some of the growers to tour the Mexicans' villages. "We flew to Guadalajara. They took us on a tour of Tequila, and we sampled tequila and all that wonderful stuff. Which is real interesting for a group of Baptists away from home, so they got mellow. They were treated royally." The Mexicans showed off their homes and were careful to point out their microwave ovens, their televisions, the rooms they had added on to their houses—all as a result of the money they had earned working in Kentucky. The Kentucky farmers were amazed at the poverty they witnessed. "They had never thought about how poor some of their workers are and how much they're really helping them by bringing them to Kentucky and how much the workers appreciate it."

The process for obtaining an H2A visa is complicated. The grower must show that no U.S. citizen wants the work, then solicit workers in

Mexico, usually through an intermediary who acts as a fixer. Once a deal is made, the worker goes to the American consulate and secures the visa. The grower must provide transport from the border to the job site and back, along with food and housing during the period of employment. The worker cannot change jobs and must return home when the crop is harvested. A tiny minority of Latinos working in the United States do so with H2A visas, well under a hundred thousand among the millions.

Immigration lawyer Barbara Hines says the H2A visa is unpopular with both employers and workers. "An H2A is for seasonal agricultural work, and it has all sorts of restrictions. The problem with an H2A is that it only gives you permission to work for a certain contractor. If you find a better job or you want to move to Chicago, you can't. These temporary visas are employer-tied. That raises all sorts of issues about labor conditions."

Another unpopular alternative, says Hines, is the H2B visa. "An H2B is a temporary visa that allows you to work in any industry—but it must be a temporary job. So if someone wants to hire you as a dishwasher in a restaurant, you don't qualify for an H2B because the employer needs a dishwasher year round. An H2B limits the worker to things like landscaping and seasonal hotel work. Yes, if you're in a resort area where your restaurant shuts down you can hire workers with H2B visas. But an H2B does not resolve the problem for the unskilled work that most immigrants do."

The regulations are complicated for both H2 visas. "You have to have an employer willing to do it. The employer has to advertise in a newspaper and show there's no qualified U.S. worker. For most employers, it's just easier to hire somebody and pay them in cash." In addition to all that, many Mexicans cannot qualify for the H2 visas. Anyone who was caught illegally trying to get into the United States or picked up and deported must wait ten years before being considered for an H2 visa.

Another reason the H2 visas are unappealing to Latino migrants is made obvious by David Coffey's research in Kentucky. "The Latinos—I call them Hispanics*—are no longer transient. They're here. They're not

---

*"Hispanic" is the term used by the federal government for Mexicans and other Latin Americans in the United States. "Latino" is the identity preferred by the people themselves according to Coffey's research, and indicates some Indian blood. "Chicano" has been used to identify ethnic Mexicans born in the United States, and dates from the early 1900s.

going back. They're community members." That's a good thing, says Coffey, because Bowling Green, a quiet college town with a growing manufacturing base, would cease to function without its Latino workforce. But despite the growing Latino presence in Kentucky, little government support is available to help Latinos assimilate into the rural areas of the state. That's due, in part, to the fact that they barely show up on official U.S. Census data. Catholic Charities estimates that the Kentucky Latino population is seven times the number cited by the Census; Coffey figures that's much too low, and he estimates it's twenty times the official count. Since most Latinos in the state are undocumented, Census figures are a joke compared with the real population. "The Census says Bowling Green has 250. We probably have 5,000 or so." Another example he offers is the crossroads town of Albany, where the Census lists only 5 Latino residents. "You can see 35 on the square," says Coffey.

An aspect of the migration north that Coffey finds bizarre and confounding is how some Latinos who are stopped crossing the border manage to walk out of immigration court proceedings—if they have enough money sent to their lawyer. Then, instead of facing immediate deportation, they're authorized to remain in the United States.

It's simple abuse of the system, explains Barbara Hines. "If you get picked up on the border, you can bond out. There are lawyers on the border who do nothing but bond hearings. You're picked up in Laredo, you have a hearing in Laredo, and you're on your way to your family members in Virginia or Kentucky. The judge sets the bond at $5,000. Or the judge sets the bond at $10,000 and you get it reduced in front of the judge to $5,000. If you go through a bonding company, you can pay half of that plus a processing fee and you get out. Many people think that that's a *permiso*, a permission. Really the bond is to assure that you show up at your next hearing. Well, you never show up. For many of these people there's really no point to show up. That's because you're not really eligible for any relief. I have clients who say, 'Well, I paid $2,500 for my permission.' What they really bring me is a bond notice and a notice to go to court— and generally, by then, they've already been deported in absentia."

As long as the migrant does not return to court, life is no different than had he managed to get across the border without getting caught and sent to court. He's just another undocumented worker, albeit one with a U.S. court record that could haunt him if he ever attempts to apply for legal status.

"They're still in the United States," Hines points out, "and that's what they came north to accomplish. So for people who are coming illegally, it's just part of the cost of the deal. You pay the smuggler. You pay for the trip to get to the border. You pay the bond—and then you disappear into the population of the United States. This is a big issue for the Department of Homeland Security. They want really higher bonds now because they argue that a large percentage of people don't show up for their hearings."

In addition to seeking higher bonds, in early 2004 Homeland Security came up with a plan to build holding pens in the Arizona desert, huge tents to contain immigrants temporarily until they face immigration courts and deportation. The tent strategy was announced along with a plan to patrol remote sectors of the border with unmanned aircraft and another massive increase in manpower for the Border Patrol. "This is not a secure border," said Asa Hutchinson, Homeland Security undersecretary for domestic security. "Arizona has become the chokepoint. This is our current battleground."[2] And, of course, it's not just farm workers and dishwashers Hutchinson is worried about. "Any time you have vulnerabilities at the border, you have to worry about terrorists taking advantage of that too." Because of the failure of U.S. immigration policy, the southern border is another front in the war on terror.

19

DEPORTATION
MADE EASIER

~~~~~~~~

UNDOCUMENTED MIGRANTS who are arrested but not savvy enough to secure a lawyer and have no access to funds for a bond usually find themselves heading south fast. The U.S. government is doing all it can to speed their departure. Those who are caught in the act of crossing the border and choose VR—voluntary return—are held briefly, until a busload is collected. They get a ride to the line, walk back into Mexico, and regroup to try to get across again. At Border Patrol stations such as the one in Douglas, Arizona, agents photograph and fingerprint new arrivals and cross-check them against Wanted lists. On the wall in Douglas are six photographs of Middle Eastern–looking men, posted along with a note announcing "Suspected Terrorists."[1] The Border Patrol knows that the wilds around Douglas, where Mexicans cross the border en masse daily, could be appealing entry points for terrorists, along with cooks, farm workers, and nannies.

In 1986 a new federal prison was built in Oakdale, Louisiana, specifically to expedite deportation proceedings. Oakdale is a pleasant little city "where plans become realities," its motto proudly claims. "Oakdale is not Paradise," its citizens acknowledge with bizarre candor in a Chamber of Commerce brochure, but "it is a nice place to live." In the mid-1980s the Oakdale economy was struggling. The Chamber of Commerce worked hard to explain why Oakdale was a nice place to live: "Quiet cars rolling on clean, wide streets" ranked second after "Good, gray, serious mockingbirds singing from rooftops" on its list of reasons to consider relocating to a place with "solid, serious citizens going to work in modern, prosperous plants."

The Federal Detention Center was an important new addition for Oakdale, providing construction jobs and then permanent employment, initially for some three hundred guards and other workers. This was the first Bureau of Prisons lockup designed and built specifically to hold aliens awaiting deportation. But that was not all. Oakdale is not just a prison. Inside its walls are courtrooms of the Executive Office for Immigration Review. Migrants picked up by Border Patrol sweeps are detained in Oakdale, deep in the rural pinelands of Louisiana, far from the border and far from cities where concentrations of Spanish-speaking lawyers practice. There they wait until their cell doors open and they are marched before the court judges.

In a makeshift office on the sleepy Oakdale main street, shortly after Oakdale started operating, a few lawyers and social workers set up shop and struggled to meet the needs of these dislocated prisoners.

"These people are not criminals," lawyer and Catholic priest Ted Keating told me. Father Keating began helping the inmates when Oakdale opened. "They have all kinds of needs other than legal. They're basically innocent people who have been taken up off the street and thrown into a large federal penitentiary, and that creates psychological problems and social problems. They've been wrenched away from their support groups and their families, their communities. Many of them have just come across the border, and here they are in the middle of an enormous United States prison." At the time we talked, the Central American civil wars were raging and many of Keating's clients were seeking political asylum.

"These people don't come across the border with elaborately documented cases," Father Keating said. "They come with the clothes on their backs. Somehow it has to be proved that they have an objective, well-founded fear of persecution. To do that they need an attorney. Almost any lawyer looking at the system would say they need legal help. Without that, this is a deportation mill. Refugees will be sent back. Their claims will not be fairly handled. Many of them will not even have the opportunity to make that claim."

Even getting hold of Keating and his few volunteers was difficult. Inmates were required to call collect. There were no Spanish-speaking telephone operators in tiny Oakdale. When I tried placing a collect call in Spanish from Oakdale, the operator hung up. Keating was convinced the prison was located in isolated Oakdale to make it more difficult for the detainees caught to fight deportation.

Inside the prison I talked with one of the few bilingual detainees. He interpreted for several of his fellow prisoners, all waiting for their court appearances. "They feel kind of left out of everything because they don't speak the language," he said, referring to the English used in the court proceedings. Few of the guards spoke Spanish. "They don't know what's going on, and they don't know the system well enough to know they have rights as human beings not to be crowded like animals." The government was flying inmates to Oakdale for a quick court appearance that usually resulted in a bus ride to Houston and another flight south.

Since those days in the 1980s, Oakdale is no longer filling up with Central American political asylum seekers. Most Mexicans and other Latinos who are apprehended coming north are looking for work. But the increasing traffic across the border means that the immigration courts are only getting busier, and the government is becoming more sophisticated at streamlining the court proceedings required for deportation.

"It's much broader, it's much bigger than Oakdale now," says immigration lawyer Barbara Hines about deportation techniques. "The big issue now is video conferencing out of the jails. They just started this in San Antonio." Court proceedings are handled with the inmate in jail, far from the judge's San Antonio courtroom. "The access issue for immigrants is so overwhelming. I just looked at some statistics. In San Antonio, 80 to 90 percent of people are unrepresented. You can't talk to the people in the jails. They can't call out collect, you can't call in. The only way you can talk to them is to drive a hundred or a hundred and fifty miles to see people. At least we used to be able to talk to the clients before their bond hearing when they were brought to the courts in San Antonio. That's been eliminated, and everything now is done by video conferencing. So that means we go to San Antonio and can never talk to the client. The client sits in front of a video screen in Laredo or some other place. The client never comes to court. The judge never sees the real person. There are some really big due process issues, I think, about video conferencing [these proceedings]. When Oakdale was built, many of us said, 'This was built deliberately to get people away from their lawyers.' There are very few immigration lawyers in Oakdale." The new video conferencing policy only exacerbates the lack of due process.

20

ONE FARMER
WORKING BY
THE RULES

~~~~~~~~~

"THEY COME ACROSS in trucks," David Coffey says he's learned. "Ours usually come in eighteen wheelers. They have fish or fruit or ice or something, and the people are in the middle. We're talking forty to eighty people in a truck." Once these truckloads of human cargo are well north of the border, the freight is transferred to smaller vans that fan out across the country. "They usually drop them off at a truck stop in St. Louis or Memphis. They give them sixty dollars, and then they call for someone to pick them up. Family members. We have one I'm concerned about who should have been here Saturday, and he hasn't arrived yet. I don't know what happened. He may have been picked up. But eventually they get here, regardless of the law."

One of the Gringos who signed up for Coffey's language lessons and took the trip to Mexico to see his laborers' hometown was Joe Elliott, a fourth-generation Kentucky farmer. We meet on a crisp autumn day in late November, the peak of the tobacco production season. Elliott is a stocky man, and his work pants are cinched up tight against his belly. His striped work shirt shows off a patch announcing Elliotts Farms. He's wearing a windbreaker against the morning chill, and on his head is a camouflage baseball cap courtesy of the South Central Bank.

"Hey, your hands are cold," his wife Mary Sue's welcome is warm. Mexican music is blaring from the tobacco drying barn. There the crop is being sorted by type and color—the richer the golden brown, the higher the quality of the leaf. Workers are "stripping the 'baccer," pulling the leaves off the tobacco plant stalks. It is time-consuming handwork. The sorted dried leaves are stacked and then prepared for auction. The tobacco season for these workers lasts about four months. One of the Mexican workers stops stripping the leaves for a moment to explain that in those four months he'll earn what it would take him two years to make in Mexico. A sign high on the wall advises, "This farm has pride in tobacco."

"It's been real good this time." Elliott is pleased with the harvest. The Elliott farm is ninety acres of tobacco and eighteen hundred acres of corn and soybeans. It's in Owensboro, just across the Ohio River from Evansville, Indiana.

Fifteen Mexicans work the place, all in the United States legally on H2A visas. "They're really very good," Elliott says. For some of them it's a regular, if seasonal, job. Elliott has been hiring them and bringing them to Kentucky for several years. It's a business deal that only improved when he began studying Spanish under Coffey's program.

"We been to Mexico," says Elliott. "We seen their problems."

He shows off the bunkhouse he's built for the workers, quarters that meet or exceed federal standards for H2A workers. "We done insulation. We done it right, all the way around. After work hours they relax. They go fishing here on the farm ponds."

The Kentucky Housing Authority considers Elliott's operation a model for treating farm workers properly. He received a $30,000 grant from the commonwealth to expand the bunkhouse. "We ended up putting a porch on it. That was really the neatest thing."

Joe Elliott bought his farm in 1965. In those days he hired American hands. No longer. "They're not here to hire."

It's been several years since he's employed American laborers. But Elliott does not join the chorus complaining that the loss of American workers is bad news, or that Americans are turning down the work because it's demeaning, or that Americans are lazy and spoiled.

"It's not all that bad, because they got better jobs. Not a part-time labor job, full time. They got benefits. I mean you can work at McDonald's for the same money we're paying here. Anbody who wants to work has got work." But that's not all that's wrecked his native workforce. "There's another thing too. People quit having kids." He can't find a local workforce in the current Kentucky rural younger generation.

Without immigrant labor, Elliott says, his farm would be paralyzed. "Yeah, I'd be out of business." There is no consistent local workforce to work the forty to fifty hours a week needed to bring in the crops. He pulls out a newspaper clipping about "600 illegals" being caught in the United States. Elliott knows that stopping the influx is impossible; he sees evidence of that fact throughout Daviess County. "There are six million of those guys in the States." But he says he never has never liked working with undocumented workers.

"It's really not worth it. Honesty and trying to do something upfront the right way is the right way to do it. If I see forty-five loaders, and I could steal a load of corn off of every one of them, that's not the right way to do it. I like to work legally."

But problems loom for Elliott's desire to play by the rules.

"The government is either going to change this thing or it's going to force me to go back to undocumented labor. They're not trying to get along with us. With all their paperwork and regulations, they're not trying to help us at all." Elliott decided to hire legal workers after rumors started spreading through Daviess County that the INS was planning raids and would seek fines of $5,000 per day per person for any undocumented workers found working local crops. And he was disgusted with the middlemen he felt forced to deal with to hire workers with stolen or forged papers. "It got so scary that we got out of it. The people that was running the damn thing was so crooked. We was getting guys with visas that belonged to people in Tennessee. It was a whole crooked game." When he started using legal workers through the H2A program, he got a clear conscience and a steady supply of reliable workers.

"We're doing a lot of this work for the moral support of these guys. We've got families out here; we've got kids. We have a lot of things in common, you know? We know the families, their wives." Elliott's children who help him operate the farm have also traveled to Mexico. The relationship is like an extended family.

Elliott says he spends $100,000 to $120,000 a year on labor, up to a third of his gross income, and much of that money goes to Mexico. Under the H2A program rules, Elliott's responsibilities include transportation and lodging for his workers. He hires a farm labor broker in Kentucky who works with contacts in Mexico to find workers, handles the logistics of bringing them to Kentucky, and satisfies the U.S. government rules and regulations. The broker arranges for visas and passports at a cost of a couple of hundred dollars for each laborer.

"I have probably a few more than I need," Elliott says. "But I don't mind. One of my workers, Alex, stayed home five months and worked construction about ten hours a day. When he finished each day, what he could find to eat somewhere he cooked on the job site. He got cardboard and slept on the job site. For a dollar an hour. He's up here working for $7.20. You think he ain't happy? Now he's got a new baby who was born two months early, who needed lots of care. Where was he at? Right here. Did he want to go home? Yes. Could he go home? No, he needed the money. It cost him $1,500 [for the postnatal care], so he's lost just about everything he's made up here just because of the baby."

On the Elliott farm there are two concrete bunkhouses for migrant workers. Beds are separated with shelves and a clothes rack, offering slight privacy enhanced by curtains. The industrial-looking particle-board walls are punctuated here and there with ad hoc decor: an image of the Virgin of Guadalupe, for example, alongside a calendar featuring Old Glory blowing in the wind.

A couch and an easy chair face a television set in one of the bunkhouses. When they're not working, the farmhands watch Spanish-language programs via satellite. "That's another forty dollars a damn month," grumbles Elliott, but he knows the value of such entertainment for people who need to hear their own language.

Joe Elliott tries to educate his neighbors about the value of Mexican migrant workers. "The people that's fighting them are breaking their own dinner plate. The biggest issue I see is they think the Mexicans are going to take their jobs." But Elliott is convinced that is a fatuous line of reasoning. "Down at Fields Packing Company here at their local processing plant, there's 20 percent Mexican people. They do the job." He says local people hire on and then leave after a few days because "they don't want to do the work. Perdue chicken farm, same thing. Or Tyson's. They got all these Mexican people. It could be stopped if the American people wanted to stop it. You don't feed your neighbor's dog unless you want him to be in your yard. If you feed him, he'll come and see you. So if you give these Mexican workers the opportunity to work they want to work and they will take over your job."

But the belief that Mexicans are taking jobs from native-born (and white) Kentuckians is not the only factor fueling prejudice against the migrants. "Race is one of them. They think they don't need 'em over here. They just don't want 'em here. I been here a long time. When I was working these guys on some farms and the owner needed workers, he was glad to see me with the Mexicans. Once he got his pension check and he didn't need no more money, he was wanting them to leave the country. That's the game."

Elliott downplays claims that Latino migrants abuse U.S. social services. "We've had different things—operations that cost $4,000 to $10,000. The hospital has to take care of that. I can't pay it, the Mexicans can't pay it. An operation for appendicitis is $8,000. They can't pay it. They're going to die. What are you going to do? Let 'em die? In Mexico— I saw it when I was down there—you die. You don't have the money, you die. Here that's just another advantage of being an American."

David Coffey says his research confirms that abuse of social services is minimal, and he points out that even those migrants without documentation who are bold enough to apply for government help are eligible for few programs. Families benefit most through subsidized school lunches, emergency Medicaid, and immunization opportunities. These programs are primarily for young children and pregnant women in need of prenatal care. Social welfare programs for single male migrant farm workers in Kentucky are nominal.

Fear plays a role in the fostering of negative attitudes toward the foreigners. Farmer Elliott hears complaints about Mexicans congregating in public places, like the Wal-Mart parking lot. He says his experiences in Mexico help him understand why his workers like to hang out together.

"You've got to learn the different lifestyles, the different thinking, how they do things. When you learn their culture a little bit, you can understand why they gang up. They're just being friendly. Are the Mexicans, just because they get together, any more dangerous than the folks you find at some sports bar where they got fifteen TVs and the thing is crammed? Are they dangerous too?"

Coffey agrees. "Wal-Mart is the nearest thing to a *Mercado*"—the community marketplace in Mexico—"that we have in most areas." He wants the farmers to look at the crowds from the perspective of the laborers themselves. "Perhaps they need to socialize after a week in the fields." Coffey offers the farmers and their families other questions to ponder. "Are they not like the rest of us," he asks, "or is the reality that people of different skin color and a different language fuel our fear and ignorance to invite racism, prejudice, and xenophobia? Do they roam in gangs after innocent women, or is the reality that they roam in gangs because one member can speak, read, or count in English? Are they taking our jobs, or is the reality that their strong backs work hard and long hours at jobs that everyone else is either too lazy to work or that they think are beneath their dignity?"

Whatever the answers of his neighbors, Joe Elliott sees Owensboro changing around him. "They have filled in all the spots that nobody else wants," he says about Mexican migrants. And he favors them over the locals. "We had whiteys that could tell you every basketball game in the last ten years: who won, who played, scores. But they couldn't count six 'baccer plants in one pile at any one time. They was thirty workers out of Owensboro here and there wasn't any of 'em could drive a stick shift. Grown men."

H2A workers can only stay in the United States for nine months at a stretch. On the Elliott farm the goal is to finish the tobacco work by the Christmas holidays. "We work our butts off to make that happen, because we understand that any family man that ain't seen his family for four months, it's time for him to go see his family. That's just how it is. We pay their bus ticket all the way back to their house." Elliott is required to buy a ticket only to the border.

He's heard stories of Mexicans getting drunk on the weekends in Kentucky and being rolled for their cash, or losing their earnings on the way back to their hometown when Mexican police stop the bus and shake down the passengers. Improved banking opportunities between the United States and Mexico are making it easier and cheaper for his workers to ship their money home instead of carrying it back as cash. "We finally got a Mexican store that's wiring most of the money back to Mexico. On Saturday they may have $25,000 in there. They only wire back cash money. They don't accept no checks. The police department, they keep a damn close eye on that store."

La Reina de Mexico is the little Owensboro general store catering to Latinos. *"Tienda, taquería, y carnicería 100% mexicana,"* it advertises under a big Mexican flag over its front door. Store, taco stand, and meat market 100 percent Mexican. The storefront is a community bulletin board. The front windows are plastered with billboards selling through tickets on buses running direct to northern Mexico cities, money-wiring services, and Spanish-language music CDs. *"Bienvenido,"* says a flyer taped to a window. *"Aprenda el inglés. ¡Gratis!"* Welcome. Learn English. Free. Another offers a 1997 Plymouth Breeze for $3,900, complete with air conditioning and a CD player, with just 66,000 miles on the odometer. And the *carnicería*, the butcher, is promoting his tripe for only $1.59 a pound.

Inside La Reina de Mexico the shelves are lined with products from Mexico. *Masa* for tortillas, Charras brand tostadas ("The REAL Mexico Flavor"), vibrant blue bottles of Fabuloso to clean floors just like at home, and tall candles in glass holders decorated with dramatic illustrations of Christ and the Virgin of Guadalupe. On one wall the flags of the United States and Mexico hang side by side, along with a huge sombrero topping some of the stars-and-stripes.

The lessons of the Elliott farm, Owensboro, and farm work in rural Kentucky are clear to David Coffey. "We've not accepted the fact that we have a labor force that is no longer transient and is doing most of our work. We haven't accepted the fact that they are going to become part of the community. We need to help them assimilate." But, at least as important, is the other half of the equation. We also need to work on "our assimilating to them. This whole idea of them being illegal—undocumented— scares a lot of people, and we don't know what to do with them."

Meanwhile an underground and subservient labor force continues to grow. "We have forced most of them to stay here," Coffey points out one of the unexpected affects of post-9/11 border controls. "Although they can still cross the border and get here, we're forcing them to stay here, and they really want to go home." They fear they won't be able to get across the reinforced border, or they can't afford the inflated prices *coyotes* now command. "They would love to go home and see their families, see their wives and children, their parents. And have some kind of legal documentation that would enable them to come up here and work and then go home for the holidays. But since they're illegal, they don't exist."

"Since they're coming anyway," I say, "why not just allow them free passage?"

"Wouldn't that be wonderful," he says, "and logical."

21

WHO WANTS
THE BORDER
CLOSED?

WHO ARE those Americans afraid of immigrants? I've found some of them on the radio while hosting talk shows. One fascinating show during which I took notes was based on seeking callers from a California audience who were considering leaving the state, moving out permanently. I asked them why they felt the California Dream had failed them.

I received a steady stream of calls and letters after the show aired. One of those was from a trucker named Marty Kemmeries. "I put it to you," Kemmeries wrote, "that you are naive and uninformed as to the facts about the financial state of our state. I put it to you further, that you will come to the realization that Caucasian America is sick of minorities, foreigners, and deviates." Marty Kemmeries wrote to me in late 1991. During the 1990s, according to government figures, the undocumented immigrant population in the United States increased by several hundred thousand each year. More migrants without proper papers arrived than left, died, or became legal residents.[1]

"Possibly I can enlighten you as to some facts that are staring us in the face," wrote Kemmeries. "You must remember that the immigrants of today are from cultures diametrically opposed to the culture that has arisen with the entrenchment of the Caucasian European settler, who established this country with intelligence and the work ethic. . . .

"In the early days of this country there were not the social programs in place (as we have now) to insulate the original settlers from the consequence of laziness, and a lacking of the ability to, or desire to, apply themselves. These (now in place) programs assure the immigrating Mexican that he can reproduce without personal consequence, or the necessity to support, discipline, or educate his offspring. Look around you at the graffiti, check the arrest records in Fresno County as to the predominate race incarcerated for driving under the influence. Are you aware that food stamps were made available to illegals, who could obtain them without fear of arrest or deportation?

"I could elaborate further, but suffice to say that the behavior, birthrate, and cultures of minorities and immigrants are destroying our daily lives with a mosaic of graffiti, foreign language, irresponsible behavior, violence, and intimidation. These (lately known as people of color) are at the same time burdening the taxpayer to the breaking point with their continuing and expanding dependency on the working Californian."

Marty Kemmeries signed his letter, "Looking forward to leaving this state, and hoping to find real America," with his name and address and telephone number, adding, "You have just read a letter written to you by a professional trucker, an owner-operator, running intrastate California. If you have any questions or comments, my office is seventy feet up ahead."

A couple of weeks later I aired another show, this one dealing specifically with Mexican immigration into California. I quoted from Marty Kemmeries's letter, and he wrote back to me. He carefully deconstructed the radio show, critiquing the callers and my conversations with them. Here's an example:

"To another caller you said you believed that those that wanted to assimilate into our society would learn our language. I say that the predominate number of our Hispanic residents do not want to assimilate into our society, but rather would prefer to re-establish California as a Mexican colony. In the event this ever happened, these people would be biting the very hand that feeds them."

Kemmeries then suggested that I write a book "on the minority, immigrant, and deviate, and expound on their social and financial impact on our state and indeed across the nation." If I took on this project and wrote about Mexican immigration into the United States, he offered the following as fodder:

"Why is Interstate 5 being modified down by San Ysidro to make it safer for illegals to enter at this common spot for border running? These modifications are being done at taxpayers' expense, while there are sections of Interstate 5 that shake and bounce a trucker and his rig all over the road. This year the disgraceful condition of Interstate 5 caused a numbness in my foot, later found to be a pinched nerve in my back, and the constant rough ride shook the inside of the factory stereo in my big truck apart. I also had to replace the steering tires on my big rig twenty thousand miles sooner than normal, just because of the condition of Interstate 5. These big truck tires are $350 each. And yet we spend money to make it safer for Hispanics to violate our borders, this idiotic endeavor supported by our Hispanic lawmakers, interested only in perpetuating the Hispanic here on our shores." He was referring to the fencing put in place on I-5 in an effort to reduce the number of migrants moving north who were hit by cars and trucks as they ran across the freeway seeking hiding places and paths around the authorities. Special signs were posted on I-5 at the time showing the silhouette of a desperate family running across the road, erected to warn drivers of the unusual hazards and potential victims on I-5 near the Mexican border.

Kemmeries asked me, "How is it that Mexicans can seemingly work for much lower wages than an American?" And then he answered his own question: "The Mexican is used to, and indeed thrives on, living conditions we find unacceptable. Living in garages and tool sheds, and fifteen or twenty people to a house originally designed and constructed to house a family of four, these people can do well on small individual incomes pooled together. Much of this income is sent to Mexico to smuggle still more of their people here. Those that live here soon learn to rely on food stamps, subsidized health care, rent subsidies, welfare, unemployment, and workmen's compensation."

Kemmeries urged me to "talk to people in neighborhoods where Mexicans have moved in. You will hear of constant illegal construction to make room for more border runners. You will hear of the raising of fighting cocks and dogs. You will hear of Hispanic girls having babies at very young ages, the birthrate of these children insuring still more income for the Hispanic resident of California."

And Kemmeries told me he was offended by what could be seen from the window of his truck. "Listen as the trucker tells you of constantly seeing Hispanics urinating alongside the highway, making little effort at modesty. This type of behavior is manly to the Hispanic. However, this type of behavior is illegal and deviant, and further it is the type of behavior that embarrasses any male that deems himself intelligent and civilized."

Truck driver Marty Kemmeries ended his assignment sheet to me with this sweeping charge: "The largest number of Mexicans and Negros [*sic*] lack personal integrity. This is reflected in their daily lives, openly violating common sense and common decency. We need to face the fact that there are intellectual and cultural differences that have made them, and continue to make them, a social and financial burden."

The April 2000 U.S. Census alone officially contradicts many of Marty Kemmeries's fears and racist charges.

I live in Sonoma County, California. Our local economy is largely based on tourism and the wine industry. We are filled with bedroom communities of commuters who struggle daily down Highway 101 toward jobs in Marin County and San Francisco. Industrial parks between Petaluma and Santa Rosa are home to what we call Telecom Valley, high-tech telecommunications companies that suffered after the dot-com bubble burst. But overall Sonoma County thrives in good and bad economic times, with low unemployment and a fast-growing Latino community.

According to Census Bureau figures,[2] Latinos hold most of the lowest-paying jobs in Sonoma County. In the decade since the Census in 1990, few Sonoma County Latinos managed to break into higher-paying managerial jobs and professional careers.

Here's how the numbers work out. About 37,000 Latinos are counted as workers in Sonoma County, in a workforce of 239,000. A striking 88 percent of agricultural workers are Latino. Well over half of all the county's maids are Latino, as are close to half the cooks. Yet Latinos make up only some 15 percent of the county workforce. And, of course, these percentages are based on official census figures. Many—if not most—of the people who are in the United States illegally are not going to trust Census takers who come knocking on their doors. They avoid them or provide them with false information. Consequently the percentages of Mexicans engaged in these low-paid, unskilled jobs is no doubt higher than officially reported.

The 183,000 white workers make up about 77 percent of the workforce in Sonoma. Ninety percent of grammar school teachers are white. Eighty-nine percent of the registered nurses are white. Eighty-nine percent of business managers are white.

The skewed list goes on. The Census Bureau breaks Sonoma County workers into five categories: white, Latino, Asian, black, and Native American. Latinos were the only group to see per capita income drop during the prosperous 1990s. Half the Latinos counted by the 2000 Census in Sonoma County were foreign born, and most of those immigrated during the 1990s, coming north to take the low-paying jobs left unfilled by other categories of workers.

"The University of Mexico grads don't come to the United States," shrugged George Ortiz after studying the figures. "It's the ranch hands and the poor guys who are trying to find a job that are coming here in large numbers." Ortiz is president of the California Human Development Corporation, a Santa Rosa organization that provides support services to Latino immigrants. "They're the latest influx of immigrants, and it takes time to get ahead."

Those 37,000 Latino workers in Sonoma County, and their counterparts across the United States, hardly pose a threat to the Marty Kemmerieses who came to this country before them. "The farmworkers are, I'd say, 90 percent Latino, mostly Mexican," says Ortiz. "Nobody else wants those lousy jobs. The border is porous as hell—the government is looking in the other direction—because they know that the people are needed here. They're not taking anything from anybody. On the contrary. They're the volcano that keeps the whole system up."

George Ortiz serves on the Mexican government's *Consejo Consultivo*; he's an adviser to President Fox on issues relating to farmer workers in *El Norte*. Especially irritating to him is the charge that Mexicans in the United States without proper papers are criminals, are lawbreakers who have entered the country illegally. "Who's doing the hiring?" he asks. "These guys aren't coming in to vacation or fool around. They're coming to find work, and somebody's giving them work. It's the needy getting jobs from the greedy. Let's talk about how these peasants, these workers, are helping the general economy. They're paying taxes too. They're contributors."

The restrictions against Mexicans at the U.S. border will disappear, Ortiz is convinced. "I predict it will happen within the next ten years. It's an economic imperative. We're talking about billions and billions of dollars," he says about trade between the United States and Mexico. "The second-largest trading partner to the United States is Mexico. The largest trading partner with California is Mexico. California would be in really bad straits if commerce stopped." He points out that money sent home from Mexicans working in the United States is Mexico's second-largest source of income after petroleum, estimated at close to $15 billion. "Green is the color that we see most of all. When we have great commerce between ourselves, it brings all kinds of peaceful solutions to all kinds of things, because that's the way it is."

But it isn't just the statistics in my county that refute the attacks of trucker Marty Kemmeries. The Rand Corporation, the Santa Monica–based think tank, published a study in 2003 that devastates the racist fears of people like Kemmeries. The economist James Smith is the author of the study. He poured over Census figures and supporting documents covering the twentieth century, and tracked the progress of Latino immigrants in comparison with those coming to the United States from Europe. Using education and income as measures, Smith concluded that "across generations, Latinos have done just as well as the Europeans who came in the early part of this century, and in fact slightly better."[3]

"There's a widespread view among both scholars and the general public that the Latino experience has been very different than the European experience," said Smith. "That view is just wrong."

Ruben Navarrette, Jr., who frequently writes about Mexican immigrants in his *Dallas Morning News* column, lauded Smith's research, using his own family as an example of one that went "from the grape fields to graduate school" after just three generations in the United States.

"Regardless of ethnicity or nationality or economic resources," Navarrette wrote, "immigrants are the same the world over. That's because a big part of what shapes their character is not the country they come from, but the fact that they leave it in the first place, risking whatever they have—including their lives—in search of a better life. Once here, they work hard in any job they can find. They instill in their children an appreciation for education and teach them the value of a dollar."[4]

Deep in Mexico, on the Yucatan peninsula, is another example to crush Marty Kemmeries's theories. There the small city of Peto has lost thousands of its young men to Marin County in California, where they can make four and five times more an hour than in a twelve-hour day back home. "It's necessary," says Felipe Acosta Díaz about the migration north and his four sons who work in Marin. "The young are obligated to go to the United States." His neighbor Carlos Ruiz agrees. "Is it any wonder that the boys leave?" he asks. Three of Díaz's sons work in Marin restaurants, sending back *migradollars* to help support the family. "It's sad and we miss them, but they must go."[5]

22

BURDEN OR

BENEFIT?

A WAVE OF anti-immigrant fervor swept the United States in the 1980s and 1990s. Many of the almost three million illegal aliens who had received amnesty and legal status under the so-called Immigration Reform Law of 1986 decided to remain in the country permanently. The law allowed them to bring their families. As usual, more undocumented workers were coming north. Political refugees headed north across Mexico to escape the civil wars in Central America. "The simple truth is we've lost control of our borders," President Ronald Reagan announced at the time, "and no country can afford that."

About 1.5 million migrants are caught each year trying to cross into the United States illegally, most of them Mexicans. Estimates vary regarding the numbers of those who make it safely across, but they are obviously huge. Also in dispute is how many are commuters and return to Mexico. One thing is certain: since the September 11th attacks, many Mexicans in the United States without proper paperwork are loath to return home, fearing that increased security at the borders will make it more difficult and more expensive to get back to their job sites.

Not only would free passage for Mexican workers into the United States make it easier to secure the southern border against intruders who may have a more nefarious intent than getting a job, it would also make it possible to begin to account for those Mexicans already in the United

States without official approval. If those millions did not fear deportation, most would likely feel more comfortable about registering their status and normalizing their residency.

That's the point Mexican Interior Secretary Santiago Creel made during a Spring 2003 meeting with U.S. Secretary of State Colin Powell. Creel came out of his meeting with the usual diplomatic platitudes. "What this trip proved," he said, "was that, though both countries had different views on Iraq, we can work together closely and intensely in many areas. We reaffirm not only our neighborliness but our commitment to free trade and our friendship."

In reality, Mexico's decision to oppose the U.S. war on Iraq only exacerbated frustrations between the two countries that had been building since September 11, 2001. Radio news commentator Paul Harvey mocked Mexico's position against the Iraq invasion by reinforcing anti-Mexican stereotypes during a broadcast to his huge audience. "Vicente Fox drinks water in Mexico every day," announced Harvey with his trademark singsong delivery. "He can't be worried about a little thing like biological weapons."[1]

After the attacks, hopes on both sides of the border for solutions to the Mexican migration crisis were extinguished as the Bush administration attempted to secure U.S. borders. Secretary Creel saw that the two goals were not mutually exclusive.

"I think to a point," he said during his Washington trip, "the U.S. internal security depends on knowing who its people are. And an important part of that population is four million Mexicans. It's not known who they are, where they are, whom they work for. If we're talking about security, we have to talk about the security of immigrants as well, giving them documents."[2]

By legalizing a victimless crime, such as migrating north for work, you can, as Secretary Creel pointed out, control it. You can also protect the migrant from ludicrously expensive border-crossing charges inflicted by predatory *coyotes*. It is less likely that employers will take advantage of workers who are in the United States legally. That means fewer cases of inappropriately low paychecks, poor working conditions, and forced overtime. Legal workers will be less inclined to keep quiet since they won't fear deportation.

As the United States responded to the September 11th attacks—bombing Afghanistan, invading Iraq, and dismissing the United Nations and many of its traditional allies—it all but ignored Mexico and Vicente Fox's ambitious proposals designed to lead to an open border. Fox had made opening the borders and concern for Mexicans in the United States critical planks of his election campaign platform. He had called for the free flow of labor across the U.S.-Mexico border. A few weeks after he won the presidency, ending seventy-one years of one-party rule in Mexico, Fox again spelled out his solutions to the border crisis. Writing in the *New York Times*, he suggested that "negotiations should begin with a view toward providing humane working conditions for Mexicans already in the United States, and for exploring new and imaginative mechanisms to organize and regulate future flows. These should include institutional guarantees of the human and civil rights of Mexicans and reduction of tensions along the border." Fox made it clear that he intended to change the status quo. "The violent deaths of my countrymen on the border are simply intolerable."[3] Ultimately he wanted legal status for all Mexicans in the United States. "It isn't fair to consider them illegal when they are employed, when they are working productively, when they are generating so much for the American economy," he said. "They shouldn't have to walk around like criminals or stay hidden."[4]

In fact, as his six-year administration passed its halfway point, matters only worsened. But initially Washington was enthusiastic about the new politics in Mexico. Fox traveled to the United States to meet with candidates Al Gore and George W. Bush. Gore labeled Fox as a man with "very large ideas" while Bush called him "an interesting man, a big, strong man, a charismatic fellow."[5] Candidate Bush was more circumspect when he was asked about Fox's open-border proposal. "I don't think he's fully explained open borders," Bush said. "As you know," he told reporters, "I believe we ought to enforce our borders."

After his meeting with Fox, President Clinton too rejected an open border. "Obviously, we have borders and we have laws that apply to them and we have to apply them, and so do the Mexicans," Clinton said while leaving the door open for change. "But I think over the long run our countries will become more interdependent."

During his U.S. trip, President Fox made it clear that he didn't envision a solution to Mexico's economic problems simply by sending all its workers north. "How can we narrow the gap on income on both sides of the border?" he asked. "How can we in the long term equal the levels of development between our countries so that we become real friends, real partners and real neighbors? How can we build up the opportunities in Mexico so that our kids, 12-, 14-year-olds, don't have to leave home, don't have to move to the United States looking for opportunities?"[6]

When Fox suggested in Washington in 2000 that the border could open in about ten years, House International Relations Committee member Mark Sanford, a Republican from South Carolina, called the border so porous that it was already essentially open. But he couldn't imagine changing official policy. "It would be incendiary," he said. "You've got a lot of the conservative base [of the Republican party] who see it as a threat to American sovereignty."[7]

President Fox hosted President Bush at his Guanajuato ranch in February 2001, the first foreign visit of Bush's presidency. Fox spoke in English to his fellow rancher, "Know that we consider you a friend to Mexico, a friend to Mexican people and a friend of mine."[8] Bush suggested the feeling was mutual.

Early in September 2001, President Bush announced, "The United States has no more important relationship in the world than our relationship with Mexico." Less than a week later the World Trade Center and the Pentagon were in flames. Washington scratched Mexico off its to-do list. Interior Secretary Creel expressed the frustration of his government: "Mexico has shown a willingness to work on drugs. Mexico has shown a willingness to work on security. But when Mexico asks the United States to work on migration, we have not seen the same willingness."[9]

In late 2003 Fox returned to the United States, again campaigning for changes in U.S. immigration policy. In speeches across the Southwest he identified undocumented Mexicans in the United States as a "complex phenomenon," not a problem, a phenomenon to be addressed from "a perspective of shared responsibility" and one that "entails major opportunities for the two countries."[10]

The exact number coming north is relatively unimportant. Whether visitors overstay the time limits on their visas, or the desperately poor run across the frontier, hiding along the route like animals, people keep coming for the American Dream. Nothing—not U.S. laws, fences, or the Border Patrol—stops this migration. Whether one believes in unlimited immigration or tight controls over who and how many people can move to the United States, there is no question that allowing this illegal immigration is bad for almost everyone involved—except for the *coyotes* and exploitative employers.

One of those who advocated strict restrictions on immigration in the mid-1980s was Colorado Governor Richard Lamm, who insisted that the Melting Pot was full. "Just like every house, every country has to have a border," Governor Lamm repeated in his anti-immigration stump speeches.[11] "There's 159 countries in the world, 158 of them control their borders. It is only the United States that lives under the illusion that we can be a borderless country."

Lamm ridiculed the relevance of the famous message on the base of the Statue of Liberty. "There's going to be a billion people added to this world in the next eleven years," he predicted. "Eighty-eight percent of them are going to be born in the Third World. To say that we can accept everybody that wants to come here is absurd. It's impossible to absorb all of the world's homeless yearning to be free." Lamm continued to champion his anti-immigrant message two decades later at the Sierra Club, where he campaigned for club office in the early twenty-first century, arguing that restrictions on immigration were needed to preserve the environment.

In 1986 Congress passed the now-discredited Immigration Reform Law in an attempt to deal with the illegal immigration that had already occurred, and to control the future flow of migrants. Wyoming Senator

Alan Simpson was a co-author of the law, which offered a one-time amnesty to those already in the United States illegally and provided for penalties against U.S. employers who hired undocumented workers. We talked while his bill was being debated in the Capitol.

"We're not looking for perfection," Simpson acknowledged. "Anybody who is looking at this bill for perfection is off the wall. I don't know whether it will work. But I think it will be the best approach before we try a military presence at our borders." Lawmakers hoped the one-time amnesty for illegal migrants already in the United States would encourage foreigners to return home when their jobs were finished, then return north only when there was new work. The reality showed the flaws in the argument that Mexican immigration is not an assimilating immigration. Many of those granted amnesty not only stayed, they used their new legal status to move family members into the United States legally, and to leave farm work for better-paying and more stable jobs in cities. That exodus opened a labor void filled by new and often illegal immigration from Mexico. In addition, it was relatively easy for immigrants who did not qualify for the amnesty to generate forged papers that indicated they met the criteria for legal status. Consequently many more Mexicans became legal U.S. residents because of the law than Congress had anticipated.

Alan Simpson is another who invokes the Emma Lazarus poem when he talks about immigration. "The Statue of Liberty doesn't say on it, 'Send us everybody you've got, legally or illegally.' That's not what it says."

No, not in those exact words. But what the Emma Lazarus poem does say, essentially, is "Send me everyone in need." "Keep ancient lands, your storied pomp," are the words that Lazarus hears the statue crying out to the world, a statue she calls Mother of Exiles. Next follow the oft-quoted lines, "Give me your tired, your poor, your huddled masses yearning to breathe free, the wretched refuse of your teeming shore." But less frequently quoted are these closing lines of the poem: "Send these, the homeless, the tempest-tost to me, I lift my lamp beside the golden door!"

The Statue of Liberty herself is an immigrant. Most Americans probably know she was a gift from France, but few must be aware of the fact that she is a hand-me-down. She was originally designed for Port Said,

at the entrance to the Suez Canal in Egypt. French sculptor Frédéric-
Auguste Bartholdi had the idea of placing a woman at that spot to represent progress, or "Egypt carrying the light of Asia," as he put it at the
time. But the Egyptian government decided she was too expensive, and
the project eventually was diverted to New York harbor.[12]

Plenty of American citizens fear the surge of Mexicans coming north is a
threat to their society. "It's getting more in your face," says Gordon Lee
Baum, an executive with the racist activist group Council of Conservative
Citizens (a headline in their web-based newsletter reads, "Non-White Immigration Will Ruin America"). "All of a sudden people see it happening
in their community. They wake up one morning like the people at the
Alamo and say, 'Where did the Mexicans come from?'"[13] Perhaps Baum
skipped history class the day the Alamo was taught. The Alamo was first
a Spanish mission, then a Mexican fortress. It was the Texas insurgents
who occupied it and refused to give it back to the Mexicans. The Mexicans were there first. Such details do not infiltrate the Council of Conservative Citizens' mission statement: "The C of CC also stands against the
tide of nonwhite, Third World immigrants swamping this country."[14]

In the mid-1980s Immigration and Naturalization Service Director
Alan Nelson told me that as many as twelve million people were in the
United States illegally, and that they were taking jobs away from U.S.
citizens. Just as so many Mexicans working in the United States are undocumented, so were the statistics waved by Nelson. They were based on
guesses and theories, just as such charges of job losses to immigrants are
undocumented today. Since no one knows for sure how many undocumented Mexicans are in the United States, it is not clear how many, if
any, take jobs from workers who are citizens or who have papers allowing
them to work.

But the late free-market economist Julian Simon told me he didn't
believe the huge numbers published repeatedly as estimates of the number of illegal Mexicans. "The volume of illegal immigration now," he said
in the mid-1980s, "may be zero. That is, as many illegals may be going

home in the average year as are coming." Of course, since the September 11 attacks, there are no average years. Government figures indicate that more migrants without documents stayed during the economic boom years of the 1990s than went back to Mexico. This new dynamic dates what may be an apocryphal story told in the days when slipping across the frontier was more routine than it is today. Asked what would happen if she were caught crossing into Texas, a maid at a McAllen, Texas, motel is said to have replied simply, "I would be late for work."[15] Comedian Diane Rodriguez used the routine of border crossing in her act during the campaign against Proposition 187 in California. "Oh, the trials and tribulations of American life," she told her audience in a monologue of Latina experiences. "Today I had to get my hair done. I broke a nail, and then I got deported again."[16]

The refrain that the United States cannot survive without Mexican labor is familiar and can be traced throughout the troubled history between the two countries. In the 1930s, for example, Fred H. Bixby, a businessman representing agriculture and cattle operations, was moved to define his industry's need for Mexican workers with this pre–politically correct litany of complaints: "If I do not get Mexicans to thin those beets and to hoe those beets, I am through with the beet business. We have no Chinamen. We have not the Japs. The Hindu is worthless, the Filipino is nothing, and the white man will not do the work."[17]

But Julian Simon was not seeing the humor when he said, "The INS has advertised wrong and false information on the subject." His research convinced him that immigrants do take some jobs that would otherwise be held by Americans. "The number, however, is relatively small." Simon was from the camp convinced that immigrants—legal and illegal—improve the economy. They open businesses, spend money, pay taxes, and often do not use social services because they fear getting caught and deported. Simon was convinced that open borders would not inundate the United States with immigrants. And he had a simple example: "If that were so, how come all of Puerto Rico doesn't move to New York?"

Many of them do, warns George Borjas, Harvard professor of economics and social policy. "The Puerto Rican experience may be instructive," he writes. "Puerto Ricans are American citizens who can move freely within the United States, and the differences in economic opportunities between Puerto Rico and the mainland are quite large. Not surprisingly, about 25 percent of Puerto Rico's population moved to the United States in the last fifty years."[18] Borjas argues that Mexicans do take jobs that U.S. citizens and legal residents would perform if the wages weren't deflated by the availability of desperate illegal laborers.

Of course a counterargument, and a strong one, is that New York doesn't suffer from this influx of Puerto Ricans. It thrives on it.

Rogers, Arkansas, and other chicken-processing cities in northwest Arkansas provide another counterargument. In the early 1990s these plants were hungry for employees because local laborers were rejecting the low wages offered by the chicken industry. Mexicans inundated Rogers, Fayetteville, Springdale, Bentonville, Bella Vista—not only directly from Mexico but from the American Southwest. They filled jobs at the chicken-packing plants and added vibrancy to the local economy with grocery stores and restaurants, newspapers and video rental shops serving the new Spanish-speaking population.[19]

Many economists consider a 1997 study conducted by the National Academy of Sciences to be one of the most comprehensive attempts to determine whether immigrants cost the United States money or fuel economic growth. The report's conclusion is that over a lifetime, immigrants provide economic stimuli that exceed any use of social services. "Immigration benefits the U.S. economy overall and has little effect on the income and job opportunities of most native-born Americans," according to the report. "Only in areas with high concentrations of low-skilled, low-paid immigrants are state and local taxpayers paying more on average to support publicly funded services that these immigrants use."[20] The study concluded that immigrants without a high school degree tended to sap the economy of about $13,000 each over a lifetime. Plenty of illegal immigrants head north without finishing school. But that $13,000 number just measures the direct relationship between taxpaying and using services. The NAS made clear in its study that crucial industries such as agriculture, restaurants, and clothing "would not exist on the same scale without immigrant workers." It estimated as much as $10 billion in added annual value of immigrant labor to the U.S. economy, and stated without equivocation, "The vast majority of Americans are enjoying a healthier economy as a result of the increased supply of labor and lower prices that result from immigration."

Statistics are used by all those who are involved in the immigration controversy, often announced without documentation and impossible to verify or negate. During the 2003 gubernatorial race in California, Lt. Gov. Cruz Bustamante cited a positive accounting, saying immigrants "pay $1,400 more a year [in taxes] than they receive in benefits."[21] But since no one knows for sure how many illegal immigrants are in the United States, none of these related numbers can be considered accurate, only educated guesses at best. Official estimates of the number of undocumented immigrants in the United States range from 8 to 10 million, with 70 percent or more probably coming from Mexico. The U.S. government extrapolates its estimates by counting the migrants it deports and trying to figure out how many it misses. Using the high figures, that's less than 5 percent of the total U.S. population. The NAS study guessed that 200,000 to 300,000 more undocumented migrants come and stay each year. But without accurate figures it is impossible to determine how much illegal immigrants pay in taxes versus how much they use of the minimal public-funded social services available to them. Both sides in the immigration controversy use the statistics that are convenient for bolstering their arguments.

23

THE ROAD FROM
CHIAPAS AND
CHIHUAHUA

IN MEXICO'S impoverished regions, desperate *campesinos*, peasants, must decide whether to scratch out a marginal income or take a chance with *El Norte*.

The sprint from the U.S. border at Juárez to the city of Chihuahua, deep into Mexico, is on a high-speed, four-lane toll road, a little more than three hours across the dry lakes and past the dunes and mesas of the Chihuahua Desert. Chihuahua looks like Los Angeles—it takes another half-hour of stop-and-go driving to get through the sprawl of car lots, strip malls, and traffic to downtown. Cars, trucks, and buses spew out their acrid smog, a choking mix of untreated exhaust and burning oil. Most streets, stores, and houses suffer from a combination of incomplete construction and poor maintenance. Paint peels, windows crack, concrete breaks, rebar waits to reinforce. These are the common denominators of the Third World: incomplete construction and poor maintenance—here in Mexico decorated with its distinctive clashing pastel colors and punctuated by the sound of blaring baa-boom-boom-ba music from car speakers, bars, and street-corner kiosks.

Pancho Villa's sprawling Chihuahua mansion is now a museum, proudly documenting his attack into New Mexico during the Mexican Revolution.

From Chihuahua, the highway to the Tarahumara Sierra climbs up to the plains cultivated by transplanted Mennonites. The Mennonites immigrated to Mexico during the First World War following conflicts with the U.S. government over their refusal to serve in the military. The Mexican government offered them refuge and land in return for lessons in modern farming techniques. Today the descendants of these immigrants are distinctive in the Chihuahuan market towns—their fair skin and clothing give them away. The women wear bonnets or scarves that recall their northern European roots, but they protect themselves from the harsh Mexican sun with a *sombrero* over their head cloth.

Three hours of climbing brings the traveler to Creel, a strip of shops and hotels along the highway and railroad that prides itself as the jumping-off point for tourists visiting the wilds of the Tarahumara Sierra—its canyons, its railroad ride through the Copper Canyon to the Pacific, the opportunity to meet the remote and indigenous Tarahumara people. The businesses along the main street crank out steak and burritos, dolls and baskets, beer and Coca-Cola. On weekend nights the local teenagers cruise in cars, on horseback, some still strolling on the sidewalks—making eyes at each other and giggling.

Some Tarahumara women in Creel—dressed in their unique eye-catching costumes (typical: turquoise and red, chartreuse and pink ruffled full skirt with puffed-sleeves blouse, solid-color socks matching one of the colors of the skirt, all topped off with a scarf of some random, nonmatching print of flowers or paisleys in more bright colors)—send their children to meet tourists, peddling colorful woven belts and elegant, intricate basketry. Farther up the railroad line from Creel are the luxury resorts of the Copper Canyon, surrounded by the impoverished camps of the Tarahumara and the encroaching international lumber harvesters, along with marijuana and opium poppy cultivators who take advantage of the isolation to do their dirty business.

The Mexican army is now on patrol throughout the region, charged with protecting cash-fat tourists and chasing narco-farmers. Hints of the complications caused by the army presence may be seen in the posters dominating the foyer of the small Catholic church on the square in Creel, posters explaining to the Tarahumara their human rights guaranteed by the Mexican constitution, posters advising the Tarahumara what to do if they are harassed by the army. Posters in the windows of the state government building on the square report a missing thirty-five-year-old man, announce the cassette and CD released by a local band, advise citizens to exercise their right to vote, "the key to democracy."

Driving fast, fast, fast across the Sierra, it's almost three hours to Guachochi. It's a spectacular and exhausting trip through canyon wilderness, punctuated by overhanging sheer rock walls towering over the highway—with pieces of rock littering the two-lane blacktop adjacent to FALLING ROCKS warning signs. Maguey, piñon, and nopal line the way. The lonely road surprises periodically with its decorations of the Tarahumara in their colorful costumes appearing seemingly out of nowhere from side canyons. They're toting plastic bags, herding cows, or sitting by the side of the road.

Kilometer after kilometer click by with no services: no phones, no gas stations, no Starbucks, and nothing on the radio.

Finally a Pemex station looms at the bottom of a hill, its familiar green sign welcoming me to a cold Coca-Cola. It's shuttered. Out of business. Whoever labeled US 50 across Nevada "the loneliest road in the world" never made the Creel-to-Guachochi run.

Guachochi is a windswept market town on the edge of the Tarahumara Sierra, dominated by a harsh-looking stone prison and ramshackle single-story houses with rusting corrugated tin roofs. Nearing Guachochi, I searched the radio dial for evidence of XETAR, the local station, and heard only static at 870 AM, its frequency. I saw the telltale transmitter tower on the horizon on the outskirts of town and beat my old rented Chevy over the rutted dirt roads to the site. Passersby directed me to an anonymous-looking house. On the building were two signs: one advising that this was indeed XETAR, *La Voz de la Sierra Tarahumara*, the voice of the Sierra Tarahumara, the other a simple, *Cerrado*, closed. I banged on the door. No answer. That's when I went over to *Los Piños* restaurant and ordered a Coke. I asked the proprietor what was wrong with the radio station. "Technical problems," he told me. I borrowed his phone and called the station. The fellow who answered said no one was available to talk because the station was off the air, and he hung up.

I looked frustrated, I'm sure, and that's when the proprietor suggested I visit his friend across town, Petronilo González. González owns another restaurant in Guachochi, *La Cabaña*, and he works at government-owned XETAR as an announcer and engineer. I found him asleep in front of a TV in his empty restaurant. "*¡Pase, pase!*" he said when I woke him. Come in, come in. I sat down and we talked.

The station was off the air, he told me, because a relay had failed and there were no spare parts available in Guachochi. The station is plagued by its old equipment, he said. "We need new equipment, but it is not forthcoming from the government." How important to the community is the station, I asked him, how serious a problem is it that XETAR is off the air? "*Es muy importante*," he said. It provides many of the Tarahumara with their only source of communication with the outside world. It is, he said, the only radio station within two hundred kilometers. I knew that to be true—I had been looking for a radio signal since leaving Creel. "There is no other communication for the indigenous people who do not have money. *No hay nada*," he said, nothing, no newspapers, no TV, nothing but XETAR for people who live out in these wilds of Chihuahua, the largest Mexican state.

As we talked in *La Cabaña*, President Fox appeared on the TV, praising the pending access-to-information law in Mexico.

"God willing, we'll find the part in Chihuahua Monday and we'll be back on the air," Gonzalez said with confidence as we said good-bye.

On this trip I'm reading the book *A Fortune-teller Told Me*, an account by the journalist Tiziano Terzani of the year he spent without any travel by airplane. Terzani writes, "There is one aspect of a reporter's job that never ceases to fascinate and disturb me: facts that go unreported do not exist.

How many massacres, how many earthquakes happen in the world, how many ships sink, how many volcanoes erupt, and how many people are persecuted, tortured, and killed? Yet if no one is there to see, to write, to take a photograph, it is as if these facts never occurred, this suffering has no importance, no place in history. Because history exists only if someone relates it. It is sad, but such is life; and perhaps it is precisely this idea—the idea that with every little description of a thing observed one can leave a seed in the soil of memory—that keeps me tied to my profession."[1]

Terzani was musing about the critical importance of journalism during a reporting trip to Burma. He could just as well have been writing from the relative journalistic void of Creel and the Tarahumara Sierra. Of course there is a corollary to Terzani's remarks. When journalists draw attention to a remote locale such as Burma and Creel, one frequent result is not necessarily advantageous: tourism. Without attention and its following tourism, Creel would not attract the Tarahumara from the hinterlands to beg and try to sell trinkets in the streets. What to make of the impact of the tourists with their short pants, loud voices, video cameras, and one package-tour margarita at sunset? Probably overall the influx of tourist-fueled capital is a healthy thing, and when news reports highlight problems, it is more difficult for the villains to go unpunished, the crises to be ignored. Visiting rural Chihuahua and Chiapas, studying Mexico's urban slums and impoverished hinterlands, helps make it clear why so many Mexicans go north.

San Cristóbal de Las Casas is a slow, two-hour propeller-plane ride over the mountains south from Mexico City. As the plane descends toward the new airport, the Mayan highlands are close enough to view the poverty of the villages: ramshackle housing, humans as cargo bearers.

San Cristóbal de Las Casas is idyllic Mexico. The town square features a two-story gazebo. The evening I first arrived it was filled with the final fiesta of a week of Easter partying, this one dedicated to peace, as hope continued that Fox and *subcomandante* Marcos would become the *"amigos"* Fox called them, and that the indigenous rights bill pending in the Congress would be passed and prove satisfactory to the Zapatistas. The bill was passed. It was not satisfactory.

A marimba band filled the *zócalo* with a mood suggesting the Buena Vista Social Club. Couples were hugging and kissing, kids were playing, the wonderful aromas of foods that I probably shouldn't eat filled the square.

This is the city Marcos and the Zapatistas took from the Mexican military in the surprise attack in 1994 that began the current incarnation of a conflict that goes back to the Conquest. The Chiapas rebellion was launched January 1, 1994, the same date that NAFTA went into effect. Thousands of armed Indians took control of San Cristóbal and several other municipalities in the state, demanding land reform, indigenous autonomy, and cultural rights. One of their slogans was "NAFTA is Death!" The Zapatistas' protest and their charismatic leader *subcomandante* Marcos found some initial enthusiastic support in Mexico and throughout the world. But the Mexican army reacted to the Zapatistas with counterassaults that left at least 145 Indians dead. Demonstrations in Mexico against the military response helped lead to a ceasefire by mid-January. Throughout the nineties the fragile ceasefire barely held, violated by the army and paramilitary groups who fought—and killed—to disrupt the political efforts of the Zapatistas. After Vicente Fox was elected president, the Mexican Congress passed the indigenous rights law that Zapatistas called inadequate. The standoff continues.

The second part of San Cristóbal's name honors Las Casas, the first bishop of San Cristóbal and an early activist for indigenous rights who wrote and spoke actively against the oppression of the Spanish conquerors.

Soon I was twisting up the Chiapas Mountains in Onésimo Hidalgo's jeep, heading for San Andrés Larráinzar. Hidalgo is director of the Centro de Investigaciones Económicas y Políticas de Acción Comunitaria. CIEPAC is an organization that Hidalgo proudly labels as without government, religious, or political party connections. We were en route to a most basic and efficient news broadcast, with Hidalgo as newscaster and *campesinos*—peasants—assembling from villages even more remote than San Andrés Larráinzar as the initial audience. As we worked our way toward San Andrés Larráinzar, a village now claimed by both the Zapatistas and the longtime governing political party as under their jurisdiction, Hidalgo explained his and CIEPAC's chores.

"We work with the poorest," he said, pointing out that the war had had devastating effects on the poor indigenous population in the Chiapas highlands. CIEPAC, he told me, is working to rebuild the infrastructure of the isolated highlands and repair society in newly polarized communities. In the process, they are attempting to create models for a society based on equal rights in a region where the indigenous people have been treated by the ruling classes as second-class citizens since the days of Las Casas.

Hidalgo is a sociologist and a graduate of the National Autonomous University of Chiapas, a Chiapas native. He titles himself an investigator, analyst, and popular educator with extensive experience in the *campesino* and indigenous movement. Much of his work is to assemble data from primary sources about the Mexican military's presence in Chiapas and the activities of paramilitary groups. This, and other news, is posted weekly by CIEPAC on its website[2] in both English and Spanish, material that he says is heavily used by Mexican and foreign journalists for their coverage of the Chiapas crisis.

Onésimo Hidalgo agrees that radio is the most important medium for news and information in Mexico, with television a distant second. In rural zones such as San Andrés Larráinzar, he cites figures of over 70 percent illiteracy. "There are not enough schools," he says. "Children must work. They are too poor to go to school. They must work to live. There is no time for school." As we turn still another mountain curve, Hidalgo points to a group of little kids by the side of the road. "Look at these *niños*," he says, "they must carry water and wash clothes." They look about five years old. "How can they go to school?" And past the colorful costumes of these indigenous children with roots in pre-Columbian Mayan culture, the reality is shocking to watch as they struggle alongside the highway with heavy loads of firewood and other goods, slung from a support cloth pressed against their foreheads, leading a scattered little herd of goats.

But despite the penetration of radio into the highlands, Hidalgo says the information on most stations is not credible because "the chiefs of radio are the people of power."

Much of Onésimo Hidalgo's work is to travel to remote enclaves such as San Andrés Larráinzar and meet with assembled *campesinos*, listen to them report to him what is going on in their villages, and then present a day-long lecture on current events—specifically current events that relate to their lives. This grassroots reporting augments the little other audio media available: government and commercial radio stations, shortwave broadcasts from abroad. The government jammed Radio Zapatista off the air in 1994. It periodically returns as its clandestine transmitter is moved from place to place, sending out news, Zapatista ideology, and music. Also in 1994, the Zapatistas occupied XEOC in the city of Ocosingo and programmed it for about fifteen days before the facility was stormed and retaken by the federal army. The Zapatistas continue to maintain a website filled with news and propaganda.[3]

An open army truck passes us on the highway as we near San Andrés Larráinzar, the site of the peace talks between the Zedillo government and the Zapatistas that resulted in a truce in the 1994 shooting war. The truck is filled with uniformed soldiers, guns at the ready. "Look," says Hidalgo, "the government says soldiers are no longer in this region, and there they are." He pulls the jeep into the churchyard, and we move to a low classroom building with whitewashed brick walls under a corrugated metal roof adjacent to the church. There we're greeted by a couple of dozen smiling *campesinos*. There are no women in attendance. The chatter of greeting from the crowd is in Tzotzil; fewer than half the Chiapas population speaks Spanish. The dress is straw cowboy hats, slacks, and *huaraches*. It has been a month since the group last met. Through a Tzotzil translator they report the news to Hidalgo. He listens and takes notes, asking questions. These men, called *catequistas*, are chosen from volunteers in their villages to be the oral news gatherers and reporters under a program organized by the Catholic church. Most take out their notebooks and write in detail as Hidalgo makes his own day-long presentation. Once back in their local communities they will repeat the process, each of them taking the teacher position before a group assembled from even more remote localities. This church-supported oral news medium has been ongoing in Chiapas for several years.

Onésimo Hidalgo makes his presentation in front of an old wooden-framed blackboard hanging on nails, using it to scribble detailed notes and charts. "We're going to speak about neoliberalism and Fox," he says, "and what this means to Chiapas and Mexico." Over the next several hours Hidalgo discusses NAFTA (the North American Free Trade Agreement), the connection between Mexico and the European Union, the Plan Puebla Panamá (the program for economic cooperation between Mexico and Central America), and the impact of these events on *campesino* life. The meeting is taking place during the week of the Western Hemisphere summit in Quebec City, and Hidalgo uses a newspaper he bought that morning in San Cristóbal as a teaching aid. He talks about the effects of globalization on family farms and explains *"transgénicos,"* genetically modified food. He condemns Monsanto, the U.S.-based purveyor of genetically modified corn seed.* It is a remarkably detailed and balanced report, and in this primitive-looking remote classroom, these *campesinos* are thoroughly analyzing world trade and its effect on local control. "All this," sums up Hidalgo, "includes the large companies and excludes the poor *campesinos.*"

We break for lunch in the churchyard. Lucky for me, it is a *campesino* meal: vegetarian, and I do not need to make up an excuse for rejecting the meat. We eat rice, eggs, cabbage, potatoes, beans, and tortillas—all well cooked, *gracias a Dios.* During lunch, José de Jesús Londín García, the parish priest at San Andrés Larráinzar, gives us a tour of the church, explaining the hybrid religious activities of the indigenous Catholics in his congregation. He too points to radio as the primary medium for news in his region. He suggests that the informed questioning during the lectures

*By early 2004 the Commission for Environmental Cooperation, a unit of NAFTA, warned that genetically modified corn was contaminating Mexican native varieties and threatening the survival of some sixty types of native corn, despite a ban on the GM seed imposed by the Mexican government in 1998. GM corn feed is not banned and is likely used by some farmers as a cheap alternative for seed.

is in part the result of the exposure some *campesinos* have to foreign broad-casters such as the BBC. "*Campesinos* must work," says the priest. "With TV you must sit and watch it, and you cannot work."

The students indicate that they want to reconvene the meeting. They have traveled for as long as four hours to reach San Andrés Larráinzar, and they want to take advantage of the day. After another hour of lecture, Hidalgo invites their participation, taking questions and stimulating discussion, finally asking this concluding question of the group:

"Why is it important for us to talk?"

And he gets these answers:

"Because it is how information is transferred."

"Because it is important to know what is happening in our country in order to construct a better life."

"Because it is important to have information about what is happening in our country and the world."

Hidalgo tries to persuade the *campesinos* in his class to stay in Chiapas and work for change, not head north for jobs in the global economy. It's much the same argument voiced by American vigilantes who advocate ordering the Marines to seal the border. "We're being sacrificed on the altar of globalism," is the chant from Glenn Spencer, the founder of American Border Patrol. "You have big corporations who want no barriers to the making of their profits."[4]

Ten years after NAFTA was approved by the United States and Mexico, it's blamed for pushing Mexicans north. NAFTA calls for the free—or at least freer—movement of capital and goods across the border. But not labor. The elimination of the trade barriers that Glenn Spencer complains about means that U.S. agribusiness can sell corn in Mexico for less, much less, than the subsistence amount of pesos local farmers earned for their crops before open competition from the United States was allowed. Kentucky farmers export much of their white corn to Mexico for the manufacture of tortillas. This corn trade is a disaster for the Mexican family farmer. "The prices seem to go down and down each year," reported Tlacuitapa farmer Maurilio Márquez. "If it weren't for my family in California sending money, we wouldn't have any choice but to go north and join them."[5]

Mexican government studies report that since the inception of NAFTA, corn prices have dropped an astounding 80 percent.[6] The numbers add poignancy to an editorial cartoon that shows a Gringo businessman in a big car asking a Mexican farmer with a burro what he'd like to trade. "Places," answers the Mexican.[7] Proponents of NAFTA continue to say that in the long term, Mexico and most Mexicans will thrive because of increased trade with the United States, even if the family farms never recover.

But it isn't only the farmer in Mexico who is suffering from the effects of NAFTA. Businesses seeking U.S. investment have fired workers in an attempt to improve their profit margin and appear more inviting. More workers lost jobs when U.S.-owned factories operating on the Mexican side of the border slowed production during the recession beginning in 2001. Ten years after NAFTA was signed, the average wage at these border plants was unchanged—at about $4.02—not per hour but per day. A gallon of milk in Tijuana costs about $3.[8] These kinds of numbers can make a border crossing look quite seductive, especially to workers already living on the edge.

The gross difference between most personal incomes in the United States and those in Mexico forces migration north. NAFTA promoters promised the agreement would result in a reduction in this disparity between wages paid in the world's largest economy and those paid in its Third World neighbor. In fact the opposite has occurred, and the wage gap increased more than 10 percent during NAFTA's first ten years. Even many of those Mexicans who try to deal with the wage inequity by crossing the border face a downwardly mobile lifestyle. "Recent moves in California to prevent illegal immigrants from receiving driver's licenses and medical care have been a depressing sign that conditions for Mexican immigrants in this country are getting worse," wrote Columbia University economics professor and Nobel Prize laureate Joseph Stiglitz in a critical appraisal of NAFTA on its tenth anniversary.[9]

On my second trip to Chiapas, to San Andrés Larráinzar, I met again with the parish priest who spoke freely of his difficulties in trying to continue his work under the jurisdiction of the new Chiapas bishop. Priest José de Jesús Londín García (known locally by his nickname Chuy) receives me in his modest office. He's wearing jeans and a T-shirt. We talk just before Sunday Mass. He acknowledges violating the desires of the new bishop and making himself available for interviews with the foreign press. The bishop wants all information disseminated from the centralized church authority. But Chuy says that expressing his opinion about local conditions is an integral aspect of his work as a priest.

Chuy uses his pulpit and the bully pulpit of his position as priest to report the news as he sees it, and he preaches the same sermon as Onésimo Hidalgo: globalization is adding to the crisis for Chiapas *campesinos* as severe social and economic problems persist. The bishop wants him to go to Rome to study. Chuy is resisting the reassignment, which he is convinced is designed to silence him. In his office are stacks of political literature.

The congregation gathers in the churchyard. Men in their traditional garb: pointed straw hats adorned with multicolored ribbons with colored pom-poms trailing over white headcloths, grey serapelike suits tied with a red sash over white shirts with red sleeves. Women in dark blue cotton skirts with white blouses embroidered in wild colors with complementary sashes—often carrying one or two babies wrapped in white.

Inside, the church is decorated with blue and white banners illustrated with images of doves. Elaborate assemblages of candles, flowers, peacock feathers, figures, and paintings of saints are surrounded with pots filled with burning incense. Mirrors hang from the necks of the figures, perhaps to reflect any evil in the parishioner so that it doesn't enter the saint, but the origin and purpose of many such rituals are no longer known for sure, they're simply repeated. The sanctuary fills with the incense smoke. The women sit on the pine needles covering the floor and chat, breast feed, tend the incense while the prayers drone from the altar. The men stand.

"Peace is a gift of God, but it is also something we have a responsibility to build together," says Chuy as part of the service.

On one wall, the Virgin of Guadalupe looks out from a tiled altar in a frame featuring flashing Christmas-tree lights. Behind the main altar are glass-covered cases lit by fluorescent tubes and filled with figures of the Virgin Mary and Christ. Recorded popular music from the Sunday market outside drifts into the church, competing with the service.

The mainstream mass media in Chiapas and the world report improvement in Chiapas since the peace talks, or report nothing at all. But Chuy says problems continue and must be addressed.

As I leave San Andrés Larráinzar, a drunken man lies across the road as if dead. Sunday is market day, church day, and drinking day—potent *posh* is a popular knockout.

On the twenty-second day of every month there is a memorial service in Acteal, another Chiapas highlands community, commemorating the massacre perpetrated by paramilitaries in the village on December 22, 1997. The memorial service is both a religious event and a news report, another example of the Mexican oral tradition for reporting news.

In a packed open-air chapel under an orange plastic tent roof, Father Pedro Arriaga—in a long speech—announces the news to the congregation. He reiterates the story of the massacre, reports that justice is unfinished regarding the perpetrators, and connects the massacre to the problems caused Chiapas by globalization. He identifies Plan Puebla Panamá—the Central America–Mexico economic cooperation plan that includes controversial infrastructure development, such as the proposal to build a land bridge across Mexico to compete with the Panama Canal—as an unjust sop to capitalists. His speech is intended as a news presentation. Father Pedro offers the handful of foreign visitors a hard copy of his remarks and tells the group, "These words are for the international press." His words are translated into Tzotzil.

Simple wooden crosses decorated with colorful ribbons adorn the dais.

The news reporting continues regarding problems in Colombia and their similarities to circumstances in Chiapas: narcotics trafficking, paramilitary atrocities, displaced *campesinos*, and human rights violations by the army.

An indigenous music group plays: trumpet, drums, harp, and violin. An elder chants a droning prayer while the congregation kneels on the dirt floor covered with pine needles. A picture of the Virgin of Guadalupe hangs below a bell on a pole. Incense burns, Calla lily blossoms peek from plastic buckets—one of the buckets is red and features the Coca-Cola logo.

The chanter drones on. One of the visiting priests on the dais pulls a camera from his robe and snaps a picture. The droning continues and the chanter's eyes glaze. Periodically the assembled priests prostrate themselves.

A local Chiapas parish priest, Father Marcelo, the first Tzotzil priest, begins the homily. It too is news reporting. He says he has two goals in the Mass. One is to come together as a community for a traditional religious meeting. The other is a remembrance of the massacre and a concern for the future. He says a good pastor makes clear what is needed in a community. And then he announces his "lead" story: "It is very dangerous when one's enemies are quiet, because you don't know when or where an enemy will attack." He refers to the day's news—or lack of news—in Chiapas. "Here attack is not theoretical," he says. Then he warns, "There is more danger when you cannot hear the shooting. So it is imperative to be attentive." In a void of believable traditional news media, this is the newscast. "Jesus is a good shepherd who can protect sheep from wolves," preaches Father Marcelo, adding as an explanation of his activist role, "Priests and nuns—like Jesus—must take care of the sheep God gave them."

The Mass continues. Father Pedro returns to the podium to explain social problems in the Dominican Republic. He provides a positive review of a new book about the former Chiapas bishop Samuel Ruiz. Ruiz championed this type of amalgam in the church: current events and religion, Catholicism and native beliefs. His successor rails against such use of the church and favors a strict, dogmatic Catholicism.

The names and ages of the massacre victims are recited: fifteen children, twenty-one women, nine men.

An electrified music group alternates selections with the traditionalists. A couple dozen members of the congregation leave the tent and return from a nearby house, forming a procession into the tent. They parade in a clockwise circle around the altar and give an offering: corn and beans in shallow baskets, flowers, a poster about human rights in the Dominican Republic, the new book about Don Samuel Ruiz.

Following the Mass I am invited to a communal lunch of eggs and tortillas with coffee. The combination of poverty and violence makes it easy to understand what motivates these *campesinos* to move north; the warmth of their community makes it just as easy to understand their homesickness.

Not far down the highway from Acteal, in the last main city before the Guatemala border, Comitán, a local commercial radio station blasts its programming—popular music—from loudspeakers in the *zócalo*. A small group of teenagers gathers to listen; an ice cream vendor provides them with refreshment from his cart. At a video arcade, teenagers are sweating on the Dance Dance Revolution machine, working out to the latest hits from *El Norte*, the lyrics still another form of news consumption. In front of the arcade's open doors, out on the sidewalk, little kids mimic the dance steps of their teenage elders, learning the rituals of the global pop community.

Millions of desperate people seeking relief from poverty, and a two-thousand-mile land border inviting them with one step to cross over from the Third to the First World guarantees trouble on the U.S.-Mexico border until a fair's day work will earn a fair day's pay on both sides. My friend Víctor Reyes, a journalist and translator in Marin County, California, writes regularly about the life of Mexicans living in Marin and Sonoma counties. Over the years he's been my Spanish-language *maestro*. We often talk about the border crisis and the migration from Mexico. Víctor is one of the fortunate migrants. Born in Puebla into a middle-class family and educated at the university there, he could choose to come north for a visit legally, and eventually he chose to stay, again legally. But he sympathizes readily with *campesinos* struggling to cross the border and decode life in the United States.

"All those people are usually way more vulnerable because of the lack of sophistication, the lack of understanding, the lack of education. So when you get those people here and they face the sophistication of American culture, they are easy victims of the system." Even if these new arrivals come north to reunite with friends and family, Víctor knows that migrants, especially those from rural Mexico, are a disadvantaged underclass both at home and once they arrive in the United States. "Sometimes they are taken advantage of by other Mexicans who have been in the States longer."

Víctor Reyes uses the number of one thousand Mexicans crossing the border illegally every day, and growing. "It's an escape valve for Mexico, to avoid the collapse of the economy." He blames NAFTA and globalization for the continuing economic difficulties in his home country, and is convinced the influx of Mexicans into the United States—legally and illegally—only benefits the U.S. economy. "They are better consumers than others," he says about his countrymen living north of the border, "because this is the first time they have the experience of being consumers. They are naive consumers. They buy anything." He throws out more statistics. "Mexicans send money back to Mexico—the second-largest source of income in Mexico after oil. Foreign investment is around eleventh or twelfth. You know how much those immigrants spend in the United States? "Five hundred billion dollars. So that shows you how good it is for the American economy to have all these guys up here, and how good it is for Mexico."

Víctor decided to stay in *El Norte* for the way of life. "You can survive much better here." That's not all. Víctor's now ex-wife is a Californian, and they have a son. "Originally I just came here to visit and to stay for no more than one or two years. But later I realized—and that's not a secret, and it's even more radical for an average Mexican—that you can live better here. An average Mexican who can make no more than five dollars a day, can make ten or twenty here—per hour, not per day. It's much better because most of them must send money back to Mexico."

Víctor appreciates the fact that he's living not just the American Dream but also the California Dream. Life for him in Marin County is free of the prejudice many Mexicans face throughout the fifty states that are their diaspora. Mexicans and things Mexican are well appreciated in Marin County; the electorate overwhelmingly votes against the anti-immigrant initiatives that periodically appear on the California ballot.

But he insists he's only around for the convenience, that he's still invested south of the border. We argue about his attitude regularly.

"Are you an American or a Mexican?" I ask him.

"I'm a Mexican," he says without hesitation.

"But you're an American citizen now."

"So what? I'm a Mexican citizen too. I'm an American citizen because I could remain being a Mexican citizen. That's just a piece of paper. That means nothing."

"You're a Mexican in your heart?"

"Oh, absolutely. I couldn't be an American. I know how to be here. I know how to relate to Americans. But I cannot be American. I can't. It's an identity. You cannot change your identity. You are who you are. That's the tragedy of the second generation of immigrants who don't know who they are. I know a lot of folks like that, very intelligent people. They struggle because they don't speak Spanish very well. They know how to become Americans, but everybody calls them Latinos. They have no defined identity."

My father suffered none of Víctor's inner conflicts about living in one place and belonging to another. He was an American as soon as he passed through Ellis Island, an American by choice, and he never looked back longingly at the Old World. Distance may well play a role in the difference between the assimilating immigration from Europe and the commuting migrations from Mexico. It was not feasible in those days before air travel to move regularly back and forth between Middle Europe and New York. Coming to America was a one-way commitment. The proximity of Sinaloa to California, Veracruz to Kentucky, Sonora to Arizona means that a Mexican can taste and test the United States knowing he can go home *mañana*. But that opportunity to stay in close touch with the homeland does not mean Mexicans don't assimilate into the U.S. mainstream. Many do, and without losing contact with their native land.

Directly along the border, from Tijuana to Brownsville, are Mexicans and Americans who deal with this mélange of cultures. "Nothing is sacred," is how Daniel Rivera, a deejay who calls himself Tolo, explains border life. "Every day new people come to Tijuana with new traditions, languages, and religions. All the icons arrive. If you don't like one, you discard it for another. There is no nationalist pressure. You don't know where your Mexican authenticity ends and your Gringo influence begins."[10]

A Mexican who has lived most of his adult life in California approached the question of identity poetically in an interview with a *San Francisco Chronicle* reporter. "If a *nopal* [a cactus used in Mexican cooking] is planted here or there," said Ramón Mezquita, "it's still a *nopal.*"[11] Or, as Víctor Reyes wrote in his newspaper column after we talked about his identity struggle, "*Soy mexicano simplemente porque no puedo ser otra cosa.*"[12] I am Mexican simply because I am unable to be anything else. Nonetheless, even as he argues against it, Víctor knows he's melting into the American pot. In e-mails to me now he refers to himself as "your *seudo gringo amigo,*" and "*el gringo nuevo,*" and "*mexigringo,* or vice versa."

24

BEST FRIENDS

TOWARD THE END of 2003, many of those who favor normalizing the status of Mexicans living illegally in the United States were surprised to find Homeland Security Secretary Tom Ridge appear to ease closer to their position. Speaking to a crowd at Miami Dade College in Florida, Ridge was asked about amnesty for immigrants in the United States without proper documents. Wouldn't such a change in their status make it easier for the government to keep track of them and thus aid homeland security? Ridge allowed as how that might be true.

"I'm not saying make them citizens, because they violated the law to get here," Ridge said. "You don't reward that type of conduct by turning over a citizenship certificate. You determine how you can legalize their presence, then, as a country, you make a decision that from this day forward, this is the process of entry, and if you violate that process of entry we have the resources to cope with it."

That was what the 1986 amnesty was supposed to do. Instead, because sanctions are so rarely enforced against employers who hire undocumented labor, and because the border remains porous, Mexicans keep coming north. Despite the insistence of Secretary Ridge, the United States hasn't the resources to cope with the border crossers or chooses not to do so.

But Ridge was simply being pragmatic when he pointed out that the government "had to come to terms with the presence of 8 million to 12 million illegals" and must "afford them some kind of legal status some way, but also as a country decide what our immigration policy is and then enforce it."[1] His comments stirred the melting pot.

Internet bulletin boards and chat rooms exploded with venom, like this note posted by a writer who identified himself or herself only as The Crusader:

> Absorbing 300,000 European immigrants yearly into our mainstream society was a pleasure and a great benefit to America. They easily assimilated into our Westernized culture and already understood our Christian faith. They willingly and eagerly learned enough English to get by, and they wanted their children to master English. They called their country of origin the old country and were pleased to have a new land to call home. Today they pour uncontrolled into our country from every "Third World" rat hole like starving rats into a dumpster and call themselves "Mexican-Americans," or "African-Americans," or "Arab-Americans," or whatever, proudly placing their country of origin before America. As for your utterly assinine comment about Mexicans not being a threat, you seem to completely fail in your ability to understand that throughout history countries got weakened and undermined by means other than military victories. Because of the ridiculous liberal mentality that pervades America today our schools are producing borderline morons as we continue to lose scholastic ground each year to other nations. Our health care and our standard of living were always tops in the world throughout most of my lifetime, but now it's all eroding as other nations surpass us in almost every category except militarily. We are squandering the great blessings that were bestowed on us by God with laziness, liberal incompetence, unchecked immigration, international trade regulations that harm American manufacturing and American workers, forced "tolerance" of sin and corruption like homosexuality, and the suppressing of Christianity. But most of all the suicidal practice of unchecked, uncontrolled immigration is what's undermining our society in this age of terrorism. Our great weakness is our insane urge to kiss the a$$ of every minority or immigrant at every turn and smile some bizarre Pollyanna smile, while madmen and butchers like Osama bin Laden use our self-defeating policies to walk

boldly into our society and carry out their sinister plans. Immigration is good for America; unchecked, uncontrolled immigration is suicide on the installment plan.

Whew.

Someone identified as Winker checked in with another assault:

Well now we know who is in bed with Vicente Fox! This Mexican Gambit is as Anti-American as it comes! If the Congress goes along with this sick plan for upwards of Twenty Million Illegal Criminal Border Jumping Terrorists by welcoming them with open arms the time for drastic impeachment action is called for. If necessary we need to sweep clean all those who vote to approve amnesty. Secretary Ridge has succumbed to the Dark Side if he authorizes this action. We The People must ensure "OVERSIGHT" is in place from this point forward if we are to believe this report. I am thinking that Ridge needs to be the shortest-tenured director in the history of Homeland Security. For this very reason this is why we were forced to go to Level Orange and now possibly we will see RED ALERT status because of absolutely no effective control of our borders NORTH, SOUTH & COAST to COAST!

That rant was followed by an unsigned simple and caustic "National Security or Cheap Lettuce. Guess we can't have both."

"It is scary to have someone such as Ridge in charge of Homeland Security," wrote Dante3, who wanted to know, "Is he this stupid, a sleeper agent, or simply blackmailed and/or bought off?"

"Remember, citizens," cautioned Captain Paint Ball, "as we permanently change the demographics and direction of this once-great nation, and as this once-great nation"—and here he steals a line from the author Paul Theroux—"becomes a turd world nation, it is important to be vigilant, be prepared!!!"

But it wasn't just the anonymous on the internet who reacted quickly. George Abruzzese from Bohemia, New York, wrote to the *New York Times*, arguing, "The *Times*, like so many supporters of illegal immigrants always reminds us that illegal aliens do the work regular Americans won't do:

pick crops, bus tables, clean hotel rooms, and so on, because these jobs don't pay enough. But the absence of illegal aliens would force employers to pay higher wages to get those jobs done, and then in true American fashion the rising tide would lift all boats. I, for one, would be willing to pay higher prices if in return our borders were secure and the people who live and work here do so legally. The wages of legal citizens are held down artificially by the presence of illegal employees in the workplace."[2]

On the editorial page of the *Sierra Vista Herald*, published just down the highway from Tombstone in Arizona, Jim Behnke bellowed, "What? Has Tom Ridge, the guy in charge of homeland security, lost his mind? Did he really say that?"

Behnke proceeded to attack Ridge's vague proposal as an invitation to terrorists.

> Of course, he was thinking of the illegal Mexicans in this country and therein lies the flaw. You cannot grant legal status to one group of people without granting it to all. Such an amnesty—or whatever they wish to call it—would show racial preference. You cannot exclude the Pakistani, Saudi Arabians and others who are here illegally. If such an amnesty were granted to Mexicans only, the Pakistani, Saudi Arabians, Afghanis, etc., would soon file suit in Federal court charging racial bias and racial preference. Such a limited amnesty would immediately be struck down by the courts because it is, quite simply, unfair. The courts would rule that amnesty must be granted to all living in this country illegally—not just one group of people. And that's where the terrorists come in. There are probably 5,000 al-Qaida terrorists living in this country illegally not to mention thousands more who believe in their cause. They, too, would fall under this amnesty because it must be granted to all—not just a few. Anyone living on U.S. soil would be eligible. This also would include the al-Qaida prisoners in Guantanamo Bay as that is also U.S. soil by international law."[3]

Perhaps Tom Ridge's remarks were designed by the White House to soften up the target for a well-rehearsed announcement a few days later that came with official pomp. President Bush assembled members of his cabinet, and a carefully selected group of Latinos, in the East Room for the announcement of his plan to deal with undocumented immigration. During his short speech he initially placated those frustrated by the inequities of U.S. immigration policy. He identified the crisis honestly and correctly.

"As a nation that values immigration and depends on immigration, we should have immigration laws that work and make us proud," Bush said, looking ahead to the November 2004 elections and the huge block of Latino and other immigrant voter blocs. "Yet today," he acknowledged, "we do not. Instead we see many employers turning to the illegal labor market. We see millions of hardworking men and women condemned to fear and insecurity in a massive undocumented economy. Illegal entry across our borders makes more difficult the urgent task of securing the homeland. The system is not working."

The president succinctly assessed the problem. But his proposed solution was vague and filled with traps for immigrants working in the United States. The Bush plan is not another amnesty for workers who have been contributing for years to the American economy and culture. It is not a plan for the immigration of settlers who become American citizens. Nor is it a plan for the free flow of people across the U.S.-Mexico frontier. The Bush plan is a guest worker proposal, with all the inherent benefits such programs reap for employers and all the discrimination they heap on employees. And with the European model for guest workers in mind, it is clear that such programs leave a legacy of social problems for future generations.

"I propose," the president said, "a new temporary worker program that will match willing foreign workers with willing American employers when no Americans can be found to fill the jobs."

That statement means that foreign workers would not, under Bush's proposal, be invited to enter the U.S. labor pool. They would be restricted to jobs that employers considered impossible to fill with American workers. Such a system is a double threat. Not only is the foreign worker reduced to a second-class status, the American worker is subjected to job offers designed for him or her to refuse because they are so poor, allowing the employer to plead the need for foreign replacements.

Next Bush explained, "This program will offer legal status as temporary workers to the millions of undocumented men and women now employed in the United States and to those in foreign countries who seek to participate in the program and have been offered employment here."

This broad "offer" from the president of the United States to people—that they might end a life underground and worried about deportation—cruelly sent out false hope to millions. As vaguely defined, the president's proposal offers legal status only for three years at a time, and only as long as the foreigner is working for the employer whose offer of a job allowed him to stay in or come to the United States. That fact alone skews the dynamic of the boss-worker relationship perversely in favor of the boss.

"Don't like it?" yells the boss at the recalcitrant worker. "I'll fire you and call the *Migra* to send you back to Mexico." Under the president's plan, the worker would have no right to remain in the United States under such circumstances and would be forced to go back underground or return to Mexico. And of course, though the president's plan refers to "foreigners," it is designed primarily to deal with Mexican workers and the ease with which they slip across the U.S.-Mexico border. And what about all those desperate workers who have no deal with a specific employer? What will encourage them to stay in Mexico rather than jump the border? Nothing. And what about the wives? There is no provision for maintaining family unity. So much for fostering family values.

"The legal status granted by this program will last three years and will be renewable," announced the president as he explained his deal, "but it will have an end."

How different such harsh language—"it will have an end"—is from the embracing welcome on the base of the Statue of Liberty. This proposal is no invitation for assimilation into the American dream. And it carries a nasty threat.

"Participants who do not remain employed, who do not follow the rules of the program or who break the law," said President Bush, "will not be eligible for continued participation and will be required to return to their home."

Immigrants tend to develop acute street smarts quickly, otherwise they could not survive. This is especially true of undocumented immigrants who constantly fear deportation. What motivation could there be to sign up for a program so weighted against them unless they enjoyed a fine relationship with an employer? The slightest digression in the workplace, the slightest misstep in public, and the *Migra* knows exactly who they are and where to find them. It sounds remarkably close to a variation of an old American immigration tradition, indentured servitude. Accessed in this harsh light, living underground as an undocumented worker may seem a much better deal to many workers, especially casual workers, day-to-day unskilled laborers.

"Employers must not hire undocumented aliens or temporary workers whose legal status has expired," Bush proclaimed about his proposed program.

Well and good to say with authority from the East Room, but impossible to enforce. We know because the same is true today: it's illegal to hire so-called illegal aliens. Yet employers readily hire undocumented workers. There is almost no policing of the workplace for such violations. The manpower doesn't exist; there is no budget for such work. And employers are not required to verify workers' documents, so if the papers are false, as long as the employer can credibly deny knowing about the fakes, only the worker is liable for prosecution. Besides, the law includes a giant loophole for agribusiness. Growers and ranchers are exempt from penalties if they hire laborers indirectly through labor contractors.

The U.S. economy would all but collapse if employers had no workers; many employers would have no workers if they had no undocumented workers. But the law and its enforcement is moot regarding documentation when you can buy a fraudulent Green Card in three hours in Bowling Green, Kentucky. Employers are not trained to detect counterfeit Green Cards. Even if they were, they have no motivation to use that training. They can just smile and tell the cops and their neighbors that they checked. They thought the guys in the fields or the kitchens were legal.

In case there is any misunderstanding that the Bush proposal is a welcome to join the American Dream and not just a device to obtain cheap labor, the president stated, "This program expects temporary workers to return permanently to their home countries after their period of work in the United States has expired."

It couldn't be said any clearer unless Bush said, "Come here. Work cheap. Go home." But the proposal includes specific devices to make sure the guest workers don't imagine there is a welcome mat at the border. "I will work with foreign governments on a plan to give temporary workers credit when they enter their own nation's retirement system for the time they have worked in America. I also support making it easier for temporary workers to contribute a portion of their earnings to tax-preferred savings accounts, money they can collect as they return to their native countries. After all, in many of these countries a small nest egg is what is necessary to start their own business or buy some land for their family." In other words, here's some cash, just get out.

Aside from the crassness of the Bush immigrant labor proposal, the European experience shows that guest-worker programs are not the tidy solution that the president proposes. Four generations later, Germany is still attempting to accommodate its Turkish minority, workers who fueled the postwar economic miracle yet were treated as legal and social second-class citizens. After the Berlin Wall fell, a united Germany was forced to deal not only with the Turks but with guest workers brought into East Germany, some sixty thousand socialist brothers from North Vietnam. When the East German economy collapsed, their jobs disappeared. In 1995 Germany made cash deals to get rid of the Vietnamese. It provided Vietnam with $140 million in development aid. In return, Vietnam agreed to repatriate some forty thousand workers. No one asked the displaced workers for their opinions.[4]

The Bush plan was designed to accomplish three basic goals for the U.S. economy: exploit labor, control labor, send labor home. And it was designed to achieve those goals while gaining Bush votes from immigrants among whom it generated false hopes of residency for friends and family. The electioneering Bush guest-worker plan was a variation on a variety of other proposals offered by concerned lawmakers in Congress. None appreciate the obvious: it's impossible to prevent unauthorized immigration from Mexico.

Woody Guthrie posed the still-unanswered germane questions when he wrote his agonizing song "Deportee" after a planeload of Mexican workers sent south crashed in California. "Is this the best way we can grow our big orchards?" he asked. "Is this the best way we can grow our good fruit? To fall like dry leaves to rot on my topsoil, and be called by no name except deportees?"

Critics were quick to vilify the Bush plan. "A guest worker bill isn't enough," said Katherine Culliton, a lawyer for the Mexican American Legal Defense Fund. "It doesn't provide equal worker rights, family unity, or a path to citizenship. Unless this plan is changed, it will produce a permanent underclass."[5]

"Look, our immigration policy has to show some consistency," insisted Congressman Luis Gutierrez after the Bush speech.[6] The Democrat from Illinois provided a stark example of what he considers unfair about U.S. priorities, pointing out that just as those who favor the laws that provide immediate legalization of refugees from Cuba "would find it unacceptable for all Cuban-Americans to return to Cuba after Fidel Castro is no longer there, we should find it unacceptable that Mexicans that have come to this country, that have worked hard, pay their taxes, want to be Americans, fight in our wars should have to return to their country. Have their children here and then return to their country. Work here and then return to their country. No, America's immigration policy has always been blessed with one thing: that if you work hard and pay your taxes and you show good moral character, we accept you genuinely and completely into our great American society."

But Colorado Congressman Tom Tancredo was disgusted by the Bush plan for other reasons. "People who are here illegally, they need to be deported," he said. "People who hired them need to be fined. If they keep doing it, they need to be sent to jail. It's against the law."[7]

Mexican President Fox, all but ignored by the White House since the September 11th attacks, replied with caution, insisting that Mexicans laboring in the United States should have "the rights that any worker in that country has, even though they are not American citizens."[8] His caution came from his bitter experience of being courted and rejected once by

Bush. But since addressing the crises for Mexican nationals at work in the United States was one of Fox's early campaign promises, he grabbed at Bush's proposals, hoping they would reflect positively on him and his administration's efforts on behalf of migrants. Fox had been looking for openings to remind Bush that they had been best friends in the recent past—before Mexico opposed the U.S. attack on Iraq. Several weeks before Bush's immigration reform speech, Fox fired Mexico's ambassador to the United States, Adolfo Aguilar Zinser. Zinser had fueled the conflict between the two countries in a speech blasting Washington for seeking a "relationship of convenience and subordination" with Mexico, and claiming the United States simply "sees us as a backyard."[9]

The flurry of Washington interest in border problems dissipated quickly. A couple of weeks after Bush made his proposal, he delivered his third State of the Union message. Buried in rhetoric about Iraq, his war on terror, and the "sanctity of marriage" was a single short paragraph reiterating his vague immigration reform plan.

A sad result of the president's proposal was not only to raise the hopes of immigrants in the United States without papers. While applause from cabinet members and invited guests was filling the East Room, scam artists were busy figuring out how to turn the Bush proposals into a hustle. Lawyers, and others posing as experts, offered their services to migrants, suggesting they could help Mexicans apply for legalization under Bush's program. But Bush was just musing, suggesting, brainstorming, electioneering. Only Congress can change the law. Nonetheless, typical was an ad in the *Diario de Juárez* offering, "Guest workers under the immigration reform by Fox-Bush. First consultation free."

Watch out, warned the Texas attorney general. Jesus Sandoval, the El Paso lawyer who placed the ad, insisted his motives were pure. "I'm advising people for them to prepare," he explained. But the attorney general's office was convinced that nefarious actors were poised to make money from desperate migrants, particularly susceptible because of the vast differences in the American and Mexican political cultures. Arturo

Vázquez, a lawyer working both sides of the border, said the official look of Bush's speech led to misunderstandings that opened the door to con artists. "In Mexico when the president says something, it's law," he explained. "So Mexicans think it's a done deal."[10]

Problems were created far north of the border too. The *Denver Post* reported that so-called immigration counselors operating out of storefronts in predominantly Mexican neighborhoods were selling advice on how to get the visas suggested by President Bush. More aggressive predators were going door-to-door offering to help migrants get the new visas. "The fraud appeared immediately," announced the frustrated acting Mexican consul in Denver, Juana Roberto González. His office produced a television advertising campaign warning of the hoaxes.[11]

The day after the Bush announcement, American newspapers were understandably filled once more with immigration stories. The White House brought the issue of migration across the U.S.-Mexico border back to the front pages. But the interaction between the two countries was perhaps best presented on a double-page spread of the *New York Times* on January 8, 2004. All the news on these two pages dealt with Bush's proposal and immigration policy. A wide photograph showed the president in the East Room receiving a standing ovation from Homeland Security Secretary Tom Ridge, Commerce Secretary Donald Evans, Attorney General John Ashcroft, and Secretary of State Colin Powell (the *Times* made a prominent note of the fact that Powell's parents had immigrated to the United States from Jamaica). Under the photo were a couple of charts, one showing the distribution of undocumented immigrants throughout the States, as compiled by the Immigration and Naturalization Service in the year 2000. California was estimated to be home to the most, more than two million. Texas was next with a million. New York and Illinois followed with just under half a million. The other chart showed that, also according to the INS, more undocumented immigrants entered the United States throughout the 1990s than went home, became legal residents, or died. Another photograph showed Mexican President Vicente Fox in his Los Piños office, shaking hands with Senate Majority Leader Bill Frist.

But whether it was planned or just magical realism, the two pages were decorated with a half-page ad filling the space under the Fox and Frist photo, an advertisement for a place called One & Only Palmilla. In the ad is a photograph of a lagoon and the view past it to the ocean and on out to the pristine horizon. The picture is framed with palm trees. The focal point of the photo brings our eyes to a woman sitting on a rock in the lagoon. She wears shorts and a skimpy white top. We see only her back; she is looking out to sea. She is sitting in the lotus position. The copy for the ad floats above her, typeset as verse:

If you could taste the sun,
If you could drink beauty,
If you could touch joy,
You would understand Palmilla.
Live the moment.

There are a few other lines of copy. "After an $80 million transformation, the eagerly awaited One & Only Palmilla is now open," the ad informs us. For those of us who were not eagerly awaiting this news, there is a hint of what's being sold. "Spend four nights and receive a complimentary fifth night." Ah, a hotel, some sort of resort hotel. And under the name One & Only Palmilla, the location: Los Cabos, Mexico.

It's difficult to imagine how the *Times* could have done a better job of pinpointing the inequitable but symbiotic relationship between the two countries than what its editors did with the composition of these two pages. Five stories on the desperate migration of workers into the United States adorned with the ad for the ultimate getaway for rich Gringos: a Mexico so different from the one the workers are fleeing.*

One George W. Bush policy for immigrants guarantees immediate citizenship. During the Iraq war, some thirty thousand U.S. troops were foreigners, including Mexican David Cuervo, a Texas resident who emigrated

---

*The One & Only Palmilla offers rooms at a base rate of $685 a night (tips included!).

from Tampico. He died in Baghdad, victim of a bomb attack two days after Christmas 2003 and two days after he called his mother to tell her he missed the smell of his favorite American food, the Whataburger. Mike Villasenor and David Cuervo were classmates in school in Texas. Villasenor told a local newspaper in the Rio Grande Valley that he missed his friend. "He was so proud," he remembered. "For a Mexican national, he had a lot of pride in America."[12] U.S. Army Private David Cuervo is buried in Texas, as an American. Under an executive order the president signed in 2002, any immigrant who joins the U.S. military and is killed in combat is eligible for immediate posthumous citizenship.

Foreigners interested in legal U.S. residency can also skip the long line if they offer the government enough money. In 1990 Congress passed a little-known law designed to encourage immigration by rich investors. The Investor Visa Program reserves up to ten thousand Green Cards a year for investors and their immediate families. Applicants must agree to invest at least half a million dollars in a new or existing U.S. business, an investment that will generate at least ten jobs. These Green Cards are supposed to be provisional for two years in order to give the government adequate opportunity to verify that the investment has been made and that the ten required jobs are filled.

U.S. citizenship is thus for sale to high bidders: your money or your life.

EPILOGUE:
A PRACTICAL
BLUEPRINT FOR
NORMALIZING
THE BORDER

THERE ARE no longer any real national borders. From the incursions of wetbacks pulling themselves out of the north bank of the Rio Grande to the global business conducted by international conglomerates, people have transcended the artificial constructs of national borders. Communication has played a key role in punching through the walls built by those who try to control migration. First radio magically proved uncontainable, spreading Mexico into the United States and vice versa. Now the internet virtually destroys the remnants of borders. What's left—especially along the U.S.-Mexico line—is, aside from the deadly games being played out during these last days of the border, a nominal irritation for the truly motivated. Despite the heavy-handed efforts of the U.S. government, people prove that they move as they always have, particularly when they are motivated by financial or family desires and needs.

So what are the possible solutions to the border crisis?

Further enforcement along the border? Unworkable. Neither the funds nor the national desire exists for such an attempted solution. Anyone who has ever eaten in a restaurant or watched a field hand at work knows how much the United States depends on Mexican labor.

Create an autonomous zone, an independent political entity along the border? Politically impossible for both the United States and Mexico. Besides, undocumented workers would still slip out of the zone and head north.

Militarize the border and create a two-thousand-mile Berlin Wall? Politically impossible. The United States cannot condemn Israel for fencing out the Palestinians while creating the same sort of monstrosity along the entire U.S.-Mexico line. Besides, it wouldn't work. Migrants already scale such a wall where it exists here and there along the border. They scale it and jump over, with a laugh at the vain attempts at keeping them out of *El Norte*.

Opening the border to the free passage of Mexicans who wish to come north is the only reasonable and long-term solution. Open the border to the people who are coming no matter what we do—people we want and need, no matter how much we may say otherwise. Once the Mexicans travel north freely, the real bad guys can no longer hide in their shadows. Over time Mexicans and Americans will learn to blend, not collide. And once Mexicans can again travel north freely, the U.S. government will know that the people in the tunnels and jumping the fences and running across the desert are the villains, not the fuel of the U.S. economy.

There is no question that the United States' southern border will be more secure if law-abiding Mexicans are allowed to pass freely. At present the bulk of the huge Border Patrol force and budget is used for chasing Mexicans. Once Mexicans no longer feel the need to sneak north, most of them undoubtedly will be happy to register with American authorities and carry whatever documents the United States requires for them to move between the two countries via official ports of entry. After that change occurs, the Border Patrol and other U.S. government agencies will be facing a trickle instead of tidal wave of illegal border crossers. With their advanced detection equipment and huge staff, the Border Patrol will then be well prepared to arrest and detain most of those who still try to cross into the United States illegally. Because of the new neighbor-friendly policy, U.S. authorities will no longer be chasing Mexican workers needed and wanted in the north; they can pursue unwanted—and potentially dangerous—border violators.

Although frustrated Central and South American workers will continue to attempt to cross Mexico en route to the United States, their numbers will be minimal compared with the Mexicans coming north, and continuing cooperation by the Mexican authorities in securing their own southern border, along with word of mouth reaching travelers about the now-secure U.S. border, will help control that illegal immigrant flow. Gangsters and drug traffickers, terrorists and spies seeking to infiltrate U.S. borders will be left alone in the spotlight without the protection offered them now by the cover and chaos of hoards of desperate Mexicans violating the border.

But there is more. Almost overnight the status of millions of Mexicans vis-à-vis the United States will change. No longer wanted criminals, they will become wanted and invited guests. By making Mexicans feel officially welcome and protected by police and society instead of afraid, Mexicans will likely be willing and active participants in helping keep those who endanger the United States out of the country.

Whether we work to make this policy happen, or just allow events to overwhelm us, now or later the artificial line separating Mexico from the United States (and Mexico's former land) will disappear.

As I made clear with the notation of my father's passage through Ellis Island, I am prejudiced to favor immigrants. It remains obvious to me that welcoming Mexicans who wish to come north to work and play is the pragmatic solution to the crisis along our border. But I'm not just prejudiced to favor immigrants; I'm prejudiced to favor Mexico and Mexicans. Perhaps it comes from growing up in California, where I was surrounded by the food, the music, the costumes, the language of Mexico. I appreciate the influence of Mexico and Mexicans on my culture. I savor Mexican evenings like one in San Cristóbal de Las Casas, Chiapas, when I ended a workday with a colleague listening to a guitarist at a local jazz club.

After we said good night, I strolled toward my hotel. In the distance I began to hear the comforting sound of a marimba band. The melodies grew louder and I followed the music, straying from my path to the hotel.

There on Avenida Cristóbal Colón, a full marimba band—six marimbistas, a bass player, and a drummer—were set up in the street, playing Chiapas classics under the glowing street lights. The bassist cautiously moved aside when the periodic late-night taxi cruised by. The traffic lights seemed to flash in time with the music.

I leaned against a nearby shop wall listening: all older men, playing for themselves—and me. The magical rattle of the marimba reverberating against the pastel walls of the stucco buildings lining the narrow streets: the Mexico of my dreams.

All I needed was my girl to dance with me on the gleaming paving stones.

NOTES

CHAPTER 2. STILL LIFE ON THE BORDER

1. "Border Town Marks 5th Migrant Day," *Miami Herald*, September 8, 2003, international edition.
2. "In Border Town, Migrant Crackdown Rankles," *New York Times*, June 5, 2003.
3. "Sonora Priest's Shelter Helps Cut Desert's Human Toll," *Arizona Daily Star*, December 26, 2003.
4. "On Trips to Mexico, Some Americans Bring Back Mexicans," *Wall Street Journal*, November 17, 2003.

CHAPTER 3. ON GUARD

1. "Battle at the Border," *San Diego Union Tribune*, August 21, 1997.
2. Mary Jo McConahay, "Human Smuggling Deaths," *Dissident Voice*, May 20, 2003.
3. Joseph Torres, "Nearly 1,200 Perish in Three Years Attempting to Cross Border," *Hispanic Link Weekly Report*, August 18, 1997.
4. Bob Moser, "Samaritans in the Desert," *The Nation*, May 26, 2003, p. 13.
5. Testimony of Representative Silvestre Reyes to the House Subcommittee on Immigration and Claims, February 25, 1999. Reyes was calling for more funds to pay for more Border Patrol personnel.
6. "At the Frontier of Irony, Border Patrol Ranks Swell with Hispanics," *Wall Street Journal*, October 22, 1998.
7. "Clinton and Dole's Dueling Immigration Ads," *San Francisco Chronicle*, July 7, 1996.
8. "Border Patrol Agent Kills Immigrant," *Los Angeles Times*, September 28, 1998.
9. "Agent Shoots Man in Second Border Killing," *Los Angeles Times*, September 29, 1998.
10. "Youth's Death Puts Focus on Border Tensions," *USA Today*, June 10, 1997.
11. Robert Draper, "Soldiers of Misfortune," *Texas Monthly*, August 1997.
12. S. C. Gwynne, "Border Skirmish," *Time*, August 25, 1997, p. 40.
13. "In Marine's Killing of Teen-ager, Town Mourns and Wonders Why," *New York Times*, June 29, 1997.

14. "Immigrants Flood Border in Arizona, Angering Ranchers," *New York Times*, June 18, 2000.

15. "Crackdown Forces More Migrants into Desert Crossings," *Santa Rosa Press Democrat*, July 29, 2000.

16. "Immigrants Flood Border in Arizona, Angering Ranchers," *New York Times*, June 18, 2000.

17. "50 More Immigration Agents to Fight Smugglers in Phoenix," *USA Today*, November 11, 2003.

18. National Public Radio, December 1, 2003.

CHAPTER 4. DEATH ALONG FOR THE RIDE

1. "Deaths of Immigrants Uncover Makeshift World of Smuggling," *New York Times*, June 29, 2003.

2. "7 Days of Desperation Along Mexican Border," *Washington Post*, May 25, 2003.

CHAPTER 6. WHAT IS A BORDER?

1. "A Wasted Land," *New York Times*, March 31, 1996.

CHAPTER 7. FAILED BARRIERS

1. William Truni, "Kids Going It Alone," *Barcelona Metropolitan*, June 2003, p. 14.

2. "Refugees Died Fighting for Air," *Dover Mercury*, June 29, 2000.

3. "Let's Hear It for Dover!" *The Express*, June 29, 2000.

4. "The One-Fence Solution," *New York Times*, August 3, 2003.

5. "Very Long Division," a chart in *National Geographic*, January 2004.

6. "Cyprus Dividing Line Opened for Day Trips," *Washington Post*, April 24, 2003.

CHAPTER 8. ANNEXING HALF OF MEXICO, TEMPORARILY . . .

1. *Economist*, August 16, 2003, p. 18.

2. Carol and Thomas Christensen, *The U.S.-Mexican War* (San Francisco, 1998), p. 41.

3. *New York Morning News*, August 13, 1845, cited in Frederick Merk, *Manifest Destiny and Mission in American History* (New York, 1963), p. 25.

4. Christensen, *The U.S.-Mexican War*, p. 19.

5. Ibid., p. 43.

6. Eugene Irving McCormac, *James K. Polk: A Political Biography* (New York, 1965), p. 373.

7. McCormac, *Polk*, p. 381.

8. *National Intelligencer*, August 5, 1845, cited in McCormac, *Polk*, p. 377.

9. From the June 10, 1847, edition of the *Chronicle*, under the title "Rough and Ready," quoted in George Winston Smith and Charles Judah, eds., *Chronicle of the Grin-*

gos: The U.S. Army in the Mexican War, 1846–1848: Accounts of Eyewitnesses and Combatants (Albuquerque, 1968), p. 12.

10. Christensen, *The U.S.-Mexican War*, p. 62.

11. Ibid.

12. Ibid.

13. Allan Nevins, ed., *Polk: The Diary of a President, 1845–1849* (New York, 1968), p. 83.

14. Polk's message to Congress was delivered May 11, 1846.

15. From President Paredes's proclamation of what he called a "defensive war," April 26, 1846, cited in McCormac, *Polk*, p. 413.

16. *New York Morning News*, July 7, 1845, cited in Merk, *Manifest Destiny and Mission in American History*, p. 50.

17. *New York Sun*, November 20, 1847, cited in Merk, *Manifest Destiny and Mission in American History*, p. 122.

18. Christensen, *The U.S.-Mexican* War, p. 90.

19. Ibid., p. 101.

20. Ibid., p. 111.

21. Belton's letter to his wife and son quoted in Smith and Judah, *Chronicle of the Gringos*, p. 191.

22. Ibid., p. 192.

23. John Ross, *The Annexation of Mexico* (Monroe, Me., 1998), p. 68.

24. May 29, 2000, at the Memorial Day service at Arlington National Cemetery.

25. Elijah Wald, *Narocorrido: A Journey into the Music of Drugs, Guns, and Guerillas* (New York, 2001), p. 35.

26. "La Tumba del Mojado" is on the Los Tigres del Norte collection *Internacionalmente Norteños*, released by Fonovisa.

27. "El Deportado" is collected on *Corridos & Tragedias de la Frontera*, released by Arhoolie/Folklyric.

28. "Los Mandados" was written by Jorge Lerma and can be found on the Fernandez compilation CD, *Los 15 Grandes Exitos*, released in 1990 on CBS Discos.

29. Tortilla Industry Association market research study, "The State of the Tortilla Industry Survey: 2002." The study concluded that 32 percent of U.S. bread sales are in the tortilla category, just 2 percent below white bread, the nation's most popular breadstuff.

30. "Developing a Taste for 'Gringo Food,'" *International Herald Tribune*, January 1, 1997.

31. "Mexican Wealth Gives Texas City a New Vitality," *New York Times*, June 14, 2003.

CHAPTER 9. EARLY CONTROL OF THE BORDER

1. "Early History of the Border Patrol," U.S. Department of Justice, Immigration and Naturalization Service, fact sheet prepared by their Office of Public Affairs.

2. Jorge L. Chinea, "Ethnic Prejudice and Anti-Immigrant Policies in Times of Economic Stress: Mexican Repatriation from the United States, 1929–1939," *East Wind/ West Wind*, Winter 1996, p. 9.

3. Leo Grebler, *"Mexican Immigration to the United States: The Record and Its Implications,"* Ph.D. dissertation, University of California, 1965, pp. 25–26.

4. *Congressional Record,* "Immigration from Countries of the Western Hemisphere," House Committee on Immigration and Naturalization, 70th Congr., 1st Sess., 1928, pp. 7–10.

5. "Says 400,000 Aliens Are Here Illegally," *New York Times,* January 5, 1931.

6. Gardner Jackson, "Doak the Deportation Chief," *The Nation,* March 18, 1931, p. 295.

7. U.S. Bureau of the Census, Sixteenth Census of the United States: 1940.

8. *The Handbook of Texas,* Texas State Historical Society, online.

9. John O. West, *Mexican-American Folklore* (Little Rock, 1988), p. 36.

10. Wald, *Narocorrido,* p. 176. The song "La Discriminación" can be found on the Los Norteños de Ojinaga album *Corridos Pa' Mi Pueblo,* vol. II.

11. Jorge L. Chinea, "Economic Stress: Mexican Repatriation from the United States," *East Wind/West Wind,* Winter 1991, p. 11.

12. Boye Lafayette De Mente, *Dictionary of Mexican Cultural Code Words* (Chicago, 1996), p. 123.

13. *El Bridge,* published by the Bridge Center for Contemporary Art, El Paso, Spring 2003, p. 18.

14. "Braceros Seek Justice," *San Diego Union Tribune,* November 26, 1999.

15. "Former Braceros Oppose Bush Plan," Associated Press dispatch, January 14, 2004.

16. *Wetbacks* was released in 1956, directed and produced by Hank McCune.

17. "San Quentin Prison was His Art School," *San Francisco Chronicle,* July 23, 2003.

CHAPTER 11. AN UNWELCOMING PROPOSITION

1. "California's Anti-Immigration Initiative Is Reviving Age-Old Economic Questions," *Wall Street Journal,* November 4, 1994.

2. "Can SOS Be Stopped?" *SF Weekly,* August 24, 1994.

3. "Auntie Immigration," *San Francisco Chronicle,* August 29, 1994.

4. In an interview with Bill O'Reilly on "The Radio Factor," March 16, 2004.

CHAPTER 12. AMONG THE VIGILANTES

1. "German Town Admits Role in Firebombing of Immigrant Hostel," *Washington Post,* February 13, 1997.

2. "Berlusconi's Immigration Policy Rings Alarm Bells," *Financial Times,* April 1/2, 2000.

3. From www.americanpatrol.org.

4. Austin Bunn, "Homegrown Homeland Defense," *New York Times Magazine,* June 1, 2003, p. 22.

5. "Police Investigate Killings of Illegal Immigrants in Arizona Desert," *New York Times,* October 23, 2002.

6. "Arizonans Watch Line in Sand: Armed Civilians Enforcing U.S. Border," Associated Press dispatch, February 10, 2003.

7. "3 Arizona Killings Are Linked to 9 Others," *New York Times*, November 25, 2003.

8. "Arizonans Watch Line in Sand," Associated Press dispatch, February 10, 2003.

9. www.aztlan.net.

10. "Do You Hire Illegal Immigrants?", *New York Times*, August 30, 1999.

11. *Bisbee Observer*, February 13, 2003, p. 16.

12. Representative Tom Tancredo speech to the House, September 16, 2003, from his website: www.house.gov/tancredo.

13. Representative Tom Tancredo speech to the House, April 8, 2003, ibid.

14. Representative Tom Tancredo speech to the House, March 6, 2003, ibid.

CHAPTER 14. THE POROUS, SHIFTING BORDER

1. "Equal Opportunity in Mexico City; Counting on Women to Be More Honest Than Men," *New York Times*, August 15, 1999.

2. "The Bribes That Bind Mexico," *Washington Post*, April 18, 2004.

3. "How to Handle an Accident in Mexico" is printed and distributed by the insurance company Seguros Comercial América.

4. *Tourist Guide Tijuana*, published by the Fondo Mixto de Promocion Turistica de Tijuana, 2001.

5. *The People's Guide to Mexico*, John Muir Publications (Santa Fe, 1990).

6. "Man Says Mexican Police Robbed Him," *San Diego Union Tribune*, January 1, 2004.

7. "More Women in U.S. Say They Were Raped by Tijuana Cops," *San Diego Union Tribune*, December 19, 2003.

8. Carlos Fuentes, *The Crystal Frontier* (New York, 1997). This citation is from the chapter titled "Río Grande, Río Bravo."

9. Tom Miller, *On the Border* (New York, 1981), p. 125.

10. *Pacific Sun*, May 29–June 4, 2002.

11. "Tensions Persist at RP School," *Santa Rosa Press Democrat*, January 31, 2004, p. 1.

12. "The O'Reilly Factor," Fox News Network, February 6, 2003.

13. "O'Reilly Gives State Views on Presidency," Iraq War, *Allentown* (PA) *Morning Call*, January 5, 2003.

14. www.michaelsavage.com.

CHAPTER 15. CROSSING THE BORDER THROUGH THE ETHER

1. "How to Build an Empire of the Airwaves," *Wall Street Journal*, August 14, 2001.

2. Details of Mussell's work can be found on his website: www.well.com/~dmsml/. The particulars of his Mexican border radio studies are at www.well.com/user/dmsml/xlnc/index.html.

3. "A Case of Receiving Mixed Signals," *Los Angeles Times*, August 25, 2000.

4. *Border Radio*, Limelight Edition (New York, 1990).

CHAPTER 16. THE DRIVER'S LICENSE DEBATE

1. "Unlicensed Drivers in 1 Out of 5 Fatal County Crashes," *Santa Rosa Press Democrat*, November 25, 2003.

CHAPTER 17. ILLEGAL AMERICANS

1. "Illegal Immigration Sometimes Goes South," *San Antonio Express-News*, October 19, 2003.
2. "Gun Charges and Trouble South of the Border," *New York Times*, October 23, 1998.
3. My interviews with Americans in La Mesa were conducted for an NBC News documentary about Americans imprisoned in foreign countries, and were included in my book *Nightmare Abroad* (San Francisco, 1993).
4. "Busy as Sin in Mexico, Tending to Straying Sheep," *New York Times*, May 12, 2003.

CHAPTER 18. ON THE KENTUCKY BORDER

1. "Border Patrol's Trap, Transplant Program Works," *Medford* (OR) *Mail Tribune*, September 27, 2003.
2. "U.S. Takes Steps to Tighten Mexican Border," *New York Times*, March 16, 2004.

CHAPTER 19. DEPORTATION MADE EASIER

1. Dan Baum, "On the Border," *Los Angeles Times Magazine*, March 16, 2003.

CHAPTER 21. WHO WANTS THE BORDER CLOSED?

1. "Immigrants are Divided on Bush Proposal," *New York Times*, January 8, 2004.
2. "Census: Latinos Dominate County's Lowest-Paying Jobs," *Santa Rosa Press Democrat,* June 2, 2003.
3. "Immigrants Then and Now," *San Francisco Chronicle*, May 28, 2003.
4. Ibid.
5. "Mexicans Look to San Rafael for New Lives," *Marin Independent Journal*, September 4, 1994, p. A3.

CHAPTER 22. BURDEN OR BENEFIT?

1. "Paul Harvey News and Comment," ABC Radio Network, October 28, 2003.
2. NPR broadcast "Morning Edition" report by Gerry Hadden, May 8, 2003.
3. "A New Kind of Neighbor," *New York Times*, August 25, 2000.
4. Vicente Fox radio address to Mexico, July 28, 2001.
5. Associated Press dispatch by George Gedda, *San Francisco Chronicle*, August 25, 2000.
6. "Mexican President-Elect Warmly Greeted in Washington," *New York Times*, August 25, 2000.
7. "Fox's Open-Border Proposal Shot Down," *Chicago Tribune*, August 25, 2000.

8. "Two Presidential Pals, Until 9/11 Intervened," *New York Times*, March 3, 2003.

9. "Mexico Struggles for the Attentions of a Preoccupied U.S.," *New York Times*, October 13, 2002.

10. "Fox Calls on Mexicans in U.S. to Work toward Migration," *Dallas Morning News*, November 5, 2003.

11. "The Promise of Liberty," Peter Laufer, NBC News documentary, 1985.

12. Anthony Humphreys and Siona Jenkins, *Egypt*, (Melbourne, 2002), p. 257.

13. "Anti-Migrant Backlash Brews Across U.S.," *Mexico City News*, August 4, 2001.

14. From the Frequently Asked Questions page of the group's website, www.cocc.org.

15. "Slamming the Golden Door," *Louisville Courier-Journal*, July 3, 1994.

16. "Auntie Immigration," Roberto Rodriguez and Patrisia Gonzales, *San Francisco Chronicle*, August 29, 1994.

17. Jorge L. Chinea, "Ethnic Prejudice and Anti-Immigrant Policies in Times of Economic Stress: Mexican Repatriation from the United States, 1929–1939," *East Wind/West Wind*, Winter 1996, p. 11.

18. "Mexico's One-Way Remedy," *New York Times*, July 18, 2000.

19. "El Barrio de Fayetteville," *Economist*, September 19, 1998, p. 39.

20. *The New Americans: Economic, Demographic, and Fiscal Effects of Immigration* (Washington, D.C., 1997).

21. "Easy Question Doesn't Have Simple Answer," *Santa Rosa Press Democrat*, September 8, 2003.

CHAPTER 23. THE ROAD FROM CHIAPAS AND CHIHUAHUA

1. Tiziano Terzani, *A Fortune-teller Told Me* (New York, 1997), pp. 46–47.

2. www.ciepac.org.

3. www.ezln.org.

4. Dan Baum, "On the Border," *Los Angeles Times Magazine*, March 16, 2003.

5. "NAFTA Gives Mexicans New Reasons to Leave Home," *San Francisco Chronicle*, October 15, 1998.

6. "Many of Mexico's Poorest Forced to Leave Homes to Work on U.S. Farms," *Miami Herald*, November 14, 2003.

7. Signe Wilkinson, *Philadelphia Daily News*, April 25, 2001.

8. "NAFTA's Legacy—Profits and Poverty," *San Francisco Chronicle*, January 14, 2004.

9. "The Broken Promise of NAFTA," *San Francisco Chronicle*, January 6, 2004.

10. "Emergence of a Hybrid Culture," *Los Angeles Times*, April 29, 1997.

11. "Family Ties Across the Divide," *San Francisco Chronicle*, October 15, 1998.

12. "¿Mexicano, Gringo o Qué?" *Point Reyes* (CA) *Light*, February 12, 2004.

CHAPTER 24. BEST FRIENDS

1. "Ridge Rapped for Immigration Views," *Washington Times*, December 11, 2003.

2. *New York Times*, December 22, 2003.

3. "Tom Ridge's Idea Will Grant Legal Status to Terrorists," *Sierra Vista* (AZ) *Herald*, December 24, 2003.

4. "Germany Set to Deport 40,000 Vietnamese to Their Homeland," *San Francisco Examiner*, October 8, 1995.

5. "Immigrants Are Divided on Bush Proposal," *New York Times*, January 8, 2004.

6. "Newshour with Jim Lehrer," PBS, January 8, 2004.

7. "Bush Calls for Changes on Illegal Workers," CNN.com, January 8, 2004.

8. "Mexico Hopes Cautiously After Proposal on Migrants," *New York Times*, January 8, 2004.

9. "Mexico Dismisses Its U.N. Envoy for Critical Remark About U.S.," *New York Times*, November 19, 2003.

10. "Bush's Migrant Plan Brings Scams," *El Paso Times*, January 16, 2004.

11. "Guest Worker Scams Arise," *Denver Post*, January 16, 2004.

12. "Salute to Pvt. David Cuervo, Mexican Immigrant Killed in Iraq," *Fort Worth Star-Telegram*, January 12, 2004.

INDEX

A NOTE ON THE AUTHOR

Peter Laufer, an independent journalist and writer, was born in New York and did his undergraduate studies at the University of California, Berkeley, and his post-graduate work at American University in Washington, D.C. He worked in radio in San Francisco and Los Angeles, and then as a correspondent for NBC News, where he covered breaking news worldwide and created documentaries, many of them award-winning. He won the George Polk Award for his documentary on Americans imprisoned overseas, and Edward R. Murrow, National Headliner, and other awards for his documentary work on immigration, drug trafficking, and illiteracy. He has also written *Exodus to Berlin*, *Iron Curtain Rising*, and *Nightmare Abroad*, among other books. His current radio work includes consulting in Europe and North America, along with hosting the "National Geographic World" talk show. He is married with two sons and lives in Sonoma County, California.